BLACK WOMEN
IN THE FICTION OF
JAMES BALDWIN

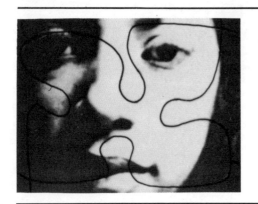

TRUDIER HARRIS

BLACK WOMEN IN THE FICTION OF JAMES BALDWIN

THE UNIVERSITY OF TENNESSEE PRESS
KNOXVILLE

The paper in this book meets the guidelines for permanence
and durability of the Committee on Production Guidelines
for Book Longevity of the Council on Library Resources.
Binding materials have been chosen for durability.

Publication of this book has been aided by a grant from the
American Council of Learned Societies from funds provided by the
Andrew W. Mellon Foundation.

Library of Congress Cataloging in Publication Data
Harris, Trudier.
  Black women in the fiction of James Baldwin.
  Bibliography: p.
  Includes index.
  1. Baldwin, James, 1924–   —Characters—Women.
2. Afro-American women in literature.   3. Women in
literature.   I. Title.
PS3552.A45Z69 1985   813'.54   84-27022
ISBN 0-87049-461-9 (alk. paper)

In fond memory
of my dear friend,
Martha E. Chew
(9 January 1941–9 October 1984)

ACKNOWLEDGMENTS

To my many friends and colleagues throughout the country who have encouraged me in this project, I offer my sincere thanks. Especially am I grateful to Professor Daryl C. Dance of Virginia Commonwealth University, who read and reread this manuscript and who encouraged me through the care of her commentary.

Residence at The Mary Ingraham Bunting Institute at Radcliffe/ Harvard during 1981–82 and again during 1982–83 enabled me to complete the manuscript. The women at the Institute, who listened to lectures and to luncheon and party discussions of James Baldwin, were unfailingly inspiring in their responses to my research. Special thanks to Linda M. Perkins, assistant director of the Institute during my tenure there, who has a unique ability to encourage by her presence and who is also an exacting reader.

Access to Harvard libraries and office space through The Bunting Institute and the W. E. B. DuBois Institute for Afro-American Research was invaluable in bringing this project to fruition. I am especially grateful to Professor Nathan I. Huggins, Director of the DuBois Institute, for his suggestions and reading time.

Thanks to the Carnegie Corporation, which allowed for my initial affiliation with The Bunting Institute. I am also thankful to the National Research Council, which, through the Ford Foundation and the National Academy of Sciences, awarded me the fellowship to affiliate with the DuBois Institute, to spend a second year at The Bunting Institute and, most important, to revise this manuscript. Such support, at a very crucial point in my career, made the difference between an idea and a book. None of this would have been possible, however, if the University of North Carolina at Chapel Hill had not granted me the release time to complete the work; I am grateful to my colleagues there.

For all the help—financial, collegial, moral—I am ever thankful. The work in its final version, however, is my own.

TRUDIER HARRIS
Chapel Hill, North Carolina
October 21, 1984

CONTENTS

BLACK WOMEN
IN THE FICTION OF
JAMES BALDWIN

INTRODUCTION

The many reactions I have received to my study of James Baldwin's treatment of black women in his fiction have encouraged me in my belief that such a work is necessary and timely. Individuals with whom I spoke who remembered the women in Baldwin's fiction were intrigued that I wanted to do a detailed study of these characters. Scholars more familiar with issues and themes than characters were concerned to know if the women were prominent enough to deserve a separate study and, if so, what I would say about them. Frequently persons less familiar with Baldwin's works could not remember the names of the female characters, and they often asked questions about which works were to be included in the study.

On occasion, I was surprised to discover that a writer of Baldwin's reputation evoked such vague memories from individuals in the scholarly community, most of whom maintained that they had read one or more of his fictional works. When I began a thorough examination of Baldwin scholarship, however, some of that reaction became clearer. Baldwin seems to be read at times for the sensationalism readers anticipate in his work, but his treatment in scholarly circles is not commensurate to that claim to sensationalism or to his more solidly justified literary reputation. It was discouraging, therefore, to think that one of America's best-known writers, and certainly one of its best-known black writers, has not attained a more substantial place in the scholarship on Afro-American writers. I am hopeful, therefore, that this study of the black women characters in Baldwin's fiction may inspire further discussions and promote additional detailed treatments of his works.

Within the limited number of critical volumes devoted to Baldwin, it is not surprising to discover that the female characters are the subjects of only a minute portion of them. Though Baldwin has been writing for over thirty years and has more than sixteen books to his credit, only three book-length critical studies of his work exist.[1] Another book-length study is primarily biographical in orientation.[2] Of these studies, none focuses exclusively on fiction, which is the genre in which Baldwin has produced most,[3] and only one was published after 1978. Two collections of critical essays have been published, both before 1978.[4] Only one critic distinguishes herself in the bulk of the criticism by giving more than cursory attention to the black women who populate Baldwin's fiction.[5] For the other critics, these women, in spite of their roles as central or shaping forces in the lives of the male characters, have been relegated to a secondary or nonexistent place in their discussions of the fiction.

Black women such as Florence and Elizabeth in *Go Tell It on the Mountain* (1953) have received the most critical exposure because parts of the novel are narrated from their points of view, but the angle of vision of the criticism has focused consistently on John and Gabriel; the women have not commanded attention in their own right as female characters. Ida, in *Another Country* (1962), has been judged a central character by two or three critics, but they have not followed through on their evaluations to give more than a few paragraphs of commentary; she usually receives only passing attention. Women in *Going to Meet the Man* (1965), even Ruth, from whose point of view "Come Out the Wilderness" is narrated, have essentially been ignored. Tish (Clementine), who narrates *If Beale Street Could Talk* (1974), has been the subject of a couple of articles, but she has also been viewed as an unconvincing narrator. Julia and other women in *Just Above My Head* (1979) have been mentioned in review articles and plot summaries. Publication dates of *Just Above My Head* and *If Beale Street Could Talk* are undoubtedly relevant in considering the quantity of criticism that has appeared so far, in terms of treatment, but most of it continues the trend of giving Baldwin's black women characters only minimal attention.

The types as well as the limited number of book-length treatments of Baldwin's works underscore the fact that a major American writer has not received the intensive and extensive evaluation warranted by his prominence. While this study is designed to fill a gap in Baldwin scholarship, it has the equally important purpose of treating characters often neglected in specific discussions of Baldwin as well as in more generalized discussions of American and black American literature. Categories I define and analyses I offer about Baldwin's black female characters are derived from careful examination of *Go Tell It on the Mountain, Another Country, Going to Meet the Man, If Beale Street Could Talk*, and *Just Above My Head.*[6]

The black women Baldwin treats in his works play a number of roles, several of which overlap. Whatever their role, most of the women believe themselves to be guilty of some crime or condition of existence that demands their doing penance. At times the women are spiritual outcasts, psychological ghetto dwellers in a familial, sexual, religious world where their suffering does not lead to redemption. Whatever her position, no black woman in Baldwin's fiction is ultimately, continuously happy, though a few, like Julia in *Just Above My Head*, reach a state of contentment. Further, few of them are spiritually healthy. Their guilt for the "crimes" that they can articulate only through suffering is often tied to their evaluations of past actions in a "sinful" life. Because of their willingness to suffer, they are therefore frequently doomed to exist in psychological discomfort, in self-accusation and repression. This book examines the sources of their guilt, its manifestations in their daily lives, and the process of extrication through which the few women who do so manage to escape their guilt.

The sense of guilt the women feel is often tied to their desire to break away from roles that have been defined for them, or to their failure to fulfill a role. Almost all of the roles in which we find black women in Baldwin's fiction are traditional ones—mothers, sisters, lovers, wives—and almost all of them are roles of support for the male characters. The most prominent women we associate with Baldwin's fiction are those who are solidly within the tradition of the fundamentalist church as it exists in black communities. These women may be classified as churchgoers, and appear from *Go Tell It on the Mountain* to *Just Above My Head*. The women in this category come closer to being stereotypes than perhaps any others in Baldwin's works. They are usually described as large, buxom, very dark-skinned, and middle-aged or older. Their long years of faithful attendance and their tending to the souls of younger church members have won them a respectable status in the church. Usually models of Christian faith and actions to nonmembers of the church, these long-suffering women are best exemplified by Praying Mother Washington and Sister McCandless in *Go Tell It on the Mountain*. They remind us of the matriarchal Mama Lena Younger in Lorraine Hansberry's *A Raisin in the Sun* in the unwavering quality of their faith and in their concern that other members of their immediate or church family should come into or remain within the fold of the church.

These women, like Mrs. Hunt in *If Beale Street Could Talk*, may be almost fanatical in the fervor with which they carry out their commitment to the church and to God. Deborah, in *Go Tell It on the Mountain*, clings to the church as if it is her last chance for life. Although she is younger than the other women, her life experiences have aged her prematurely, and she is therefore as "old" in faith as Praying Mother Washington. She is consistent in witnessing for the Lord, in attending to the sick and the dead, and in fervently uttering "amens" in response to Gabriel's and other preachers' sermons. These fanatical church women may on occasion make the very example of their piety a threat to those around them. People who would make fun of Deborah's plainness or of the fact that she has been raped are awed into silence by the faith she exhibits. Mrs. Hunt specifically becomes a threat to the young people around her, as do Sister Mc-Candless and Sister Daniels in "The Outing." These women may also become so single-mindedly dedicated to the church that, like Mrs. Hunt, they neglect their families in a literal adaptation of the biblical injunction to sacrifice even husband, son, and daughter for one's belief in God.

A subdivision of the category of churchgoers, represented by women slightly younger than those described above, would be the one into which Elizabeth Grimes fits in *Go Tell It on the Mountain*. By virtue of the fact that her husband is a preacher and a deacon, Elizabeth *must* have a role in the church. She is torn, therefore, between what form demands and what she knows her own heart to believe. She is certainly not without faith, but she is not as believing or as committed as Deborah and Mrs. Hunt are. She tries to find the blend of raising her children within the church and minding her own soul; she does not reject one in favor of the other. She is much more silent and passive than the first category of churchgoers. Although we see her on her knees praying in church, we never hear her so much as utter an "amen" during the services she frequently attends. On rare occasions, these women in the church extend their roles beyond those of support to ones of leadership. Praying Mother Washington has a recognized position of respect in *Go Tell It on the Mountain*; she is "a powerful evangelist and very widely known."[7] Sister Daniels, a member of the same church, has been "blessed" with a "mighty voice with which to sing and preach," and she is "going out soon into the field" (p. 57). The most prominent of the female leaders in the churches that appear in Baldwin's works, however, is Julia Miller in *Just Above My Head*. As a seven-year-old child prodigy preacher, she is responsible for bringing many souls to Christ.

As leaders and as supporters, the women in the church subdivide into true believers and hypocrites, which in turn affects their portrayal as women. Even among the true believers, some are presented more seriously than others; Deborah is portrayed straightforwardly, but Sister Daniels is sometimes presented in slightly derogatory ways. Mrs. Hunt is obviously a hypocrite at whom we are encouraged to laugh. How the women are presented is affected in part by the period in which the work appeared and by the nature of Baldwin's politics at the time.

Baldwin's portrayal of mothers overlaps with his portrayal of churchgoers. Indeed, many of the women in the church who have no children of their own assume the role of mother to the young people in their churches. Several of the mothers, like the churchgoing women, are long-suffering. They range from hypersensitive Elizabeth, from whom her son John must sense her moods and desires, to supportive Sharon Rivers in *If Beale Street Could Talk*. The atypical portrait of the mother is Mrs. Hunt, also in *Beale Street*, who rejects her son. The most attractive mothers are the ones who would give everything for their children, either in quiet ways, as Elizabeth does with John, or in very vocal, aggressive ways, as Sharon Rivers does with her daughter Tish. Mrs. Hunt, by contrast, is most unattractive as a mother because she fails to support, because she refuses to allow sacrifice for her family to become part of her personality.

Women as sisters are also important to Baldwin. They range from Florence in *Go Tell It on the Mountain*, to Ida in *Another Country*, to Ernestine, Adrienne and Sheila in *If Beale Street Could Talk*, to Julia in *Just Above My Head*. Sisters, like mothers, are most attractive when they are in helpful roles to other members of their families,

particularly the males. Florence believes she has trouble partly because she feels she has mocked her brother Gabriel's ministry, while
Ernestine is a positive image because of the sacrificial nature of her
support for Tish and Fonny. Adrienne and Sheila are superficial fluffs,
mere window dressing, because they care more for aristocratic manners than for their brother Fonny. Julia initially causes many problems for her younger brother Jimmy, but later redeems her role as
sister by being especially helpful to him.

As lovers, Baldwin's women are always engaged in heterosexual
affairs; lesbianism as a concept does not surface in his books. In their
roles as lovers, therefore, the women are to be evaluated on the basis
of how well they complement, satisfy, and work toward the happiness
of the men in their lives—or, in the case of the fanatical lovers of the
(masculine) Lord, the extent to which they are committed to Him.
Just as mothers are to sacrifice for their children, so are women to
sacrifice for their men. The women almost invariably allow the men to
determine their paths in life, whether it is to be a part of the church,
as with Elizabeth, or to shape her conceptions of beauty and worth,
as with Tish. Julia is the only female in Baldwin's fiction who finally
seems to lead a reasonably happy life without a man; when men are in
her life, however, she is acutely destructive in sublimating her desires to theirs.

Lovers make up one category of romantic or sexual involvements in
Baldwin's fiction, but there are others. Several women are pictured as
having "loose" or questionable morals. The first of these is Esther in
Go Tell It on the Mountain. Though Gabriel is basely attracted to
Esther, he nevertheless tries to picture her as wanton because of the
numerous young men he sees escorting her to and from work. She is
outside the traditional moral values as exemplified by the members of
Gabriel's church, but she is not as morally confused as Ruth in "Come
Out the Wilderness." Ruth sleeps with more men than Gabriel suspects Esther of being involved with. Neither woman is presented as
being emotionally stable—although Esther is certainly more mentally healthy than Ruth.

Esther and Ruth are the more "innocent" of the women with loose
morals. Both Ida in *Another Country* and Julia in *Just Above My
Head* are more seasoned in the liberties they take with their bodies.
Ida can be described as an elevated whore; she makes a conscious
decision to use her body in an effort to become a successful singer.
She concludes that the only way of dealing with the exploitative

system under which she must live in New York is to become the
"biggest, coolest, hardest whore around."[8] Julia, on the other hand,
is the saint/whore, the daughter who willingly engages in incest with
her father and the "sister" whose brother revels in the delights her
body offers him. She is debased, but she is also a source of elevation; ultimately, she is able to extricate herself from degrading
circumstances.

Few women in Baldwin's works are able to move beyond the bounds
of the traditional roles that have been cut out for them and in which
the use of their bodies is the most important factor. There are, nonetheless, a few iconoclasts. Florence expresses more independence
than is usual with anyone in Baldwin's early fiction, and Sharon Rivers
is certainly unusual in her cursing, nonreligious approach to sacrificing for her children. Ernestine, as a community activist, also moves
her role beyond strict confines.

In terms of the work they do, though, few women in Baldwin's
works are nontraditional. Even Florence, who values independence
so much, still has a very traditional job as a domestic. Ida, in her bid
to be a singer, has a profession that started in tradition and has moved
beyond it. Like many women in Baldwin's works, she started out
singing in the church; her desire to be a blues singer in nightclubs is
the added dimension. But it is Julia who has the atypical career for
women in Baldwin's fiction; she is a model. Mention of her work
seems more a device for allowing Julia and Hall to meet again than to
emphasize the intrinsic value of the work; but it is different from that
in which most of the other women engage.

Different categories can mean that the black women are treated
differently and that Baldwin has varying degrees of positive or negative responses to them. However, no woman is ultimately so acceptable to Baldwin that she is to be viewed as equal to the prominent
male characters. It is a function of their guilt as well as of their
creation that most of the black female characters in Baldwin's fiction
have been subordinated to the males; they are in a supportive, *serving* position in relation to the males and the male images in their
lives. They serve their neighbors; they serve their children and their
husbands; and they serve God. The serving position reflects the
central fact of their existence: they are incomplete without men or
male images in their lives because wholeness without males is not a
concept the majority of them have internalized.

Such evaluations also apply to the black women characters treated in Baldwin's dramas. Sister Margaret Alexander, pastor of the church in *The Amen Corner* (1954), is most like the women in the fiction in her desire and ability to serve. Though she leaves her husband, she replaces him with the church and God, and with the possibility of making her son David as unlike her husband Luke as she can. In her adherence to scripture, she is one of the most fanatical of Baldwin's black women characters. Yet in her recognition of the unrelenting antagonism between males and females, she voices the plight of all of the church-based women: "The only thing my mother should have told me is that being a woman ain't nothing but one long fight with men. And even the Lord, look like, ain't nothing but the most impossible kind of man there is."[9] Juanita, in *Blues for Mister Charlie* (1964), asserts early upon Richard's return to their small Southern town that she views it as her responsibility to save him—from the whites as well as from himself. She determines not to let Richard "go anywhere without" her.[10] At times an outspoken, feisty civil rights marcher, Juanita still experiences the most thoroughly satisfying time of her life when she is with Richard. Black women in the dramas may act differently at times because of the demands of the genre and Baldwin's political/religious statements, but in the guilt they feel and the burdens they bear, they are often strikingly akin to their novelistic sisters.

How the characters in the fiction are revealed to us is important for understanding Baldwin's progression in the treatment of them as well as for seeing more clearly the place he has assigned to them. Most of the women are revealed through omniscient narration or through male narrators in a third-person, limited point of view. The only female who narrates a story or novel is Tish in *Beale Street*. Like Hall Montana in *Just Above My Head*, she often ventures into an omniscience in picturing scenes at which she is not present, in recreating conversations she has not heard, and in revealing thoughts of other characters when those thoughts have not been verbalized to her. For the male narrators, it is often necessary to consider their personalities and sympathies as well as what they present about the women characters who appear through their narrations. Black women we see in Baldwin's fiction, then, are usually at least twice removed—by way of Baldwin and his narrators—and are sometimes distanced through other layers as well.

The women presented in this study progress from trying to find sanctuary in the church to realizing that it affords none. They progress from condemning themselves for their trespasses against other human beings and against God to taking advantage whenever it is necessary and to pushing God into the background, if not completely out of their lives; community replaces church, and secular, social commitment replaces traditional religion and the hope of heaven. The women generally move out from under the shadow of their own guilt and doubt about their humanity to singing praises to life and living. Their sexual attitudes change from the pristine to the carefree and sometimes to the outrageous. They move from individual family concerns to extended and communal family concerns. Yet for all this growth and progression, for all this freedom of action and movement, the women are still confined to niches carved out for them by men whose egos are too fragile to grant their equality; and, for their own part, there are still flaws in their characters that enable them to accept those external definitions. Even the freest of Baldwin's black women, such as Ernestine in *Beale Street* and Julia in *Just Above My Head*, are initially not free of conformity, and, at some level, to male definitions of them. Finally, and most important, they are not free of the creator who continues to draw in their potential for growth on the short rein of possibility.

CHAPTER ONE

WILLING SCAPEGOATS FOR THE MALE EGO

Go Tell It on the Mountain

The black women in James Baldwin's *Go Tell It on the Mountain* (1953) are all limited in the emotional relationships they form with the men in their lives. Their limitations spring from two sources—how they have been shaped by the women who had responsibility for their formative years, and how, through these older women, the force of the church has been driven into the minds of the younger women. Their predicament illustrates the major critical problem in evaluating women here, and it is one that permeates most of Baldwin's fiction: the black women are conceived against the backdrop of the fundamentalist church within the black community.[1] Setting them against such a backdrop, whether or not Baldwin ultimately approves of that church, is too restricting a model for complex development of characters; lines are too sharply drawn in terms of good and evil. Through the church, the women are very early taught to accept their places as wives, mothers, and sisters, and to feel guilty if they do not. They are taught to be other-centered, to be preoccupied with the things that form a part of their lives beyond themselves and too little occupied with their own hopes, dreams, and aspirations.

Indeed, within the framework in which they are conceived, it is almost impossible for them to think of themselves as vibrant human beings who have needs; failure to put God and others, especially men, at the centers of their beings makes them suspect. The women in the novel, therefore, find themselves guilty when they have actually committed sins and guilty when they have thought only of themselves. They are at the beginning of a progression of women in Baldwin's fiction who will never be free until they free themselves of both the secular and the sacred male domination of their lives. As long as they see themselves as women who can define themselves only in relation to men or within the male/God-centered church, they will be limited in terms of how they can grow and how interesting they can become for critical evaluation. The story of Baldwin's treatment of black women is really the story of that process of freeing them from the church, of extricating them from the limitations that so restrict their development as characters.

We do not have many opportunities in the novel for viewing women interacting with other women, but for those in which we do, the picture is not a particularly happy one. Nor is it one in which we can see the possibilities for any more positive images than the ones that we are given with the women interacting with the men. Several female/female contacts give us points of reference for pursuing how women perpetuate guilt in other women and how women support women in an attempt to overcome the guilt-inducing or otherwise restricting situations in which they find themselves. First of all, there is the relationship between Florence Grimes and her mother, in which the mother seems to perpetuate the strictures on her daughter's development that the male world does. There is also the relationship between Elizabeth and her aunt, again one in which the older woman attempts to impose upon the younger one a male-dominated vision of the world. There is the relationship hinted at between Florence and Deborah, the nature of which must be surmised from evidence rather than examined directly. Finally, there is the relationship between Florence and Elizabeth in the portion of the novel relating to John's life; here is the only sustained glimpse of a positive relationship between two women, one in which they provide mutual comfort and support to each other. In all of these relationships, men provide for the major topic of conversation and concern for the women, which suggests that how they view their lives, even when not in the presence of men, is still informed by male-centered directives that they seem unable to escape. The relationships are nevertheless revealing for commentary on Baldwin's conceptual framework for the treatment of black women in his works.

Florence and Elizabeth are both initially seen in the role of daughter to the older women in their lives, Florence literally and Elizabeth by reason of her mother's death. Both are touched by the problems of generational differences that have made the older women retreat into the safety of the church. Rachel, Florence's mother, has experienced slavery and knows what it means to be completely helpless against forces over which one has no control. As a woman who has borne children and seen them sold into slavery, she wants the best possible protection for the children who remain with her; to her, her vulnerable daughter can find sanctuary in a marriage that will be infinitely more secure than the fragile unions in slavery. Her experiences in slavery have not given the mother the powers of imagination to conceive of lives for women beyond the very mundane and practical. The limited vision she sees for Florence is only a natural outgrowth of the limited vision to which she has been exposed.

What Rachel wants for her daughter Florence is in direct contrast to what she wants for her son Gabriel, a fact that reveals her male-centered approach to life. Women, her experiences have taught her, have only had as much value as they had worth to the men in their lives, whether husbands or masters. Rachel therefore brings to her daughter a devalued conception of herself that can only mean a similar devaluation for her daughter. How Florence manages the perceptiveness to escape that slot is perhaps more surprising than her actual journey to New York. The chain of being is such that women keep other women in place for men.

Rachel has waited many years to be delivered from slavery, realizing throughout her bondage that she "had only to endure and trust in God."[2] Such trusting makes her passive, and she teaches her daughter the same passivity. She finds the will to walk off the plantation when freedom comes, but she has no desire to escape from the South; she is willing to trade her bondage for a different kind of slavery as long as she has dwellings visibly separate from the whites. Her many trials and tribulations have made her efface herself into peaceful coexistence with the whites, and she tries to instill the same in her daughter: "She was content to stay in this cabin and do washing for the white folks, though she was old and her back was sore. And she wanted Florence, also, to be content—helping with the washing, and fixing meals and keeping Gabriel quiet" (p. 72). Rachel has arrived at her stoicism as a result of witnessing the power of the Lord in His deliverance of the slaves. The need to trust in the Lord and wait upon

His intercession in human affairs means submitting oneself to whatever life offers and bearing any burden thrust upon one. Florence, however, prefers the power of the individual to change his or her circumstances, but her efforts to escape from the teachings of her mother are just as futile as her efforts to minimize the influence of God in her life.

Florence tries to escape her mother and life among the "wretched" by going to New York. At the moment of Florence's departure, Rachel uses her illness and the threat of hell in an effort to force Florence to stay. "Girl," Rachel says, "you mean to tell me the Devil's done made your heart so hard you can just leave your mother on her dying bed, and you don't care if you don't never see her in this world no more? Honey, you can't tell me you done got so evil as all that?" (p. 78). A daughter's place, Rachel reasons, is with the mother who needs her and with a husband, who should be chosen from nearby. Florence leaves physically, but she does not escape psychologically.

The effect her mother has had upon her can be seen in Florence's response to kneeling at the altar during the tarry service in Part Two of the novel. She reflects that she has traveled a long road over the past sixty years, and it has led her at last "to her mother's starting-place, the altar of the Lord" (p. 66). The influence has reached out and drawn her into the church in spite of herself, for it is not out of conviction that she comes; she comes out of fear, the fear of facing judgment that her mother has instilled in her many years before, especially on that morning when Florence walked out of the cabin to go to New York. Fear of dying and guilt for her past actions make Florence realize that she has not escaped and force her to judge herself, finally, by rules she has tried throughout her life to reject. She does not undergo any resounding conversion, but she is brought low; the only thing that prevents her salvation is her own heart, which is still weighed down by "hatred and bitterness" (p. 66) directed primarily at Gabriel. If Gabriel is the Lord's anointed, she maintains, "she would rather die and endure Hell for all eternity than bow before His altar" (p. 66). Unrepentant, she bows nonetheless, and she finds herself thereby forever tied to the mother whose influence she has tried to remove from her life.

The kind of control Rachel tries to exert upon Florence is similar to that Elizabeth's aunt tries to exert over her. The aunt is a generation out of slavery, but her notion of woman's place is not substantially different from Rachel's. To her, Elizabeth should exchange pride for

humbleness and live out her life in quiet submission to biblical teachings. The aunt senses in Elizabeth a haughtiness that will only be
punished by destruction; because the aunt cannot bring Elizabeth
low, she passes on the teachings that suggest that God will do what
she cannot, that He will punish Elizabeth for being too proud, that
she will ultimately feel guilty for the sinful life she has led.

From the age of eight, Elizabeth is brought up by her aunt in
straitlaced adherence to sermons that emphasize the threat of hell to
those who are haughty and proud. She is a constant affront to the
sacrifices her aunt claims to have made for her and to the love she
publicizes (but for which little evidence exists). Elizabeth "sensed
that what her aunt spoke of as love was something else—a bribe, a
threat, an indecent will to power. She knew that the kind of imprisonment that love might impose was also, mysteriously, a freedom for
the soul and spirit, was water in the dry place, and had nothing to do
with the prisons, churches, laws, rewards, and punishments, that so
positively cluttered the landscape of her aunt's mind" (p. 156). She
struggles quietly and obstinately against that power until she can
escape from her aunt's house and from the South.

The aunt superimposes thoughts upon Elizabeth that will haunt
her later and that she will remember when she is feeling remorseful
about John's illegitimate birth. "You go walking around with your nose
in the air," her aunt says, "the Lord's going to let you fall right on down
to the bottom of the ground. *You* mark my words. You'll *see*" (p. 156).
The aunt uses God in an attempt to bully people into a prescribed
behavior, but Elizabeth's knowledge of what she has done causes her
to feel more than the depth of guilt her aunt would have wanted.

Response to the relationship between Elizabeth and her aunt is
dictated as much by what happens between them as by what does not
happen. There is no loving, supportive, or understanding interaction
between the two; from the very earliest days of Elizabeth's arrival in
her aunt's house, the two are presented as antagonists. The aunt
expects Elizabeth to be grateful for having been taken in after her
mother's death, but Elizabeth can only blame her aunt for having put
her father out of her life. Her life has centered upon her father; she
freely admits that she never loved her mother, indeed had responded
to her mother's advances with an "unpleasant sense of duty" (p. 153).
What she has felt for the mother is transferred to and intensified with
her aunt; the mother was an obstacle to her relationship with her
father, and so is the aunt. The coldness between Elizabeth and her

aunt, then, has as its basis the reaction to a man. Reflecting an ingrained sense of duty that is larger than childish resentment, the aunt provides clothes and shelter for Elizabeth until she goes off to be with Richard, who will become John's father. It is one of the ironies of Elizabeth's life that she must end up pursuing a sense of duty in her marriage to Gabriel that is comparable to what her aunt has done for her; the acquiescing, self-denying life that Elizabeth has railed against has now become her own.

To balance out these negative interactions between women, there are two accounts of positive relationships between black women in *Go Tell It on the Mountain*; one is hinted at early on and not fully developed, and the other is the most developed relationship we see among the women in the novel. The relationship between Florence and Deborah, as well as that between Florence and Elizabeth, develops because of an impact men have had upon their lives. Florence and Deborah become friends after Deborah has been raped. They judge all males harshly and center upon Gabriel as the personification of what they find disgusting about men; this is especially true of Florence. They witness together Gabriel's scandalizing response to his baptism and, in later years, his tomcatting backsliding to a life of sin. Both women feel threatened, Deborah because she has been raped and reduced to the tainted body that few men will ever look beyond, and Florence because her beauty has similarly reduced her to the mere function of body. Both women feel that they will forever be at the mercy of men simply because they are women in a society that has judged them to be of lesser value. Their understanding of their place in the world creates a bond between them that is also in part a function of their closeness in age.

They are drawn together in future years because Deborah plays the role for Rachel and Gabriel that Florence refused to play; she is faithful "daughter" to Rachel until her death, and she watches over Gabriel until he is safely in the fold of the church. Upon Florence's departure from the South, she and Deborah are tied together through the years by the same thing that had brought them together as girls: their sense of the wrong that has been committed against them because they are women. After Deborah's marriage to Gabriel, Florence becomes her confidante during Gabriel's affair with Esther and in the following years as Gabriel's illegitimate son, Royal, grows up unclaimed by Gabriel. Hard-working, committed, invisible Deborah sees much more than Gabriel gives her credit for seeing, and she reports what she sees to Florence. There is nothing Florence can do to assist her other than offer words of comfort, but the fact that Deborah keeps writing to her points out at least one nondestructive way in which black women interact in the novel. Deborah writes to Florence "in a rhythm that seemed to remark each crisis in her life with Gabriel" (p. 88), thereby tying them together again in a way that emphasizes the significant role men have played in each of their lives. Exemplary Deborah obviously cannot find among her fellow parishioners anyone to whom she could tell that their pastor and her husband has had an affair and produced an illegitimate son whom he has watched grow up but has refused to claim. So Florence serves a necessary function of support for Deborah; she provides thereby at least minimal relief from the mental torture Deborah must frequently have felt when contemplating the behavior of her husband.

The two women engage in a hopeless little conspiracy against Gabriel when Deborah writes what Florence hopes she can use to make him less severe in his attitudes toward Elizabeth and John. However, just as Deborah was unable to confront Gabriel directly, Florence will be equally unable to do so. Even as she uses the letter telling of Gabriel's infidelity to threaten him immediately following the tarry service, we are not convinced that she will show it to Elizabeth; and should she find the strength to do so, we are not convinced that it will make a significant change in Gabriel's behavior.

Elizabeth and Florence represent the only instance in the novel in which black women of different generations manage to get along very well. One possible reason for this is that Florence may now have reached the stage in her own life where she symbolically needs a daughter, for she is old enough to be Elizabeth's mother. They are initially drawn together, though, because of the work they do and because of the fact that they are both recuperating from the deaths of the men in their lives. Also, in their jobs as cleaning women in a Wall Street office building, they are both isolated from the rest of the workers. Elizabeth refuses to socialize over a cup of coffee after work because she must hurry home to take care of the six-month-old John. Florence has hardened into unsociability; Elizabeth sees Florence as a woman who "moved in a silent ferocity of dignity which barely escaped being ludicrous. She was extremely unpopular . . . she seemed to have nothing to laugh or gossip about. She came to work, and she did her work, and she left" (p. 177).

Perhaps it is respect for or curiosity about this woman who marches so "grimly down the halls, her head tied up in a rag, a bucket and a mop in her hands" (p. 177) that prompts Elizabeth to have a cup of coffee with Florence on that rare occasion when Florence extends the invitation. Elizabeth imagines that there is a story behind Florence's present posture; she imagines that Florence "must once have been very rich, and had lost her money; and she felt for her, as one fallen woman for another, a certain kinship" (p. 177). But the romance merely shades a gloomier reality; Florence is who she is and acts as she does because of a man. Elizabeth provides Florence with the medium for confession, just as Florence has provided Deborah with the outlet to relay her tales about Gabriel. It is fascinating to discover how Florence relates her tale, for she embues her relationship with her husband, Frank, with an unexpected aura of romance. Certainly there is some bitterness in her memories as well, but she prefers to remember her life with Frank in a slightly less than realistic way.

According to Florence's tale to Elizabeth, Frank had tended to irresponsibility, but he had "adored her . . . and satisfied her every whim" (p. 177). The Frank Florence has presented in her section of the novel differs in obvious ways from the image she recalls for Elizabeth; the new image paints her as the suffering widow who has been dealt an unfortunate hand. She does not mention that she and Frank were no longer together at his death, or that he had left her for another woman. True to her sense of pride and to her need not to confront failure directly, she only mentions how "like a man" it was that Frank would not take out life insurance because he thought he "would live forever" (p. 177). Such a picture portrays Florence even more as the elderly woman in need of sympathy because circumstances and an unthinking man have forced her out of the security of her home and into work as a cleaning woman. Elizabeth never learns that, even if Frank had taken out life insurance, Florence would probably have had to fight in order to get any of it. Instead, Elizabeth sees Florence as a wronged woman who needs the sympathy of someone who shares that "certain kinship."

Florence's surprising baring of her personal life to Elizabeth makes Elizabeth reciprocate. Initially, Elizabeth is astonished that the proud Florence is so in need of "confession," but that need is quickly mirrored in herself as she tells Florence all about Richard and John. Florence's "age and kindness" lead Elizabeth to trust her, again emphasizing the symbolic mother/daughter relationship (in its ideal state, that is) that quickly develops between the two women—in addition to the sharing of personal lives that makes them confidantes to each other; their assumed kinship also emphasizes that the act of confession, which is tied to the churches in which the women have grown up, is another dimension of their need for repentance. Elizabeth's confession that John "ain't got no daddy" (p. 181) leads Florence to her usual theme of the victimization of women at the hands of men. "I ain't never," she says, "seen it to fail. Look like ain't no woman born what don't get walked over by some no-count man. Look like ain't no woman nowhere but ain't been dragged down in the dirt by some man, and left there, too, while he go on about his business" (p. 181). Elizabeth's clarification that Richard died rather than leaving her merely brings Florence's tirade to a halt; it does not change her mind about the general position of women in the world and of men's abilities to use and abuse them. Even in death, men leave women unpleasant legacies: "The menfolk, they die, all right. And it's us women who walk around, like the Bible says, and mourn. The menfolk, they die, and it's over for them, but we women, we have to keep on living and try to forget what they done to us" (p. 182). To Florence, men are not to be forgiven either in life or in death.

How Florence presents Gabriel to Elizabeth is relevant, for Elizabeth will shortly meet him at Florence's house. Florence refuses to forgive Gabriel for any of his shortcomings, and she tells Elizabeth to be wary of him. Elizabeth can only see that a sister is not responding to her brother in a sisterly fashion; when she meets Gabriel, she believes Florence's evaluation of him has been exaggerated, for she watches him "unable to find in the man before her the brother whom Florence so despised" (p. 183). It is perhaps because Florence knows and can see more than Elizabeth that she makes such a nuisance of herself in intervening in the lives of Gabriel and Elizabeth, and perhaps out of a sense of guilt that she has brought them together. Like any mother, Florence has gathered from experience what Elizabeth can only learn by gathering from similar experiences. Therefore, Florence can only watch over her, like a powerless fairy godmother, until the daughter has seen the same things the mother has.

Elizabeth's blindness to Gabriel's true personality and her willingness to take him at face value as the dedicated preacher he presents himself as being is tied to her desperate need to find a source of comfort and support in some man, and to absolve her guilt. To her, Gabriel represents, first of all, the possibility that God has not judged her too harshly for the sin she has committed by bearing John out of wedlock. Here is a kind, gentle man, she believes, who knows of her sin but has not condemned her for sinning. Gabriel seems so understanding and good; if such a man, who is also a representative of God, is lenient in judging her, then perhaps she will not have to face eternal damnation on Judgment Day. Gabriel gives Elizabeth the hope that she can be safe from the wrath of God, just as he gives her the hope that he will provide earthly comfort and security to John and herself. The two levels of safety, both on earth and in heaven, draw her to him; she sees that safety as lying before her, "like a hiding-place hewn in the side of the mountain" (p. 186), and therefore cannot hear what the mothering Florence has to tell her. When Gabriel then gives her the formula for completing her safety—"call on the Lord . . . He'll lift you up"—she eventually responds by joining the church. Fear of the consequences of sin, remorse, and regret all bring Elizabeth to accept the role as the uplifted "handmaiden to God's minister" (p. 188); she has deliberately pushed Florence's warnings into the background in the face of a greater need within herself to have a man in her life and to escape the guilt of her past life.

Elizabeth's marriage to Gabriel perhaps ties her and Florence even more closely together. Out of respect for Elizabeth's hopes for the marriage, or for some other reason, Florence never reveals the details of Gabriel's past life to Elizabeth; nor does she show her the letter Deborah had written. Instead, Florence intrudes herself into the marriage as much as possible in an effort to blunt the effect of Gabriel's outrages and harsh judging of Elizabeth when she is only guilty of sins minimally comparable to his own. The two women become partners in their knowledge of the present unhappiness Gabriel creates in all of their lives, and they bear the burden of him as best they can. Yet both are willing to plod along, hour by hour and day by day, throughout the years, instead of trying to bring about some kind of fundamental change in their lives with Gabriel. For fourteen years, Florence observes the relationship between Elizabeth and Gabriel, and for fourteen years she keeps silent with the information that could possibly give Elizabeth some leverage in the marriage. The information would certainly allow Elizabeth to know that she is not the only one who has sinned before marriage, even if it failed to give her the strength to confront Gabriel and demand better treatment. Still, Florence keeps silent, and Gabriel stands forever as a major force in the lives of these two women. In many ways, their lives become calculated reactions to him and thereby continue the tradition of women centering their lives upon and in reaction to the men who come into most direct contact with them.

The major concerns of the two women set them up in an adversary position to the men in their lives. They form a bond against Gabriel, after the marriage, just as Florence and Deborah have formed a less tangible bond against him. Their time, but especially that of Elizabeth, must be spent in symbolic combat—what will please Gabriel, what will not, how to prevent his wrath from being evoked. The bond between Elizabeth and Florence becomes another measure of the extent to which the women in *Go Tell It on the Mountain* have their lives predetermined by that restricting framework of the church. Elizabeth endures all because she can see herself only as wife and mother, and she hopes to be forgiven for her earlier sins. Florence fails to push too far because she, likewise, can see very little for women beyond the traditional roles. If they were to confront Gabriel and bring about a divorce, Elizabeth would have to go to work. We know from Florence's and Elizabeth's early days at the office building that both, but especially Florence, hated the cleaning they had been forced into doing. To Florence, that humiliation could have been prevented if the man in her life had taken care of her as he should have. And both women know what a hard time they had (Florence alone and Elizabeth with only one child); how much more difficult it would be for Elizabeth to work and take care of four children with a fifth one on the way. The roles the women are in, therefore, are perpetuated by practical realities, realities that also define the nature of their friendship. It is wonderfully romantic to have a loving husband, wonderfully dreary to be without a husband at all. The realistic medium, not a happy one, is to have a husband who has forsaken romance and often forsakes courtesy, who may sometimes beat his wife, but who, in spite of all of that, continues to provide the necessities of life that prevent the wife from having to work.

We could, if we believed in perverse inversions, say that Elizabeth has, through her own choice, managed to make a way for herself in the world, a way that ensures her safety and the food and shelter necessary for her children. Unfortunately, such a perversion, no matter what it may net in terms of practical realities, nevertheless depicts the character in a situation where all of her actions are limited or have powerful negative consequences and where her positive potential for growth is stifled by the very limited choices she is allowed to make. If one is in prison, the fact that she can read or go out for exercise or shower or visit the dining hall does not change the basic reality that all of these "choices" are undercut by her imprisonment. Whatever good she may effect in that prison environment, however healthy she may keep herself and her cellmates, she is still confined, and all of her relationships are dictated by that confinement. Florence and Elizabeth can be only as much to each other as their narrow conception allows and within the limits it has placed upon them as female characters. They are destined to react, seldom to initiate, and their lives of reaction are always informed by the knowledge of the consequences in store for them if they should dare to become initiators of action.

How the women are presented to us narrationally affects how we perceive their characters and how we respond to the actions that they use to define their guilt. What we see of Elizabeth and Florence is first revealed through the eyes of fourteen-year-old John. Through Baldwin's use of a third-person limited point of view, we see only what John sees in the confrontations among the adults, and we can only agree or disagree with his evaluations on the basis of what is being presented to us. There are certainly points of irony in the voice, and there are points at which the sophisticated Baldwin superimposes his mature analyses upon the adolescent John. Basically, though, we form impressions in Part One of the novel through John's eyes; these impressions will be verified or gainsaid in Part Two, when Gabriel, Elizabeth, and Florence are revealed from their own third-person limited points of view in their prayer sections.

John sympathizes with the women against his father in Part One. He is perhaps somewhat awed by the spirited response his Aunt Florence has to his father in the scene following Roy's injury, for here is someone who does not quake with fear when confronted with his father's stony face and his silent judgment. Yet John is also able to see that his aunt's spirit is contained by something he does not understand. His mother gives his aunt the sign to keep quiet, showing John that his father exerts control over even those who would contend with him. And he sees, too, that even as Elizabeth motions to Florence to keep the peace in the family, his mother's mouth tightens "bitterly" and she drops her eyes. John sees enough and can surmise enough to realize that there are many levels of confrontation going on among the adults and that the women choose to postpone part of it for a while. Since John has been portrayed in a warm scene with his mother, and has not presented his aunt as a negative character—as he has presented his father—it is only logical to assume that his sympathies in the scene with Roy are more with the women in response to his father than they are with Gabriel. John, who sees Gabriel as the source of the majority of his afflictions, in turn sees the women as potential opposites from that position. His mother is as much in the church as is his father, but there is at least that ambivalence in her that suggests to John that she is not as fiery a representative of the straight and narrow path as Gabriel, not as universally exacting in her bid to keep her children within the Christian fold.

John's identification with the women, even before Gabriel slaps Elizabeth, leads us to identify with them, and to reject Gabriel even more vehemently after the physical violence. John detects from Florence's tone of voice early in the scene that the situation, the extent of Roy's wound, is not as desperate as Gabriel presents it as being. When Gabriel slaps the pregnant Elizabeth, then, we see it as an action far out of proportion to any retaliation that the situation might have warranted. And we are also shocked that this man, who has been presented to us as controlling behavior effectively with gestures, looks, and his mere presence, resorts to such brutishness. We therefore see Gabriel in his own form of desperation. Because things do not work in the ways they usually do, and because he senses that his position as the head of the household is being threatened, he resorts to the only thing he has left to retain that control: sheer physical strength.

In these, his formative years, when John spends more of his time with female adults than with males, it is perhaps only natural that the identification should be more with the females. The violent scene he witnesses, though, points out several things that may be relevant to his own development as an adult male. First of all, the women are almost completely helpless before his father. When Gabriel beats Roy for cursing him, Elizabeth cannot interfere; it is only when Florence reaches out to hold the belt that Elizabeth gathers Roy into her arms, "crying as John had never seen a woman, or anybody, cry before" (p. 49). Florence's action may be considered daring, but it has not prevented Gabriel from beating Roy. John sees, therefore, that there is a certain power that can accrue to him simply because of his gender. That possibility for his own development is toned down, however, by the fact that he has so far failed to identify with his father; he imagines choosing the path of the mind as a way of getting away from the emotional church to which Gabriel belongs and of escaping the factory job Gabriel has. He can step away from his father if he wishes, but he can also be like him in accepting the notion that power and control are masculine virtues, not feminine ones.

The extent of Gabriel's influence is also pointed out to John in this scene. Gabriel has become the center of and manages to control a group of six individuals, two of them adult women. What that could mean to John is further toned down in that he is often identified with things that are traditionally considered more feminine; he is the one who must take care of his younger brothers and sisters, he must cook and clean when his mother is indisposed, and he must efface himself in the presence of his father just as his mother sometimes does. John is also presented, in contrast to Gabriel the factory worker, as fragile, quiet, studious, and sensitive to pursuits of the mind. John knows the world, therefore, from the eyes of his father as well as from those of his mother and, during these impressionable years, the mother's view is prominent in his mind, and his sympathy toward her as woman is greater. It is therefore not surprising that he wants to kill his father for striking his mother.

John similarly sympathizes with Florence. The final image we get of her, which is rendered through John's eyes, causes us to continue our sympathy with her as well. To John, Florence has been strong, resilient, perhaps all-enduring. After the tarry service, however, he gets a sharp insight into how things are changing around him and affecting those he loves, including his aunt. He observes her approach toward the subway: "She started slowly across the street, moving, he thought with wonder, like an old woman" (p. 219). The wondering surprise that John feels about his aged aunt makes us realize as well how broken down she is. She walks away alone while the others proceed home in a group. The comment from Elisha, John's Sunday school teacher, following John's observation of Florence, that "*she* ain't going to be out to service this morning" (p. 219), reinforces the lonely, drooping image of a tired old woman. It conveys to us, again, that Florence will be powerless against Gabriel even if she chooses to use that letter she has held on to for so many years.

Through John's eyes, we have been led to sympathize with Florence and Elizabeth in Part One of the novel. When we get to Part Two, where Elizabeth's and Florence's backgrounds are revealed to us, we are already inclined to respond favorably to them as we get more information about them. The force of the description of the scene in which Florence leaves her mother's cabin encourages us to attempt to see things from her point of view, just as we have felt earlier that she was particularly oppressed in her mother's cabin because of the mother and because of Gabriel. We understand her need to leave, and we do not judge her harshly for going. We are led to be on the side of adventure and self-determination and to reject duty and responsibility. Our sympathies are guided in part because Florence becomes a parallel underdog to John, just as Elizabeth will later in her section of the novel. Florence wants freedom from her mother in the way that John wants freedom from Gabriel in Part One, and again we respond to the need in the oppressed to find release from the oppression.

We are also led to sympathize with Florence as she suffers through her failed expectations in New York. The sympathy prevails in spite of Florence's faults, for she is certainly not without them. She is rude to Frank's guests and wants him to adhere to middle-class virtues as her husband. Because we have already seen what she has left and know the circumstances that have formed her expectations, we hope that she can triumph in spite of her faults and in spite of her own indictments of herself. Unfortunately, sympathetically as she is portrayed, what we observe is a woman who destroys her marriage and harbors guilt. The guilty dilemma she wrestles with during the tarry service is a larger version of the guilt John feels for having masturbated, thinking that that sin will cause his soul to be lost unless he comes into the fold of the Saints.

Narrationally, "Elizabeth's Prayer" is also set up as a parallel to the sympathies that have been evoked during John's and Florence's sections of the novel. Elizabeth, like Florence and John, is a person in opposition to the parental authority in her life. She seeks freedom from her aunt just as John seeks freedom from Gabriel and Florence freedom from her mother. All three are drawn as victims: Florence is victimized by her mother's preference for Gabriel; John is victimized by his father's preference for Roy and hatred for him; and Elizabeth is victimized by her aunt's hatred of her father. All three are therefore put in situations where there is a natural evocation of sympathies in their favor. By contrast, what we feel for Gabriel is disgust that he is not using his privileged position of love and opportunity as wisely as he should. Florence suffers initially because of him, but he is too dense and too self-centered to realize that. John and Elizabeth suffer continually because of him, but he is again too self-centered to reflect overly long on the conditions of either one. From his point of view, children should simply obey their parents, and wives should take care of their husbands and children. Gabriel operates at a surface level with powers he thinks have been bestowed upon him by the supernatural; he seldom, if ever, operates at the level of conscience to respond to human needs in this world. His first contact with the need for repentance emphasizes the peculiar context into which he has placed that need: "He wanted power—he wanted to know himself to be the Lord's anointed, His well-beloved, and worthy, nearly, of that snow-white dove which had been sent down from Heaven to testify that Jesus was the Son of God" (p. 94). Power is always the surface action that reveals little about depths because it does not have to concern itself with such trivial things. It also identifies Gabriel with the perpetrators of victimization. Florence and Elizabeth, on the other hand, in part because they desire freedom rather than power, are ultimately reflective individuals who are identified with John in their concerns for other than the mere necessities of life.

Baldwin's identification with Elizabeth is also tied to the fact that he gives her the same nicknames he had when he was growing up. Those names, ones of outcast from his own youth, become terms of endearment between Elizabeth and Richard. At times, Richard calls Elizabeth "Sandwich Mouth," "Funnyface," and "Frogeyes."[3] Richard has the love for Elizabeth that Baldwin was never able to elicit from his stepfather. Elizabeth as character, therefore, lives out one of the fantasies that Baldwin was never able to live out as a physically unattractive, outcast adolescent. Loved and accepted not only by Richard but by her father as well, Elizabeth becomes a kind of alter ego to Baldwin—at least in these elements of her life. (I am not suggesting that Baldwin is intending to draw direct parallels; I am merely suggesting that his narrative identification with certain characters grows out of particular incidents and characters in his own life.)

Sympathy is also created for Elizabeth in the scene in which she must confront the white policemen after Richard's arrest. As authority figures, the policemen are far more potentially destructive than Gabriel, but the parallels between John and Elizabeth are nevertheless continued. Her rage and terror at confronting them and seeing how unconcerned they are about Richard is comparable to the helpless rage John feels when he is forced to confront the father against whom he has no power. For John, Gabriel might just as well be all the white policemen in the world and God the Father combined; that is the extent of control that John feels Gabriel has over his life. Elizabeth too finds herself in a situation in which she has no control and in which her physical person is threatened even as she is assaulted mentally by the insults of the officers. She is victimized more threateningly than John is and perhaps only slightly less so than Richard himself is. (In fact, in this scene, Richard is the most sympathetic of the adult black male characters presented in the novel. Notice, though, that it is precisely when he is victimized and weeping—that is, when he is evincing "feminine" features—that he evokes the most pity in us. As the swaggering, distant, aloof young man earlier, he has not drawn similar responses from us. Remember, too, that it is the sensitive qualities in Richard—his love of books and arts—that Elizabeth wants to keep alive in John; those features connected to John therefore give Richard one kind of "saving grace" by placing him in opposition to Gabriel.)

The extensive antagonism between male and female in the novel raises questions, finally, about John's sympathetic feelings for the women. The answers to the narrational problems lie in the fact that the novel is autobiographical, which clouds a pure division of sympathies solely along male and female lines. On the one hand, Baldwin has given Elizabeth some of the traits identified with himself as a young man; he has perhaps also built into her character some of the things he has identified with his own mother, such as the rapid succession of babies. These elicit sympathy from him as male in spite of the femininity attached to them. On the other hand, Gabriel is drawn in part on Baldwin's stepfather and John on Baldwin himself; therefore, from one point of view, Gabriel is the most unattractive of Baldwin's characters. Female sympathies are against him because Baldwin's sympathies are against him.

In his essays, Baldwin has chronicled the difficulties he had growing up in a household where his stepfather considered him ugly and "strange"; Gabriel often mentions John's big eyes, which he considers almost repulsive.[4] Baldwin's hatred for his stepfather, a hatred all the more intense because it had to be restrained, is unleashed upon Gabriel. Although Baldwin as author is older and wiser than Baldwin as oppressed stepson, enough of the venom remains for him to draw the villainous Gabriel sharply and clearly. With Baldwin's growth, though, and the assumption of his own role as a man, there is also enough identification with Gabriel for Baldwin to leave undisturbed some of the basic traits he identifies with masculinity. Gabriel may be oppressive from the young Baldwin's point of view, but the adult Baldwin, the writer, finds little wrong with Gabriel's inherent right to assume power; it is his abuse of that power that is the problem. Presumably, if Gabriel were benignly supportive of his wives, his children, and his sister, Baldwin would still approve of his customary role as head of the household, and of the privileges—freedom from cooking and other domestic chores, expecting his wife to care for the children, obedience from wife and offspring—that are due him as a male.

The part of the novel in which Gabriel is pictured most unattractively is the part of his life in the South, with which the young Baldwin, and the young John, are unfamiliar. On that territory, Baldwin can let his imaginative indictment take its course, remaining in a way symbolically removed from that treatment of Gabriel. Baldwin's general negative notions of the South may also be relevant here.[5] Through a fictional license, Baldwin can let his avenging imagination create a kind of wish fulfillment lowering of Gabriel's and the stepfather's positions; Gabriel literally wallows in his own vomit during that life. The power Baldwin has not had over his stepfather in real life is thus given special force in the power of the pen to reduce enemies to drunkards and whoremongers. But that is not the final portrait we have of Gabriel; John's life with him is in New York, after the Southern adventures, and when Gabriel is brutishly oppressive.

Thus, Baldwin is torn between wanting to strike out at what has oppressed him and masculine identification with the perpetrator of that oppression; and the portraits of the women get caught in this tension. It is a dilemma that occurred only in this first, autobiographical, novel. In the fictional works following *Go Tell It on the Mountain*, Baldwin would not be so torn between the forces of good and evil as they are manifested in one character. That problem is solved not only because the other novels are less consciously autobiographical, but because Baldwin allows more of his other male characters to narrate their own stories; the omniscient narration in *Go Tell It on the Mountain* forces the mediating voice to be considered with that of the character. It allows more direction of sentiments, sympathies, and evaluations, and makes Baldwin more consciously a character within his own story than he would be in some of the later works.[6]

We understand how the women have been manipulated into feeling guilty, and we understand how our sympathies are being directed in response to them. From their own points of view in the novel, however, the women are hopelessly mired in judging themselves by the yardstick of the church and by Gabriel as its most ardent representative. As objective readers of the novel, we can see that Baldwin finally intends Gabriel as a negative character. My analysis of each of the women characters, however, is predicated upon the assumption that they are too closely involved in the situation to see Gabriel in other than a victorious manner; their responses to him presume their inferiority in the face of his superiority, whether that superiority is interpreted in terms of morals, of independence, or of physical strength. The following quotation, lifted from a sermon by Gabriel, serves well to illustrate the strictures the black women in *Go Tell It on the Mountain* have internalized and the kind of criteria they shape their lives in direct reaction to:

> For let us remember that the wages of sin is death; that it is written, and cannot fail, the soul that sinneth, it shall die. Let us remember that we are born in sin, in sin did our mothers conceive us—sin reigns in all our members, sin is the foul heart's natural liquid, sin looks out of the eye, amen, and leads to lust, sin is in the hearing of the ear, and leads to folly, sin sits on the tongue, and leads to murder. Yes! Sin is the only heritage of the natural man, sin bequeathed us by our natural father, that fallen Adam, whose apple sickens and will sicken all generations living, and generations yet unborn! (pp. 103–4)

The women have an ingrained sense of guilt that is aggravated by the constant self-sacrificing choices they are forced to make. Their paths to heaven are ones in which they must willingly dissolve their personhood on the altars of the male egos around them. In the world about which Baldwin writes, women may be the ones who open church services on Saturday night with their singing, but they are not ultimately the ones who can most frequently commune with God; the men do. The women may pray, sing, shout, and admonish children, but they must defer to the minister in serious questions concerning behavior, or about organization within the church. Thus the women find themselves serving men, God, and the church, and they find subservience as the state of existence men have defined for them.

Operation within the church in Baldwin's novel presupposes that one is forever in need of a state of grace ("only rebirth every hour could stay the hand of Satan" [p. 113]), that sin is dominant in one's life, that the state of existence stretching from Adam's Fall made man, but especially woman, guilty from birth. After all, it was woman who made man fall, and it is through women giving birth that sin continues. So the guilt on the part of the women is especially acute. That prehistoric state, combined with the tradition of the black church as it was established in the community, put black women in the serving state that suggests that they are forever atoning for their mere existence—or should be.

The God of *Go Tell It on the Mountain* is not the anthropomorphic God of the black folk communities that the Grimes family resembles so much; He is the God of the Old Testament, ever ready to bring down fire and brimstone upon the heads of those who fail to keep His commandments. His potential ability to forgive is overshadowed by His ability, and what the characters believe is his eagerness, to punish. They do not harbor comforting images of the Jesus of the "Go Down, Death" funeral sermon of James Weldon Johnson, the Jesus whose bosom is like those of so many of the matriarchally stereotypical black women portrayed in Baldwin's fiction. There is no mercy in the bosom Baldwin's characters most frequently encounter; there is only the wrath that can hurl them forever into the burning fires of Hell. That threat draws them to what they fear; they do not come to God because they wholeheartedly believe that He loves them above all else. If they refuse to seek shelter in His bosom, they may find themselves in predicaments perhaps a million times worse than the ones they have experienced on earth. Imagined damnation serves as the purest motivation for crying before the altar of the Lord; the threat of Hell wins out over the promise of Heaven.

Florence, Deborah, Esther, and Elizabeth, with their biblical and biblical-sounding names, are the four women in Baldwin's early fiction who come closest to his traditional, sometimes stereotypical conception of the black woman in relation to the church. I do not mean that the women are happiest in that state; I mean they are most acutely conscious of their state of uncleanliness and work hardest to try to atone for it—or at least they work hardest in terms of conscience in shaping their lives and actions in response to the "sins" they believe they have committed. Florence, the most outspoken and rebellious of the women in *Go Tell It on the Mountain*, nevertheless shapes her life, finally, in response to how others have perceived her for breaking away from the church.

Florence's character is built in direct opposition to Gabriel's. The freedom she may have felt for refusing to remain in that traditional church in which her mother found herself and in which her brother would eventually end up is undercut by the fact that she still judges herself in terms of the values her mother and Gabriel consider paramount. What Florence knows about the shortcomings of those who profess Christian belief has still not freed her completely from those individuals and the strictures they constantly present to her. She finally undercuts her own independence by temporarily crawling back into the sanctuary that she had left so many years before.

In the scene surrounding Roy's injury, we see a Florence who is strong and secure and who appears not to be overcome with guilt; this is a sharp contrast to the burden-carrying images we get of her later on. Florence tries to force Gabriel to live up to the life he professes to believe in although she herself has lived a life outside the church. "Oh, no, you ain't," Florence tells him when he says he will have questions for Elizabeth. "You ain't going to be starting none of that mess this evening. You know right doggone well that Roy don't never ask *nobody* if he can do *nothing*—he just go right ahead and do like he pleases. Elizabeth sure can't put no ball and chain on him. She got her hands full right here in this house, and it ain't her fault if Roy got a head just as hard as his father's" (pp. 43–44). She declares that Gabriel "was born a fool, and always done been a fool, and ain't never going to change," and that Gabriel's children will do their best to keep his life from being "*their* life" (p. 44). Florence's last sentiments echo John's almost exactly, for he feels particularly oppressed by Gabriel, whose life is one of straitlaced theoretical adherence to scriptures, but a failure to put those beliefs into practice. Gabriel provides sustenance without nurturing and shelter without comfort. He lives up to the letter of his promise to Elizabeth to claim John as his own son, but the spirit is absent.

When Gabriel tries to humble Elizabeth by suggesting that his mother, Rachel, would have found a way to keep her son out of trouble, Florence again forces him to face truth instead of myth. "She was my mother, too," says Florence, "and I recollect, if you don't, you being brought home many a time more dead than alive. She didn't find no way to stop *you*. She wore herself out beating on you, just like you been wearing yourself out beating on this boy here. . . . I ain't doing a thing . . . but trying to talk some sense into your big, black, hardhead. You better stop trying to blame everything on Elizabeth and look to your own wrongdoings" (p. 47). Florence serves as Gabriel's unwanted conscience; in the face of his desire to condemn others, she reminds him constantly of his own shortcomings as a young man, many of which are faults he has not yet overcome.

To John, his Aunt Florence is a strong, independent woman who stands up, easily and defiantly, to his father. The independence and defiance have been shaped in reaction to her mother's influence and by the men in her life; they are perpetuated by her own sense of failure and by her sense of guilt. A decision she made for her growth becomes one that haunts her nonetheless. Just as her mother had escaped from her cabin in slavery, Florence had vowed that she would escape from the cabin she shared with Rachel and Gabriel when she realized she had no future there:

> Gabriel was the apple of his mother's eye. If he had never been born, Florence might have looked forward to a day when she would be released from her unrewarding round of labor, when she might think of her own future and go out to make it. With the birth of Gabriel, which occurred when she was five, her future was swallowed up. There was only one future in that house, and it was Gabriel's—to which, since Gabriel was a manchild, all else must be sacrificed. Her mother did not, indeed, think of it as sacrifice, but as logic: Florence was a girl, and would by and by be married, and have children of her own, and all the duties of a woman; and this being so, her life in the cabin was the best possible preparation for her future life. But Gabriel was a man; he would go out one day into the world to do a man's work, and he needed, therefore, meat, when there was any in the house, and clothes, whenever clothes could be bought, and the strong indulgence of his womenfolk, so that he would know how to be with women when he had a wife. And he needed the education that Florence desired far more than he, and that she might have got if he had not been born. It was Gabriel who was slapped and scrubbed each morning and sent off to the one-room schoolhouse—which he hated, and where he managed to learn, so far as Florence could discover, almost nothing at all. (pp. 72–73)

At twenty-six, Florence makes the decision to leave, but all her experiences tell her that that decision is wrong in the light of the environment in which she has grown up and that she should feel guilty for having made it. To think of herself is to step outside the mold that has been carved out for her and thereby risk public condemnation and perhaps eternal damnation. So begins a reign of guilt that will haunt Florence throughout her life; to think of herself, to achieve her independence, is to abandon those who need her. Because she has no frame of reference for self-conception other than that which is so exacting in its requirements for obedience, she is torn between her desperate need for independence and the externally imposed teachings that she should forget about herself and commit her life to others.

The forces pulling at Florence conspicuously surround her extended decision-making process. Her white employer's proposal that she become his concubine encourages her to leave, yet her sick mother and Gabriel's effort to make her feel guilty encourage her to stay. Florence is thus torn between duty and self-determination. To stay home in the South would be to dissolve into destructive routine and lost hope. To go to New York is to dare, to expect, to believe, as many blacks in that Great Migration believed, that things could be better than the predetermined slots that awaited them in the South. So Florence goes—against nature, according to her mother and brother—and makes a life for herself in New York.

Florence's decision to leave is one of the major points of Jacqueline E. Orsagh's argument that Baldwin's female characters are unlike most of those in American and English literature in that they transcend stereotypes to become believable characters who *act*. Most of Baldwin's women characters are certainly believable, as Orsagh maintains, but the ideas of their transcendence of stereotypes and their wide-ranging actions are questionable. They may act, but Orsagh fails to consider the consequences of their actions. They act, but especially for the early portraits of the black women I am studying, they are not as free or as secure in their actions as Orsagh suggests. She says "they act and are not condemned," which is sometimes true for some of the women; rather than *being* condemned, several of the black women *condemn themselves*, as Florence does. Orsagh ignores the fact that Baldwin has woven this trait into their characters.[7]

Florence's action, her decision to go to New York, leads directly to her guilt. Although she manages to cage it initially, it begins a slow process of tearing down its prison walls. Years later, as Florence is on her knees praying at the tarry service, her guilt circulates freely. No matter what her early actions suggest to the contrary, she was and is a woman acutely aware of stepping out of her place, out of the role predetermined for her. The guilt that daring breeds haunts her at sixty in the form of a dream she cannot force from her subconscious. In the dream, her mother, Gabriel, Deborah, and her husband come to curse her for her negligences and failures. She would beg forgiveness of them, but realizes her sins are so extensive that only God can forgive her; thus, she falls wailing and weeping before the altar on the night of the tarry service. Her knowledge that she is dying makes her repentance stronger, or so it seems initially.

But what, precisely, are Florence's sins? She says she has denied Rachel on her deathbed, scorned and mocked Gabriel's ministry, mocked Deborah's barrenness, and committed unnamed crimes against her husband, Frank. Her harshness in judging herself, in feeling guilty for aspiring to better things, shows that she has not escaped the traditional slot that was carved out for her, for the reality of her existence has been quite a contrast to the dream. She says her greatest sin is pride, which has caused her to reach out beyond her lot in life, but such desire seems more than tolerable and forgivable. To all those who pursue her in the dream, she has been reasonably generous. She has served Rachel for years, whether or not she loved her. The choice she made was an emotionally tearing one, but nevertheless a valid one: should a child sacrifice her life to an aged, dying parent or deny that parent and live for herself, especially when another sibling is at home? While it is true that black communities are notoriously unforgiving of children who neglect aged and especially dying parents, and that extenuating circumstances are inconsiderable, Florence's case nevertheless presents some worthy points. Her mother will use her but never value her in the ways she values Gabriel. Gabriel will use her equally and never expect Florence to want more out of life than to serve her family. If she marries one of the men "who lusted after her," she will merely "exchange her mother's cabin for one of theirs" and "raise their children and so go down, toil-blasted, into as it were a common grave" (p. 74). To stay would make Florence into a non-entity, a body defined by the functions it executes: daughter, sister, wife, mother. Leaving, though, creates an overwhelming burden of guilt and, ironically, no escape at all from the traditional roles.

How Florence could blame herself for questioning Gabriel's ministry is again a measure of how guilt has induced a dream that dwarfs reality. She has seen enough of Gabriel to know that it would be difficult to clean up such a pig and place him in a pulpit, yet her subconscious allows him to pursue her in the dream for mocking and scorning his ministry. It deserves to be mocked and scorned, and Gabriel deserves to be thrown out of the pulpit. His self-righteousness unfits him for the humbleness espoused by Jesus, and his egotistical belief that he has been chosen to father a royal line is uniquely despicable. Gabriel uses religion as a weapon to keep people feeling guilty and to maintain his superiority over them. He marries Deborah in order to nurture a perverted image he has of himself, and he marries Elizabeth for similar perversions of religious intention. Florence has seen Gabriel "vomit-covered" and drunk; she has seen him fake a conversion and practically curse through a baptizing; she knows he has been unfaithful to Deborah; she has seen him mistreat John; and she has seen him slap Elizabeth like the lowest of unconverted heathens. Yet she feels guilty, at least in the dream, for holding bad thoughts about the purity of his beliefs. Truly Florence is afraid of encountering God after death.

Her dream-guilt that she has mocked Deborah's barrenness is also fallacious when compared with reality, for there is no evidence in the novel to support that assertion. Evidence is quite the contrary—that Florence had become Deborah's best friend after the rape and that they had grown up together in trying to understand the world and the men around them. Then, too, Florence was in New York before Deborah married Gabriel and her barrenness was confirmed; how could she blame herself for that? Also, it is Florence in whom Deborah confides about her life with Gabriel and the affair he has had with Esther. Unattractive, long-suffering Deborah has only one friend in the novel, and that friend is Florence. Instead of seeing Deborah as accuser, Florence should see her as her one source of consolation in that disturbing, recurring dream.

What the dream-turned-nightmare reveals about Florence is that the many decisions she has made years before have not been free of the influence of a church-based conscience. Florence's relationship to Deborah, for example, has been very positive; that Deborah is also a part of the nightmare that haunts Florence reinforces the notion that "sinning" pervades all areas of these women's lives. Because Florence knows, subconsciously, that she has failed her mother, the guilt surrounding that one incident permeates others about which she should have a relatively positive feeling. Again, such a response is tied to that church-based evaluation; how can anyone who has sinned against one brother, so the logic goes, feel good about the good deed done for another? For the sake of one's soul, peace must be made with the wronged brother; failing that, guilt and damnation result. Because Florence feels she has failed in some areas of her life, the total life becomes a nightmare for her.

Florence's life with Frank provides the most damaging evidence that she has not escaped the traditional role cut out for her. His presence in her dreams reflects her failures as a wife. Ironically, she goes to New York to share ten years of married life that are hardly different from what her existence would have been in the South. She judges Frank's performance as breadwinner and husband against the yardstick of her expectations; when he falls short, she becomes the nagging, common wife, uglier in her outbursts, perhaps, than Gabriel in his drunkenness. She had wanted the marriage with Frank, but her guilt may encourage her to see her lot with him as her deserved punishment for all her imagined sins. Frank, surprisingly for Florence, is not unlike many men she might have encountered in the South. He sings the blues, drinks too much, refuses to attend church, and squanders his money in foolish ways.

Florence goes into the marriage with hope that quickly dissolves into the dull throbbing of an unpleasant existence. She had desperately wanted a husband to complement her romantic picture of married life, which makes her disappointment all the more acute when the romance dissolved. The pattern of Frank's habits is another burden Florence cannot escape. He will not save money to buy a house, preferring instead to spend it in ways objectionable to Florence:

> He would come home on Saturday afternoons, already half drunk, with some useless object, such as a vase, which, it had occurred to him, she would like to fill with flowers—she who never noticed flowers and who would certainly never have bought any. Or a hat, always too expensive or too vulgar, or a ring that looked as though it had been designed for a whore. Sometimes it occurred to him to do the Saturday shopping on his way home, so that she would not have to do it; in which case he would buy a turkey, the biggest and most expensive he could find, and several pounds of coffee, it being his belief that there was never enough in the house, and enough breakfast cereal to feed an army for a month. (p. 84)

Anger is Florence's response to Frank's unusual way of showing love and to his drinking to reward himself for what he considers good deeds; her shouting outbursts drive him and his drinking buddies from their home. Even as she accuses his friends of being common and littering up her living room, she sinks to the same level, just as Frank points out. She finds herself left alone with her clean house, her tears, and unplucked turkeys with the heads still on.

Florence had left the South in part to escape the fate of the "common niggers" (p. 67) she despises. She tells Gabriel upon leaving that if he sees her again, she will not be wearing rags like those he has on. Her attitude toward blacks, George Kent suggests, is one that places her in a long line of Baldwin characters who have "absorbed from the dominant culture the concept of blackness as low, contemptible, evil." He further suggests that Florence "founders in a mixture of self-hatred, self-righteousness, sadism, and guilt feelings."[8] Her guilt is certainly prominent, as is her self-hatred, but the self-righteousness pales in comparison to that Gabriel exhibits. To say that Florence is sadistic is perhaps to saddle her with more of a burden than she carries. At least one other critic, though, agrees with Kent's evaluation of Florence's attitude toward blackness. Shirley S. Allen points out that, during the tarry service, "Florence cannot empty her heart of malice, against 'niggers,' against men, and especially against her brother Gabriel."[9] We have seen her responding to her brother Gabriel and to the "low-life niggers" she accuses Frank of bringing home; her attitude toward men is further illustrated in her relationship to Frank.

She sees her destiny with Frank as that of most women in the world, and perhaps that is why she bows to it for ten years: "Looking at his face, it sometimes came to her that all women had been cursed from the cradle; all, in one fashion or another, being given the same cruel destiny, born to suffer the weight of men" (p. 83). She deludes herself into thinking that she masters Frank when he crawls into her arms, stinking drunk and penitent. At those times, she convinces herself that Frank will "come along," that he will "change his ways and consent to be the husband she had traveled so far to find" (p. 83). By the time she discovers that some people are in a perpetual state of "coming along," she also realizes the truth of her delusion that she has any mastery over Frank. Indeed, when he crawls into bed drunk and makes love to her, it is he who exerts an insistent power over her. She is drawn to him, and it is he who becomes her master.

The notion of the sexual act as a source of power and the male sex organ as a weapon is one Baldwin returns to again and again in his works. Females usually submit to the weapon of power, as Florence does here with Frank:

"Sugar-plum, what you want to be so evil with your baby for? Don't you know you done made me go out and get drunk, and I wasn't a-fixing to do that? I wanted to take you out somewhere tonight." And, while he spoke, his hand was on her breast, and his moving lips brushed her neck. And this caused such a war in her as could scarcely be endured. She felt that everything in existence between them was part of a mighty plan for her humiliation. She did not want his touch, and yet she did: she burned with longing and froze with rage. And she felt that he knew this and inwardly smiled to see how easily, on this part of the battlefield, his victory could be assured. But at the same time she felt that his tenderness, his passion, and his love were real. (p. 87)

In *Another Country*, Ida, like Florence, will also submit to the weapon of love, as will Tish in *If Beale Street Could Talk* and Julia in *Just Above My Head*. Baldwin explores the political power inherent in the sexual act in "Going to Meet the Man" and with Officer Bell and Fonny in *If Beale Street Could Talk*.[10]

In the sexual encounters between Florence and Frank, Baldwin also introduces the dual notion of man as sexual master and man as spiritual master (lord). The coaxing, conversion, baptism Florence undergoes with Frank will be acted out much more explicitly and effectively with Fonny and Tish in *If Beale Street Could Talk*. Although Frank approaches Florence in a drunken state of disgrace, he is nevertheless able to call her by the thunder of his sweet talk and change her from anger and disgust with him to sheer physical delight. She may fight with him, as many sinners do with the power of the Holy Ghost, but she ultimately gives in to him to be cleansed and renewed, and to have her faith restored.

After ten years, Frank leaves, but it is Florence who suffers. Alternating between hatred of men and guilt that her marriage has failed, Florence takes no further interest in men, although she is only in her late thirties when the marriage dissolves. (Frank later dies in France.) She indicts herself for her failures as a woman, for her inability to bear the burden of wife that a good Christian woman should. Gabriel's prediction that she would not succeed in New York makes his presence a constant reminder of her own shortcomings. Gabriel is certainly not worthy of emulation, but at least he plays the roles of father and husband that Florence has failed to play as wife and mother. For all his sins, Gabriel is at least successful as far as the outside world is concerned, while Florence, for all her higher desires, is a pathetic old woman. A tainted jealousy of Gabriel may also carry over from Florence's days in the South. As far as Florence can see, the laws of retribution that she had hoped would bring Gabriel low have not caught up with him yet. Instead, she finds that she is the one whose failing health has made her outwardly humble. It is the threat of death that brings her to her knees at the tarry service; if her good health had continued, it is not clear that she would have been so humbled. She turns to the church, as Kent suggests, "as a gesture of desperation,"[11] and, in her case, desperation can only be produced by fear and guilt.

Florence last appears in the novel walking home with Gabriel after the tarry service, during which she threatens to make Deborah's letter known to Elizabeth: "I know you thinking at the bottom of your heart that if you just make *her*, her and her bastard boy, pay enough for her sin, *your* son won't have to pay for yours. But I ain't going to let you do that. You done made enough folks pay for sin, it's time you started paying. . . . It'll make Elizabeth to know . . . that she ain't the only sinner . . . in your holy house. And little Johnny, there—he'll know he ain't the only bastard" (p. 214). Gabriel is self-righteously superior before her, maintaining that God always strikes down the enemies of His anointed. He still believes that he is in the right, that he has been chosen and will be forgiven, and he still uses religion to hammer down those who would question the authority he asserts he has received from God. Before him, Florence diminishes into a tired, sick old woman who may be well-intentioned but whose spirit will not stand the test of confronting the obstacle that Gabriel places before her. She is alone and tragic; the image of her leaving the group to take her subway to an empty house, disease, and death is truly pathetic. Gabriel, personification of evil, has family and neighbors to accompany him; he has battered thoroughly all his earthly opposition, including his sister. We feel that Florence will bring no further change in Gabriel's life. If she has held on to the letter for thirty years, she is unlikely to reveal it now. Love does not hold her back, nor does fear; but the spirit necessary to accomplish any major goal seems to have been drained from her. If her weeping before the altar was genuine, she will turn from threatening Gabriel to setting her own house in order before she dies ("Set thine house in order" is the biblical text she hears during the tarry service).[12] Sadly, this woman of so much drive, energy, and hope has been beaten down to a very traditional role for elderly black women in black communities; in compensation for her failures in the world, a possible option is for her to lose herself in the bosom of Jesus. For all her desire to escape, she could end up in exactly the same place as perhaps 90 percent of the black women who never left the South. In the greatest irony, she may become the traditional female supplicant seeking her Master, the Lover of all the lost.

Deborah, the opposite of Florence, epitomizes the black woman in Baldwin's early fiction who has not an ounce of independence or positive self-conception about herself. She lives her life as if it were predetermined from the beginnings of time; the slot was cut out and all she had to do was fit into it. She does not question her existence or the things that happen to her. The most important thing that happens to her, or at least it has the potential to be most significant in terms of shaping her view of the world and of her self, is her gang rape by a group of whites when she is sixteen. Certainly the incident makes her reflect upon men, but she does not go far beyond that. She never really blames the whites that she has been raped; rather, she quietly accepts the attack as somehow being the lot of an individual like herself. Her rape becomes a kind of cross; by having her body attacked by the white men, and symbolically destroyed the way Jesus' body was literally destroyed on the cross, she is somehow brought closer to Him. It is almost as if the degradation she suffers is itself her purification. And indeed she treats it as if it were such; after the rape, she becomes the exemplary model of behavior for the church.

Her role in the church blinds her to Gabriel's true nature, at least initially, and she becomes an example of his ability to keep the women in his life distant from him and respectful, even if grudgingly so, of his power. Deborah, who dies before Gabriel goes to New York, is revealed in part through "Florence's Prayer" in Part Two of the novel, but mainly through "Gabriel's Prayer." The composite picture of her is that of a woman who discovered early in life that there would be no silver slippers for her and settled down to being plain, faithful, and dull. Deborah's life is that of a woman victimized by racism and sexism, who finds that nature has also played a trick on her. She bears up well under multiple drab circumstances, but her life is one of interest to few and that few would be inspired to chronicle.[13]

The rape solidifies her relationship with Florence, but it also makes her seek for transcendence within the church. Her neighbors look upon her not as a woman, but as "a harlot, a source of delight more bestial and mysteries more shaking than any a proper woman could provide" (p. 73); this description will be taken up again in *Just Above My Head* with the character of Julia, who sleeps with her father and provides lustful speculation for the men who come into contact with her. For Deborah, however, it seems to be her fate never to be loved or to be respected, so she turns to the church, which does not discriminate against victims like herself. That the black community makes her a victim is testament to the power the whites have over them; blacks cannot face the reality of blaming whites for Deborah's violation, which would mean they are all subject to similar violation, so they blame Deborah and try to stay as excluded from white hatred as they can. They make her guilty, and she accepts her guilt.

Deborah wraps herself in the Word, becoming more godly than considerably older parishioners. As such, she is the thoroughly one-dimensional good character who stays safely within the church, providing a contrast to Florence and Esther. Deborah cannot contemplate the commission of an evil act or the possibility of walking out on her responsibilities. She is eminently suited to walking the straight and narrow path within the limitations of the church. It is in this state that she enters the Grimes household to feed and sit with Rachel after Florence's departure and during Gabriel's tomcatting absences. Her place in life is outlined clearly, and she accepts it. As a woman who can never have children, she becomes mothering angel to the sick and shut-in. She is apparently without ambition to change her status. Effecting the kind of transcendence Florence never could, she goes quietly, acquiescingly about the roles that have locked her away from her self. Deborah waits with Rachel, who stays death until Gabriel's dramatic conversion. Immediately after Rachel's death, Deborah becomes for Gabriel what his mother used to be and what he believes his sister should have been. She cooks his meals, washes his clothes, darns his socks, and keeps him company. It is partly recognition of the *role* she plays that convinces Gabriel to marry her.

Deborah epitomizes service, the spiritual over the physical, in that she lacks physical beauty and she seems to have found a subservient identity in life. She becomes the most pious of the pious, making those who would mock her uneasy in their evaluations. When Gabriel begins to preach, she sustains him "most beautifully in his new condition" (p. 99). For her, he becomes a personification of the righteous. She fasts with him, prays with him, graciously refers to him as Reverend, stays spiritually by his side, and believes unfalteringly in his abilities. All of those virtues add up to a colossal caress of Gabriel's ego, which has been expanded by many degrees since his conversion. Deborah's devotion and attention encourage Gabriel to see her in a new, egotistical light: "He had been real for her, she had watched him, and prayed for him during all those years when he, for him, had been nothing but a shadow. And she was praying for him still; he would have her prayers to aid him all his life long" (p. 100). Gabriel recognizes that, in Deborah, he has his own personal religious groupie. His decision to marry her thereby provides the ultimate compliment to himself.

Victimized by white men and the black community, made barren by nature, Deborah will shortly become the accompaniment to Gabriel's vision of his chosen status with God. It is only through understanding the intensity of his vision that we can understand the severity of his disappointment when he discovers Deborah is barren and when he discovers how disappointing making love to her is in comparison with some of the women he has pursued before his conversion.

Deborah keeps the faith of her marriage in spite of her inability to have children, in spite of Gabriel's infidelity, and in spite of his eventual disgust and hatred for her. She had expected nothing of life; the momentary happiness she receives will serve to balance out the years of deadly routine that follow it. It is to Deborah's further disadvantage that Esther's appearance makes Gabriel evaluate her even more harshly; he sees "how black and how bony was this wife of his, and how wholly undesirable. . . . He thought of the joyless groaning of their marriage bed; and he hated her" (p. 118). His purpose of elevation has dissolved quickly, for it is in the first year of his marriage to Deborah that Gabriel has the affair with Esther.

The letter Deborah writes to Florence tells us that she is more observant than she appears to be, and a scene in Gabriel's section corroborates the letter writing, but Deborah bears with Gabriel through his passionate pursuit of Esther and his neglect of Royal, his son by Esther. It is only when Deborah tells Gabriel of Royal's death that he finally cries and admits that Royal was his son. Willing to take the child in as her own, but hampered by Gabriel's silence, Deborah is still quiet as Gabriel, not surprisingly, indicts her barrenness and the burden of her as his wife as part of the reason he had to deny his son. When he announces that he did not "want no harlot's son" (p. 148), Deborah quietly reminds him that Esther was no harlot. Deborah has the power to forgive, the power to suffer all. From the day she is sixteen, she is already old and worn in the vineyard of the Lord. If anyone deserves heaven, certainly she does; tragically, her life has been such a conglomeration of pain, suffering, victimization, and unhappiness that the heavenly goal seems almost frivolous. While Christianity preaches denial, it never maintains that believers should be unhappy over a lifetime.

In her ability to efface herself from her own thoughts and actions, Deborah epitomizes the self-effacing stance willingly taken by many of Baldwin's black women characters for the sake of serving others, especially the males, in the novel. Deborah has lost all sense of personhood beyond that which complies with the admonitions to be humble, loving, kind, generous, and forgiving. These are not undesirable virtues; I am merely suggesting that the sustained pursuit of them makes the black women characters in *Go Tell It on the Mountain* seem trapped within a procrustean world that has chopped out their hearts and parts of their minds, particularly those parts that would have given them an iota of complexity in terms of the decisions they make about other people in their lives.

Deborah exemplifies a Christian life in the extreme, and she is everything that Esther and the young Florence are not. She is finally victimized not only by Gabriel and others, but by the very religion in which she has sought refuge. This woman, who has no sins that we can detect, could easily have gone from birth to heaven to cut out the suffering in between. Her life in the novel serves only to show a contrast to Gabriel; her Christian example makes his small, but he still wields power over her by claiming sexual and spiritual mastery. Left with little else in life, Deborah needs to believe in Gabriel and in God; at times, they are almost one to her.

Esther, as harlot/whore, the opposite of the woman who is "saved" within the church, provides the other extreme of the dichotomy Baldwin develops. By not having had a personal experience with God, and by refusing to following the rituals of the church, Esther shows the negative possibilities of the limitations of character within Baldwin's religious framework. Here is a woman who could be many things, except for the fact that she is viewed and judged solely on her lack of connection to the church. That is what causes her downfall with Gabriel and that is what, from her actions, she seems to use to measure herself after her affair with Gabriel. The life she has presumably been content with is found lacking when she measures it against what the expectations of the church might be. Apparently it is her experience with Gabriel, and the increasing sense that she is being punished as a result of it, that cause her to look at herself through his eyes and to bring the yardstick of the church to bear upon her own life. Although she remains outside the church even after her affair with Gabriel, she nonetheless feels guilty and remembers the church, or rather her absence from it, as her particular moral failure. The initial good feeling she had about herself disappears in the face of adversity and she, like Florence, is beaten down for daring to find a meaning in life beyond that of the predetermined roles governed by the safety of the church.

Esther's physical beauty makes her the antithesis of the dutiful, unattractive Deborah and shows, in her ability to destroy males—at least from their point of view—that she is not quite acceptable within the Baldwin conception of character. Certainly she serves to point out Gabriel's failings, and certainly we may be more sympathetic to her than to Gabriel, but she is not ultimately a model for emulation either. She is tainted, sinful and sinning, finally another one-dimensional cog in the wheel of progression for Baldwin's black women characters.

Gabriel succeeds not only in forcing Esther to change her mind about herself, but in overpowering her and thereby reducing her to the same level of dirt and grime that is his daily sustenance. Esther is the temptation to return to the vibrant, often funky life Gabriel has left behind when he presumably wrapped himself in the church. To Gabriel, Esther becomes the Devil who may cause one to fall, but who can be overcome if one holds ultimately to the gospel plow, which he is presumptuous enough to believe he does.

Just as Deborah epitomizes goodness, duty, and responsibility, Esther epitomizes evil and irresponsibility. She comes to represent for Gabriel the realm of the body, and the church-based war of woman's role is fought in a different arena. Youth combines with flesh and passion to make Esther especially attractive to Gabriel. He associates Esther "with flame; with fiery leaves in the autumn, and the fiery sun going down in the evening over the farthest hill, and with the eternal fires of Hell" (p. 116). Projecting this image onto Esther, Gabriel easily contrives her circumstances to be other than they are. He tells himself that he pities Esther for being lost, for not going to church, for being free with the numerous young men who wait after work to escort her home. And when she asks if a "pretty man" (p. 116) like him is really going to preach, he determines to save her; or more precisely, to bring her into the church before her presence tempts him out of it. Coaxed to attend a service where Gabriel delivers a fiery, egotistical sermon designed to bring about her conversion, Esther instead sits in bemused observation, "with a bright, pleased interest, as though she were at a theater and were waiting to see what improbable delights would next be offered her" (p. 121). Gabriel cannot raise Esther to the spiritual level he envisions himself occupying, so he falls to the burning level of flesh he sees as her domain. Not only does he fall but, in his base desires, he falls far below the Esther he considers so degenerate.

The nine-day affair with Esther is made into a holy war in which God's chosen warrior, Gabriel, eventually wins out over Esther, the

Devil's disciple. Esther is the expendable moral lesson who can be sacrificed on the altar of the masculine figures who evince more strength than she does. She does not change her mind that Gabriel is a "pretty man," but she does not try to encourage him to continue the affair. Her casual attitude prefigures her downfall; she takes life too lightly and is much too intent upon enjoyment to survive in the schema Baldwin has set up. Esther is too self-centered in terms of her reason for being; she pursues her own pleasure, not the pleasure of the male figures in her life. Because she is committed only to herself, she is as expendable as the interlude she spends with Gabriel.

Before his encounter with Esther, Gabriel has done an excellent job of convincing himself that he is good and pure and that he has escaped the life that found him drunk and vomit-covered so many mornings. It would shatter his image of himself beyond reclamation if he were to admit that he is at fault in the affair with Esther. He must therefore tell himself that he is the superior being who is being tested, who is being tempted by the luscious fare served before him. He is like Jesus in the wilderness confronted by the Devil, and it is a test of his will that he must overcome Esther's temptations. His participation in the affair pales, then, in comparison with the super-human strength with which he extricates himself from his fallen status. God, he has been taught, and obviously desperately needs to believe, is a forgiving God. If one but humbles oneself before Him, all can be erased and the backsliding sinner can begin anew with a clean slate. What Gabriel does is to twist the teachings of the scriptures in that there is more ego in his bid to be forgiven than anything else, but he succeeds in divorcing himself from the tainted state that must be his if he in any way admits that he and Esther have something in common other than their brief encounter. He therefore represses the memories she evokes in him of the life he found so attractive a matter of months earlier. As the schema is set up, he feels no remorse for Esther because she is beyond human sympathy and consideration by virtue of her allegiance to the Devil. Good is destined to win out over Evil; representatives of the Good are not to spend time worrying about the conditions of the Evil Ones they have destroyed.

The beginning of Esther's downfall can be seen in Gabriel's response to her pregnancy. He is stunned, but his ultimate concern is for himself, not for Esther, for she is outside the realm of expected caring. As an "unsafe" woman, one beyond the church, she can evoke no responsibility in him toward her. He recalls his efforts to plant holy seeds in Deborah, then thinks of his baby: "It was in the womb of Esther, who was no better than a harlot, that the seed of the prophet would be nourished" (p. 129). If Esther is a harlot, it is only because Gabriel has made her so. He has spoiled innocence (there is a kind of innocence in the fact that Esther leads a carefree life about which she feels no guilt) and destroyed a love of life, yet he blames the victimized Esther, not himself. Esther has certainly not been angelic, but there was nothing ugly about her until Gabriel touched her. Just as he projected lust onto her to cover his own passion, so too would he project filth onto her reputation in order to protect his own. He initially questions whether the baby is his, then insists that Esther is "a wicked woman" who has made him fall. Esther's assertion that she is not "the first girl's been ruined by a holy man" only brings further condemnation from Gabriel:

> "Ruined?" he cried. "You? How you going to be ruined? When you been walking through this town just like a harlot, and a-kicking up your heels all over the pasture? How you going to stand there and tell me you been *ruined*? If it hadn't been me, it sure would have been somebody else."
> "But it *was* you," she retorted, "and what I want to know is what we's going to do about it." (p. 132)

Open, honest, laughing, gay Esther is reduced to desperate calculation in the face of Gabriel's treatment of her. When he insists he can do nothing to help, she forgoes going through town and telling everybody about the "Lord's anointed" only because of what it would do to her parents. Instead, she asks for money to go away and have the baby alone.

The facts of the situation and the tone of the scene illustrate that Esther is the weaker of the adversaries and will probably lose her fight with Gabriel. She is the one people have observed being morally loose, while Gabriel has been the model preacher. She is the one who will bear the baby and people will shortly see signs of the coming birth; Gabriel's guilt will never have a physical manifestation. Then, too, Esther comes almost too humbly, nearly begging Gabriel for assistance. It is therefore already a realistic possibility that the strength and vibrancy she has shown earlier will shortly disappear.

Of prime importance, though, is the fact that the wild and bestial coupling with Gabriel—and the ensuing pregnancy—begin a season of guilt for Esther and the evaluation of herself as a "bad" girl. She has acted only in reference to herself prior to this point; now she must consider her parents and what the knowledge of her pregnancy would do to them. All of a sudden, she must face the concrete reality of not having lived an exemplary life, of not having been safe. No matter what her feelings or her true personality, the community will judge her harshly; they will see nothing good about her, and they will not be lenient in calling her a fallen woman. The full burden of guilt will fall upon her, none upon the man who has been her partner.

Esther goes North with money Gabriel steals from a hoard Deborah has accumulated, thus leaving him untainted in the eyes of his congregation and further supporting the thesis that women in the novel seem to pay more acutely for their sins than do the men. Esther disappears to loneliness, poverty, and death, growing increasingly bitter with her increasing pregnancy. What happens to her in terms of hardship and isolation contrasts sharply with Gabriel's security. He cannot begin to envision the reality of those months; nor does he wish to do so. He is snug and safe with his self-righteous image of himself. The one letter he receives from Esther rings like Deborah's and Florence's admonitions—that Gabriel had better get his life in order before he has to confront God. Esther writes:

> *What I think is, I made a mistake, that's true, and I'm paying for it now. But don't you think you ain't going to pay for it—I don't know when and I don't know how, but I know you going to be brought low one of these fine days. I ain't holy like you are, but I know right from wrong.*
>
> *I'm going to have my baby and I'm going to bring him up to be a man. And I ain't going to read to him out of no Bibles and I ain't going to take him to hear no preaching. If he don't drink nothing but moonshine all his natural days he be a better man than his Daddy.*   (p. 135)

Esther's notion that she has made a "mistake" for which she is now "paying" echoes the teachings drummed into young girls to keep their chastity before marriage. If one errs, it is certainly the woman who will pay; that is the image Esther now has of herself. She also believes in the laws of retribution, that Gabriel will also pay and one day be brought low, which are also a part of those church strictures that she has earlier refused to accept. Her entire notion of right and wrong may just as easily have been developed under the guidance of the Praying Mother Washingtons of Baldwin's fiction as derived from her own experience. Esther's claim that she will bring her son up to be a man is the last bit of defiance we see in her, but considering where she is and under what circumstances at the time the claim is made, it fails to carry force. It is an interesting aside that Esther assumes her child will be male. Considering what Gabriel has done to her, the more natural assumption would be for it to be female, or to have the sex remain unindentified. Or perhaps Esther desires to have a male child in order to raise him in opposition to Gabriel as a kind of negation of what Gabriel has done to her. Perhaps, too, it is a testament to Baldwin's politics that masculine is dominant and preferable even to females undone by masculinity.

A comparable situation, in terms of the prayer for a male child who has been conceived out of wedlock, develops in Baldwin's *Blues for Mister Charlie* (1964). After Richard's death, Juanita thinks: "Mama is afraid I'm pregnant. Mama is afraid of so much. I'm not afraid. I hope I'm pregnant. I *hope* I am! One more illegitimate black baby—that's right, you jive mothers! And I am going to raise my baby to be a man. A *man*, you dig? Oh, let me be pregnant, let me be pregnant, don't let it all be gone!"[14] Although both women are alone, Juanita has lost Richard through a brutal murder, in contrast to Esther's rejection by Gabriel. Juanita's desire for a male child therefore follows much more logically out of the circumstances in which she is involved than does Esther's. For Esther, however, Gabriel is equally "dead," and the birth of their son leads to her own death.

Esther dies and Gabriel thrives; her femininity has been her failing, and her life outside the church has ensured the possibility of that failure. She thought it was permissible to become attracted to a "pretty man" and to have an affair with him. Little did she know that the pretty man was more demon than he viewed her as being. She encounters a situation where she expects her femaleness to protect her, and it is just that sexuality that is her undoing. The freedom to indulge in an affair turns her own body into a prison that ultimately kills her. She has been mastered by the male body that has become lord of her femininity, and she has been destroyed by the weapon of that savage god.

Elizabeth is perhaps the most complicated of Baldwin's images of black women in *Go Tell It on the Mountain*, primarily because her being in the church is a role she plays without conviction. To her fellow parishioners, Elizabeth is in many ways a model wife and mother. She is usually at Gabriel's side for church activities, and several of the women comment on how well she manages to run her house and take care of her children. Yet Elizabeth lives through the

rituals, goes through the forms of being saved, without the conviction that goes along with it. She is in the church in part because it is
through Gabriel that she was able to get assistance in raising John.
She is wife and mother because she has not been taught to envision
roles beyond those. Perhaps, too, her desire to keep her nuclear
family intact is a reaction to the loss of her mother at an early age and
the separation from her father. It may also be a way for her to cling to
what she has never had with Richard, or to act out her guilt that
Richard is not alive to share her life.

Whatever her reasons for staying with Gabriel, Elizabeth has
pushed her individual concerns into the background. She stays in the
marriage for her children, or for Gabriel's image in the church, or for
her memory of Richard; she does not stay wholly for herself. She
suppresses whatever tendency to independent and individual thinking she may have had under the forms of the church and the quiet
safety that can save her from herself. She is not a bad woman, but
neither is she the truly committed woman that Deborah is; she is in
the church out of the fear of not being safe and out of the guilty
possibility that her past actions could reverberate onto the heads of
those she loves. While she seems to outsiders to believe in what she
practices, the few glimpses we get of her in Part Two of the novel
reveal that there is another component to her personality. All of her
views, though, are centered upon males and male figures in her life.

Elizabeth's life, like those of Florence and Esther, has been shaped
in part by an early unforgettable encounter with a man. Proud, unbending, quietly stubborn in the face of the moral threats and admonitions Gabriel uses against her, Elizabeth is nevertheless torn and
haunted by the memory of Richard. How she responds to his loss has
been shaped by how she responded to the loss of her father. Upon her
mother's death, her aunt actually provides the physical necessities of
security, but her father has provided those intangible supportive
components that are also necessary for the normal growth of human
beings. Elizabeth is unable to forgive her aunt for having caused the
separation from her father or for the kind of strictures under which
she is forced to grow up.

The sympathetic contrast Richard provides to her aunt, and the
allowances she makes for his sometimes rude behavior, establish a
pattern for Elizabeth that will control her emotional relationship
with Richard and that will nurture the guilt soon to be her reaction to
their affair. To the eighteen-year-old Elizabeth, Richard, a twenty-

two-year-old Northerner visiting the South, is as close a conception to Prince Charming as she can derive in her Maryland town. Generally haughty, aloof, and disdainful, with Elizabeth Richard is teasing, smiling, and playful. She soon wins freedom from her aunt on the pretext of the "greater opportunities the North offered colored people" (p. 161) and goes to New York to join Richard. Circumstances conspire against their intended marriage as they settle into working as chambermaid and elevator boy in the same hotel. Quickly lapsing into a courtship routine that had been prevented in the South by Elizabeth's aunt and by Richard's transiency, unsupervised in everyday activities, the young lovers discover sexual freedom, thus pushing their intentions of marriage further into the background.

Elizabeth has actually made the same geographical move as Florence, and she presumably has a similar potential for breaking away from the constraints that have defined her early life. That spark of independence which caused her to come to New York, however, is very quickly sublimated under feelings of guilt for having betrayed her aunt and the relative in New York with whom she lives. The external constraint obvious in her aunt's presence changes to an internal constraint as Elizabeth develops her own exacting conscience. She becomes her own greatest obstacle by losing the bit of will that has made her reasonably independent in her actions. Never again will she be so daring; she will submit to Gabriel's judgments and occasional beatings and retain only a minimal portion of her former resistance. We sense the resistance in John's feelings about his mother (that there is somehow more to her than she ever reveals), and we sense it in Elizabeth's prayer and the feeling that she is not totally repentant for her former life. Gabriel also gives her mental defiance some credibility in his feeling that Elizabeth is resisting him; however, in all of her actions, she is the model of acquiescence and straitlaced conformity. Her arrival at that state is tied to how she has acted with Richard and to how she has judged herself.

The church-centered background Elizabeth brings to bear upon her adult experiences can be seen vividly in her reaction to the people she encounters in New York. They epitomize everything her aunt has taught her is wicked: they drink, smoke, and make love, they listen to music, and they are generally thoroughly satisfied with their lives outside the church. "Not one of them ever went to Church— one might scarcely have imagined that they knew that churches existed—they all, hourly, daily, in their speech, in their lives, and in their hearts, cursed God. They all seemed to be saying, as Richard, when she once timidly mentioned the love of Jesus, said: 'You can tell that puking bastard to kiss my big black ass'" (p. 163). Her weeping and "terror" at Richard's declaration are only compounded by the examples she sees reflected back to her in the many people she encounters every day. To sensitive, fearful, guilt-conscious Elizabeth, whose only frame of reference is the church, the very air she breathes and the very streets she walks in New York reek with iniquity. She does not feel at home here, but she can only "timidly" offer Jesus as an alternative, perhaps sensing in her own hesitation that that alternative is somehow inadequate but must be held on to because she knows no other.

Initially, the guilt Elizabeth feels disintegrates before Richard's smiles and his physical need for her. Though she gives in to him, she nonetheless views her life in biblical terms: she has "fallen." Again and again, she indicts herself for the extent to which she has fallen— by deceiving her relatives, by easily giving up her "pearl without price" (p. 162), and by consciously making the choice to continue in what she considers a sinful life. Railing against her aunt has not prevented the moral teachings from causing a war within Elizabeth; she is torn constantly between what she does and what she knows she should do if she is to be considered a "good girl." She knows what the spirit requires, but she cannot resist the flesh. If she were forced to choose between God and Richard, she concludes, "she could only, even with weeping, have turned away from God" (p. 157). Not God Himself, she thinks further, could have made her turn back from the "fiery storm, of which Richard was the center and the heart" (p. 161). So the affair continues, with Elizabeth having serious concerns that she rationalizes herself out of discussing with Richard. She sees herself in many ways as a protector for the restless, orphaned young man with whom she has fallen in love. His rages against social restrictions elicit mothering responses from her; she wants to soothe him into forgetting everything that hurts him, to protect him against a cruel world.

Richard's intellectual ability to deal with the world is not matched by an equally strong emotional ability. When he finds himself in a situation where he is emasculated, and forced to respond to the world through "feminine" tears, he commits suicide. He is falsely accused of robbery, thrown into jail, beaten in a professional way, and abused beyond the endurance of his fragile intellect. Exoneration and release merely increase his self-accusation that he has somehow failed and increase his humiliation that he has been so awfully dehumanized. Back in his room, he slits his wrists and bleeds to death,[15] ignorant that Elizabeth is pregnant with John. She had withheld that knowledge in another protecting gesture; she had assumed that he had too much on his mind with the police and trying to recover from the arrest to burden him with news of his impending fatherhood. Her silence serves as another wagonload of guilt, for Elizabeth later thinks that knowledge of the pregnancy might have provided Richard with the strength to withstand the assaults on his manhood; after all, fatherhood is one of the most tangible manifestations of manhood.

What Elizabeth cannot face is the one essential truth of her relationship with Richard: she is stronger than he is. The tone of her actions conveys that she believes men should be stronger in relationships; if they are not, perhaps it is in part because their female partners have not allowed for that development. Her own strength is therefore more detrimental to Elizabeth than it is to Richard. She tells herself that she should have played a different kind of role, one that would have convinced Richard beyond a doubt that he was the stronger of the two, the one who naturally deserved to be in the leadership position. Not that Elizabeth ever tries to be first in decision making or anything else in the relationship; but at some subconscious level she knows that she is stronger than Richard, and that knowledge brings down her own judgment upon herself as woman and as lover.

Equaling Florence's ability to assume a load of guilt about men, Elizabeth never forgives herself for not being more of what Richard needed, even though she has difficulty articulating that need very precisely. Richard's final humiliation had been to cry in her arms like a child the night before he committed suicide. Perhaps, to him, this meant the ultimate reduction, to be reduced to such a pathetic lack of control before the woman he loved. As far as Elizabeth is concerned, however, there is little, if anything, wrong with Richard; his having given up on life is somehow her fault. She blames herself for being bold enough to want Richard, and she sees his death as God's way of cutting them both down, a fate also in store for John if she cannot contain his pride:

> There was a stiffness in him that would be hard to break, but that, nevertheless, would one day surely be broken. As hers had been, and Rich-

ard's—there was no escape for anyone. God was everywhere, terrible, the living God; and so high, the song said, you couldn't get over Him; so low you couldn't get under Him; so wide you couldn't get around Him; but must come in at the door. (p. 174)

To Elizabeth, the laws of retribution are an ever-present threat. She believes God will eventually make one pay for every sin committed, and if the guilty parties do not suffer sufficiently, then their innocent offspring will. But the same question can be asked of Elizabeth that was asked of Florence: What are her sins? She judges herself for the ill feelings she held toward her aunt, but those feelings are not wholly without justification. She is proud, but hardly to a fault. In the eyes of the church in which she has been raised, she does sin when she engages in sex with Richard and conceives John out of wedlock. To her mind, her sinning continues after John's birth because, even though she goes back to the church to beg forgiveness, she is not truly sorry for having known Richard or for having conceived John. Gabriel senses Elizabeth's unbending posture and pushes her all the more to repent, for he feels his own son, Roy, may be harmed if she does not: "It came to him that this living son, this headlong, living Royal, might be cursed for the sin of his mother, whose sin had never been truly repented; for that the living proof of her sin, he who knelt tonight, a very interloper among the saints, stood between her soul and God. Yes, she was hardhearted, stiff-necked, and hard to bend, this Elizabeth whom he had married" (pp. 114–15). Not once does Gabriel think that his own sins could bring damnation upon Roy.

What Elizabeth and Gabriel share is summarized in his reaction to her seeming lack of repentance: they both believe in the laws of retribution, they both believe their children could possibly suffer for sins the parents have committed. For Elizabeth, her relationship with Richard has been an example of God's exacting vengeance. Because she was proud enough to be willing to put Richard before God, she believes that was "why God had taken him from her" (p. 157). She must therefore try to humble herself and try to get John to humble himself, if they are to escape further punishment. Though Elizabeth is certainly not as fanatical as Gabriel is, she is as securely bound by those fundamentalist strictures. Her life with him is a form of perpetual atonement. She keeps trying to humble herself, but she keeps failing because she sees inconsistencies in the rules that should govern her life. Her fear of the tragedies that could engulf the lives of her children, especially John, keeps her reasonably humble, but her love for Richard and the life they shared keeps her proud; that memory will forever be vivid, partly because it serves as such a sharp contrast to her life with Gabriel. If there is to be no happiness in righteousness, there was at least happiness—initially—in loving.

For Elizabeth, then, Gabriel serves as the purest, sternest conscience she could have. If she endures him, she may perhaps escape the ultimate wrath of God. Elizabeth had met Gabriel through Florence, and her circumstances led her to believe Gabriel when he said the Lord had sent her to him as a sign. Over twenty years older than Elizabeth, Gabriel must have seemed to her like a fatherly, helpful figure when she met him. He was the epitome of kindness when they were introduced at Florence's house, and in the weeks and months following their introduction, he was respectful of her and attentive to John. Gabriel had become "her strength. He watched over her and her baby as though it had become his calling; he was very good to John, and played with him, and bought him things, as though John were his own" (p. 186). However, the birth of Roy, Gabriel's second Royal, pushes his commitment to John into the background, and Elizabeth's marriage becomes a miserable round of having babies (she has four and is pregnant with the fifth), going to church, and trying to run a household to please Gabriel. The task is especially hard because Gabriel is seldom happy or pleased. Yet Elizabeth endures through the transformation, or what seems like a transformation. On her knees at the tarry service, she thinks: "When had he so greatly changed? Or was it that he had not changed, but that her eyes had been opened through the pain he had caused her?" (p. 187). Still she stays and gives her body to be burned with Gabrel's passion and worn out with having children.

Her roles as mother and wife, in which we first see her in the novel, force Elizabeth to try to keep peace within her family, to protect her husband's image with her children and to save them, as much as possible, from his wrath. Against Roy's accusation that Gabriel is an authoritarian figure who punishes without love and holds to rules for their own sake, Elizabeth defends him as a good provider, which is perhaps the only safe topic of conversation she can have with her children about their father. When John asks if Gabriel is a "good man," Elizabeth's "mouth tightened and her eyes grew dark" (p. 24). Rather than answer the question, she chastises John for asking it. He correctly suspects "that his mother was not saying everything she meant" (p. 24). The complexity he envisions as hers causes him to speculate: "What were her thoughts? Her face would never tell. And yet, looking down at him in a moment that was like a secret, passing sign, her face did tell him. Her thoughts were bitter" (pp. 24–25).

Elizabeth defends Gabriel, who seems almost indefensible to Roy, and she simultaneously tries to satisfy the needs of her children. When everyone else has forgotten John's birthday, she produces a few coins to provide him with an outing and presents. He is overwhelmed by the gesture and his mother's comment that he is her "right-hand man" (p. 31) and that she is "counting" on him (p. 32). To John, who must decipher his mother's attitudes and feelings from what she says as well as from what she does not say, her transformation in church is instructive: "His mother, her eyes raised to heaven, hands arced before her, moving, made real for John that patience, that endurance, that long suffering, which he had read of in the Bible and found so hard to imagine" (p. 15). She represents for him the best of the Christian tradition into which he will shortly be irresistibly drawn. Yet we will discover later that Elizabeth's long-suffering comes from a completely different source than might be divined from John's evaluation.

Elizabeth's role as mother in the scene in which Roy is brought home injured reveals two important things. First of all, she plays a secondary role to Florence, thus causing us to question why. Secondly, she is very low-keyed, subdued even, in reaction to Gabriel's accusations of irresponsibility on her part. She comments only when Gabriel tries to implicate John: "Ain't nobody to *blame*, Gabriel. You just better pray God to stop him before somebody puts another knife in him and puts him in his grave" (pp. 47–48), whereupon Gabriel slaps her, Roy curses him, and the beating scene occurs. There is too much truth—both that which Gabriel admits consciously and that which he holds close to his heart (Royal has died of stab wounds)—in Elizabeth's statement for him to let it stand unchallenged. And the only challenge he can provide is that of his strength as masculine authority over his wife and children, so he slaps her back into the place out of which she has stepped.

From all we know of her, Elizabeth's actions in this scene are unusual. She has apparently developed in the years since her affair with Richard into a long-suffering, retiring individual. Initially thankful for Gabriel's attention and rescue of her from her single status, she has grown into a model of Christian behavior and motherhood. That she defies Gabriel openly is undoubtedly in part because of Florence's presence; in the earlier scene with Roy and John, she has responded to their questions as if the very shadow of Gabriel had been in the room. Too long conscious of her roles as supportive, understanding wife and mother, she must now try to reestablish them before she reaps suffering upon the heads of her children, illustrating again her preference for safety over independence and adventure. So she joins Gabriel and the others at the tarry service.

Intense physical violence serves as immediate inspiration for the reflections of the parents once they arrive at the tarry service, but thoughts of their former lives also force them to try to pray. Elizabeth wants to protect both of her sons, but Gabriel wants to protect his second Royal. When the praying culminates in John's salvation, Elizabeth is too overwhelmed with the possibility that it is a sign of her forgiveness to celebrate with the other saints. An exactly opposite interpretation could be postured, however—that Elizabeth is overwhelmed with tears for fear of the possibility that John's conversion is further indictment of her inability to humble herself. She could be crying because John has now been initiated into the same kind of hypocrisy that is her constant companion. She is a perceptive woman, and she senses the real motive in John's conversion—that it is a way for him to reduce the distance between himself and Gabriel. Her thoughts are drawn from the present back to the days when she knew Richard; her reflections are a kind of circular culmination of her fall and her being lifted up at the tarry service.[16] How positive her uplifting is or how long it will last is uncertain. She moves through the novel much as Florence does, with only a hint at the end that there may be some future change for her.

Elizabeth, for all the instances of her proud defiance, is still at the mercy of the males in her life. She has had only two "romantic" involvements, one with Richard and one with Gabriel, each of which represents an extreme. She has no knowledge of what it means to be involved in a healthy, guilt-free sexual partnership. Guilty since she was a small child who hated her aunt for taking her father away from her, she is no less guilty with Richard and with Gabriel. It is not an option for Elizabeth truly to envision a life without men. When she is alone with John, she is dragged down with responsibility and loneliness, then she ties herself to Gabriel to be equally bogged down and repressed. Graphic reality of existence replaces any delusions about romance; the image of Elizabeth, pregnant, washing clothes on a scrubbing board, with soapsuds up to her elbows, is all we need to contemplate to see the distance between romance and reality. Her role as combination mother, housecleaner, nurse, maid, and wife is what Gabriel demands most of her, and that is what she gives. Except for the brief time with Richard and the memories of her father, Elizabeth offers us no evidence that she desires more out of life. Her conscience tells her she has made her bed and that she must lie quietly, uncomplainingly, in it.

So she will continue to exist in her round of babies, mothering, and wifing. Her position would be more tolerable if there were evidence to suggest that she enjoys her roles; there is little, for the novel is not a happy one. Guilt induced by the threat of hell highlights the sins committed to an extent that each little indiscretion seems monstrous. Magnification of guilt and fear removes laughter from the lives of the characters and makes them somber, puritanical keepers of the faith whom few would choose to emulate. That John wants to become "purer" than Gabriel and use his purity to bring Gabriel low is but another indication of the perversion of true Christian belief that pervades the novel.[17]

It is the irony of Gabriel's life that all of the women with whom he comes into contact have been "violated" in some way and that the one woman, Deborah, who could have legitimately given him his first royal heir is barren. Following her rape, Deborah becomes tainted in the eyes of the black community—and in Gabriel's; otherwise, he would not view marrying her as such an uplifting function. Esther is not only not a virgin, but she is viewed as a harlot whose womb does not deserve to nurture the son of the prophet. And Elizabeth brings to Gabriel her son John, living proof that her sexual treasures have been discovered by someone else. Because Gabriel, as male, carries no physical evidence of the many violations he has committed, he can continue to believe that these women are somehow undermining his holy purpose on earth. The women, to his mind, become his punishment and his atonement. They are the burden he must bear, unwillingly, if he is truly to seek the fulfillment of his objective, and it is only through them that his royal line can be nurtured. To him, then, women are doubly obnoxious and must be dealt with at the same time he believes they are inherently weaker and can be dismissed easily. He can master them; he can triumph over them; but ultimately, he cannot live without them.

For all its shortcomings in terms of the presentation of black female characters and the limited vision allowed them in the novel, the women are equally if not more memorable than the male characters in *Go Tell It on the Mountain*. It is a paradox of the novel that the very thing that makes Baldwin's black women limited is also what makes them most human—they care for other human beings. That caring may be couched in terms of the church but, at bottom, the women do care, and they do make sacrifices which, were they not forced to be evaluated within the framework of the church, would almost be admirable. The women may serve the men, they may efface themselves, they may feel guilty for the sins they commit, but they are frequently more attractive than many of the adult male characters Baldwin presents. It could be posited, in the vein of the old argument used to discuss black women and their long-suffering, that their strength is in their very weakness. They continue; they thrive quietly within the limited space and air available to them, and they hope for better days in their children. It could also be posited that, in their seeming weaknesses, they anticipate Julia Miller in *Just Above My Head* in that they are representatives of that "vulnerability before which stone and steel give way" (p. 525); that they, though weak, will somehow outlast Gabriel's strength—if not Florence or Elizabeth, then surely some of Elizabeth's children. That, however, is taking the long view; the more immediate view leaves the women mired in their day-to-day existence, without any real power under a system that ensures that they must perpetually be resigned to their fishbowls, for the oceans are not available to them.

CHAPTER TWO

TO BE WASHED WHITER THAN SNOW

Going to Meet the Man

Like the women in *Go Tell It on the Mountain*, most of the women in *Going to Meet the Man* (1965) lead church-centered lives; they act and react according to what is expected of them. One noticeable exception anticipates the movement away from the church that will surface in greater detail in *Another Country*—the portrait of Ruth Bowman in "Come Out the Wilderness." Ruth is consciously iconoclastic in her bid to shake off the influence of the church upon her life, but she is still in the throes of struggle. Ruth looks forward to Ida, in *Another Country*, who replaces humbleness with anger and subservience with action. Not wholly without conscience, she is nonetheless not as plagued as the earlier women with the day-to-day guilt surrounding her actions. Her reasons for guilt are sometimes just as exacting as the morally based reasons the women in the earlier works have, but there are also reasons beyond the church that cause her to feel guilty for the things she does.

Four of the eight stories in *Going to Meet the Man* have black female characters who live in accordance with or in reaction to the black church.[1] In the first two stories, the women know constraint and feel guilt almost as acutely as the women in *Go Tell It on the Mountain*. The women in "The Rockpile" and "The Outing," in fact, are earlier versions of the church- and family-centered portraits in *Go*

Tell It on the Mountain, and characters appear here who are presented more fully in the novel. Gabriel, Elizabeth, John, and Roy are the same, but the younger children, no longer all female, differ in name and number from those portrayed in *Go Tell It on the Mountain*. In the novel, there are two girls, Sarah and Ruth, and Elizabeth is pregnant with her fifth child; in "The Rockpile," there is only one girl, Delilah, and no mention is made of a pregnancy, but there is a baby boy, whose name is Paul. In "The Outing," the other children are Lois, who, "saved" at nine, is sadly isolated from her peers, and an unnamed baby brother.

"The Rockpile"[2] shares several parallels with *Go Tell It on the Mountain*, but it also deviates from the novel in its portrayal of the character of Elizabeth. The story recounts in concentrated detail the incident of Roy's fight and injury which, in the novel, takes place on the Saturday of John's birthday. Baldwin apparently found the story form too constricting in what it allowed him to accomplish in the development of Gabriel's character as well as Elizabeth's. They both have features similar to those they have in the novel, but the background information on how they came to be as they are cannot be handled very effectively within the story. For example, Gabriel is presented as an angry man, but we can only speculate on the causes of his anger. Elizabeth, obviously frightened of Gabriel, similarly lacks the extensive background that would make her interaction with him clearer. As the story is written, the lines of sympathy are drawn, but they are not as clear as they are in the novel. Because Gabriel is left fumbling at the end of the story, instead of performing a conclusive act such as the slapping in the novel, we are also left hanging. We have only been told that Gabriel is a villain; we have not seen any action in the story that would convince us of that. Therefore, there is no conclusive reaction to Gabriel as the authoritarian controller of his family that he is implied to be. The novel makes motivation clearer, sets up an uncluttered division of sympathies, and brings a conclusive resolution to the scene. The story is left at a level of frustration in which extraneous factors are allowed to obscure Gabriel's true personality.

We get two pieces of evidence that let us know that religion is prominent in the lives of the characters and that therefore allow us to judge what they do and say against what they profess to be. First of all, Sister McCandless is visiting the household when the injury to Roy occurs. The fact that she is "Sister" McCandless lets us know that she is connected to a church, and the fact that she is visiting Elizabeth lets us know that these are active members of the church. Second, after the injury but before Gabriel's arrival on the scene, Sister Mc-Candless refers to him as "the Reverend." We now know that this is the preacher's house the good sister is visiting and, from what our experiences have told us about preachers, we expect a tolerant if not an unqualifiedly good man (we already have indications from John's and Roy's reaction that Gabriel is strict); her tone, however, leaves enough ambivalence for us to perhaps anticipate revising our initial expectations.

In contrast to Elizabeth, who is presented as a concerned mother, though not a frightening one, Gabriel is presented as a frowner upon enjoyment who will come home early this Saturday and "end" the boys' freedom of sitting on the fire escape; he is a force of disapproval, from the boys' point of view, from the very first paragraphs of the story. No longer mired in the soapsuds washing image we last have of her before Roy's injury in *Go Tell It on the Mountain*, in the story Elizabeth leaves Roy and John on the fire escape to go into the kitchen "to sip tea with Sister McCandless" (p. 11). Roy slips away to the rockpile across the street, where the fight will shortly occur.

Two differences in Elizabeth's portrayal are relevant here. First, the oppressive routine of work is momentarily lifted. No matter how well earned the break, that moment of seeming idleness could support, from Gabriel's point of view, the idea that Elizabeth is negligent of her children. She has gone to "sip" tea, which has sociability and lightheartedness as its connotations, not responsibility. Though she has warned her sons, especially Roy, of the dangers involved in playing on the rockpile, and has witnessed the dangerous play, she has left them in a tempting position while she tends her company. That is the kind of case Gabriel could make against her, because he disapproves of his sons sitting on the fire escape. Second, Elizabeth's realm of action in the incident is extended beyond the apartment; she and Sister McCandless run out to meet the man who picks up Roy after his injury. The action simultaneously increases her concern and heightens the guilt that Gabriel can use against her. She runs out in panic, with Sister McCandless behind her panting "Don't fret, don't fret" (p. 13). Elizabeth is "trembling" when she tries to take Roy, so the "bigger, calmer" Sister McCandless takes him instead. Though the man keeps emphasizing that Roy's injury is "just a flesh wound," that it "just broke the skin, that's all" (p. 13), Elizabeth is frantic. Her reaction borders on hysteria, in sharp contrast to the more stoic Elizabeth in *Go Tell It on the Mountain*.

The near hysteria has at its base an ever-present fear of Gabriel. Elizabeth is almost paralyzed into inactivity because of feelings of guilt probably induced by Gabriel's previous accusations and the anticipated resurgence of guilt once Gabriel arrives on the scene. Her fear combines with the comment that the boys see Gabriel as an end to their freedom to suggest that Gabriel is a terror who makes his entire family uncomfortable; he does so by evoking feelings in them which control certain parts of their behavior even in his absence. Although the scar is "jagged," which would suggest an injury more serious than is the case, it is also "superficial"; yet Elizabeth murmurs, "Lord, have mercy . . . another inch and it would've been his eye" (p. 13). That line belongs to Gabriel later in "The Rockpile" and in *Go Tell It on the Mountain*, where he exaggerates the wound in order to underscore Elizabeth's presumed negligence. Even as she makes the comment, she looks "with apprehension" (p. 13) toward the clock, knowing that Gabriel will be home shortly and that she will be held accountable no matter what her degree of responsibility.

Elizabeth's actions show that roles and expectations are more important to Gabriel than people. He values her primarily as the mother of his children, especially of Roy. She is expected to cook and clean for them, to protect them, and to know their whereabouts at all times. If she fails in her role, she must endure the consequences. Her nervous actions before Gabriel's arrival illustrate that she is perfectly aware and fearful of those consequences. She asks Sister McCandless "nervously" if Roy is going to keep the scar. The woman's response reveals a lot about Elizabeth and about Gabriel: "'Lord, no,' said Sister McCandless, 'ain't nothing but a scratch. I declare, Sister Grimes, you worse than a child. Another couple of weeks and you won't be able to *see* no scar. No, you go on about your housework, honey, and thank the Lord it weren't no worse.' She opened the door; they heard the sound of feet on the stairs. 'I expect that's the Reverend,' said Sister McCandless, placidly, 'I *bet* he going to raise cain'" (pp. 14–15).

The guilt that both Elizabeth and John feel causes them to realize that, blameworthy or not, they will both be implicated in Roy's injury. That realization comes out in John's declaration to Elizabeth that Roy's crossing the street to the rockpile was not "my fault" and his sense that Elizabeth's response that he "ain't got nothing to worry about"

(p. 15) does not bring the comfort it should. It could be speculated, in fact, that John is somewhat taken aback by his mother's rather placid response; he looks at her in a direct, questioning way, but she turns to look out the window. From past experiences, both Elizabeth and John know that Roy is Gabriel's "heart" and that injury to him is a personal affront to Gabriel. They have both apparently been made to feel that they are intruders who are suffered but not loved, tolerated but not valued. And they have both been taught to know that the fault is within themselves, that they are somehow guilty and must suffer whatever befalls them. Elizabeth's guilt probably derives from John's illegitimacy, but John himself is unaware of that fact. From nuances of speech, however, and definitely from Gabriel's actions, John knows that he is not the favored child. In his own defense, therefore, he can only plead his case to Elizabeth, who can offer no appreciable comfort because she continually sees her own unworthiness and guilt reflected in John's actions and mannerisms, in his mere presence. John becomes inarticulate and visibly invisible in ways that are parallel to the anguish Elizabeth herself feels when confronting her husband.

The same tension between John and Gabriel exists here as in *Go Tell It on the Mountain*—or perhaps it is more visible here, since Gabriel literally frightens John into speechlessness—and Elizabeth understands in both instances, but Gabriel refuses to in either. Without Florence's presence, however, the scene with Gabriel is anticlimactic. Standing up to Gabriel and forcing him to place responsibility where it belongs, Elizabeth changes character and becomes much more assertive than her trembling nerves suggested earlier. Her interruptions of Gabriel's questions to Roy and her continuing refusal to be quiet show an Elizabeth who contrasts too directly with the character we have seen earlier in the story:

> "How you feel, son? Tell your Daddy what happened?"
> Roy opened his mouth to speak and then, relapsing into panic, began to cry. His father held him by the shoulder.
> "You don't want to cry. You's Daddy's little man. Tell your Daddy what happened."
> "He went downstairs," said Elizabeth, "where he didn't have no business to be, and got to fighting with them bad boys playing on that rockpile. That's what happened and it's a mercy it weren't nothing worse."
> He looked up at her. "Can't you let this boy answer for hisself?"

Ignoring this, she went on, more gently: "He got cut on the forehead, but it ain't nothing to worry about."

"You call a doctor? How you know it ain't nothing to worry about?"

"Is you got money to be throwing away on doctors? No, I ain't called no doctor. Ain't nothing wrong with my eyes that I can't tell whether he's hurt bad or not. He got a fright more'n anything else, and you ought to pray God it teaches him a lesson."

"You got a lot to say *now*," he said, "but I'll have *me* something to say in a minute. I'll be wanting to know when all this happened, what you was doing with your eyes *then*." (pp. 16–17)

Tensions underlying this relatively controlled conversation have their basis far beyond the incident itself. Gabriel, who has been presented as a destroyer of freedom and a creator of nervous tension in his wife, is all of a sudden a caressing, considerate father who desperately tries to soothe his injured son. The posture is not inconsistent because we know, through Elizabeth, that John is illegitimate and that Roy is Gabriel's oldest son. Gabriel, who wants to show love at this point, is unaccustomed to doing so; he therefore sounds gruff and inadequate, and his efforts at soothing only increase Roy's crying panic. It is only with Elizabeth's assistance that he is able to take the bandage from Roy's face and look at the wound. John, also witnessing the scene, can see that Gabriel's gruff tenderness will never be directed toward him. Elizabeth can see that Gabriel's overindulgence of Roy will forever cause problems for this favored son of his, and she can see, too, that John, who will never give Gabriel any trouble, will always be outside the realm of concern he shows toward Roy. Ironically, though it is not clear if he is aware of it, Gabriel must depend upon Elizabeth if he is to attend Roy properly. The fight may have caused conflict among the family members, but it forces them to work together—John holds the baby while Elizabeth and Gabriel tend to Roy's wound. It is not togetherness that Gabriel wishes to dwell upon, however, for as soon as he is satisfied that the wound is not major, he resumes his accusatory stance toward Elizabeth and John.

Gabriel's anger is undramatized throughout the scene of examining the wound; it is like a volcano waiting to explode. Wondering when Elizabeth will learn to "do right," Gabriel tries to reclaim his authoritarian superiority, but Elizabeth stands firm in maintaining that no one has "let" Roy go downstairs: "He just went. He got a head just like his father, it got to be broken before it'll bow. I was in the kitchen"

(p. 17). Elizabeth's retorts force Gabriel to turn on John, who lapses into a silence that Gabriel threatens to break with a strap. "No, you ain't," Elizabeth says. "You ain't going to take no strap to this boy, not today you ain't. Ain't a soul to blame for Roy's lying up there now but you—you because you done spoiled him so that he thinks he can do just anything and get away with it. I'm here to tell you that ain't no way to raise no child. You don't pray to the Lord to help you do better than you been doing, you going to live to shed bitter tears that the Lord didn't take his soul today" (p. 18). Such spunkiness is again too drastic a change in personality from the apprehensive Elizabeth we have seen earlier in the story.

Elizabeth's comment on Gabriel's hard head and her admonition that he should do better than he has been doing neutralize Gabriel's active anger, but the silent intensity of it remains; she sees fury and hatred in his eyes, which "were struck alive, unmoving, blind with malevolence" (p. 18). The summary of Gabriel's anger, no matter how poignant, still has less force than that of a dramatization. Gabriel has no further speech in the story; he stands in silent fury as Elizabeth, leaving the room, directs John to pick up his father's lunchbox. The silence is problematic because what we know of Gabriel would suggest that it is impossible for him to be calmed into passivity. John scrambles to pick up the box, "bending his dark head near the toe of his father's heavy shoe" (p. 19), the final clause in the story and the final indication of how Gabriel would like to resolve his angry dissatisfaction.

It is easy to see why Baldwin rewrote the story. It lacks dramatization of Gabriel's fury, and it is inconsistent in the development of Elizabeth's character. It is not clear what kind of prior knowledge she would have had of Gabriel's hard head, nor is her suggestive comment that he had better pray to the Lord for improvement ultimately a forceful one. In the novel, Florence is the medium for providing information on Gabriel's background and his own sins: if Elizabeth is to have such knowledge, and present it convincingly, then that knowledge should serve as more of an equalizer in her position in relation to Gabriel; she should not be so panicky, nervous and trembling. In its delineation of character, therefore, as well as its development of motive and action, the novel is much more forceful in presenting the rockpile incident than the story is.

Elizabeth, in standing up to Gabriel, *seems* to win the argument against him. It can be argued, however, that her changed action does not suggest a substantially changed personality from *Go Tell It on the Mountain*. As a black woman who has mothered an illegitimate son and found a haven in a hardworking churchman, Elizabeth is sensitive to that haven and to her own tainted position. Her actions indicate that she does not wish to allow anything to anger Gabriel because that anger would be turned against her and toward the fact that, to Gabriel, she and John are still interlopers in a paradise that should be forbidden to them. Then, too, it is Elizabeth who leaves the room, not Gabriel. It is she who sees in his eyes his desire "to witness her perdition" (p. 18), not he who is overcome by her spoken fury. In the contest of wills and of self-imposed guilt, it is Elizabeth who finally retreats, not Gabriel. Her retreat would be all the more vivid if Gabriel had slapped her as he did in *Go Tell It on the Mountain*. For without Florence, and without Roy, who has turned into a screaming child instead of the perceptive father-hater he is in *Go Tell It on the Mountain*, Elizabeth has no other support for her position than the momentary shock of surprising Gabriel with her outburst. Her triumph, therefore, is a pyrrhic victory at best, a slinking away from the battlefield at worst.

Elizabeth has almost unconsciously used one of the children as her defense against Gabriel's retaliation for her outspokenness. After her outburst at Gabriel, she takes Delilah from John and stands looking at Gabriel as if to say, "Trust me; I have mothered your children. How can you assume that I would not want the best for them?" Delilah is her tangible shield against Gabriel's fury, and the child's presence conveniently prevents Gabriel from striking her mother. It is because of the child that the hate and anger Gabriel shows in his eyes finally changes: Elizabeth "moved the child in her arms. And at this his eyes changed, he looked at Elizabeth, the mother of his children, the helpmeet given by the Lord" (p. 18). Elizabeth must symbolically stand in wait for the change in Gabriel even as she starts to leave the room.

As in *Go Tell It on the Mountain*, then, Elizabeth and her children must live in an environment permeated with tension and potential disapproval. Gabriel's pompous shadow falls on them all, unapprovingly, whether he is present or not. Consequently, Elizabeth has as much personality, in a way, as Gabriel allows, and as much as he is willing to recognize in her role as mother of his children. By her actions and the tone of fear she conveys to us, she almost succeeds in suggesting that Gabriel is somehow correct in his evaluation of her

guilt. Her ultimate self-realization depends upon being at peace with
Gabriel, who is unquestionably the master of his house and family,
but at the end of the story that peace is not even a promise.

The church is more immediately the background against which the
characters of the black women are drawn in "The Outing."[3] Elizabeth
still does the correct things, if we judge only from the external forms
of her actions, in terms of interacting with her fellow saints, but we
are also provided with images of black women who are not a part of
the church. Significantly, too, those matronly keepers of the faith of
the variety of Praying Mother Washington are painted much more
ironically in this story than in their previous presentations. Baldwin
still has some of the women in the church, others in it but not of it,
and others completely out of it. And since the story is told less from
their point of view than from the point of view of the young people
whom they have the potential to influence, it allows for somewhat
more of an objective evaluation of their characters. Instead of seeing
what motivates them, and having our sympathies defined from that
perspective, we see them in action and must gauge our sympathies in
accordance with their actions and with how the young men view their
actions. At times, this process elicits a more direct indictment of the
strictures of the church and more direct condemnation of the perpetrators of those strictures.

Set against a Fourth of July picnic boat trip sponsored by the
Mount of Olives Pentecostal Assembly, the story focuses primarily on
Roy and Johnnie as growing adolescents, on the budding homosexual
relationship between Johnnie and his friend David Jackson, and on
the efforts of the three boys to present a birthday present to Sylvia, a
young saint. How the youngsters see their parents, and how they
respond to their "saintliness," provides commentary throughout the
story on those in the church and those who are being forced to
become a part of it. The church therefore becomes oppressive and
intolerant of youthful development in terms of playfulness as well as
in terms of sexual awareness.

The initial contrast we see in terms of insiders and outsiders as it
concerns the black women in the story involves Johnnie's reaction to
his mother, Elizabeth. Without the point of view that allows for the
introspection of the prayer scene in *Go Tell It on the Mountain*,
Elizabeth is not at all realized in the story; she remains a shadowy,

elusive entity to Johnnie, whose point of view is central, and she remains similarly elusive to the reader. She seems harassed, preoccupied, worn down by circumstances at which we can only guess. Our impressions of her are formed as Johnnie watches her come aboard for the trip:

> His mother, on all social occasions, seemed fearfully distracted, as though she awaited, at any moment, some crushing and irrevocable disaster. This disaster might be the sudden awareness of a run in her stocking or private knowledge that the trump of judgment was due, within five minutes, to sound: but, whatever it was, it lent her a certain agitated charm and people, struggling to guess what it might be that so claimed her inward attention, never failed, in the process, to be won over. She talked with Lorraine and Mrs. Jackson for a few minutes, the child tugging at her skirts, Johnnie watching her with a smile; and at last, the child becoming always more restive, said that she must go—into what merciless arena one dared not imagine—but hoped, with a despairing smile which clearly indicated the improbability of such happiness, that she would be able to see them later. They watched her as she walked slowly to the other end of the boat, sometimes pausing in conversation, always (as though it were a duty) smiling a little and now and then considering Lois where she stood at Brother Elisha's knee. (pp. 23–24)

The image is of a hollow woman who moves through social obligations as gracefully as the burdens of her soul will allow. Although Mrs. Jackson maintains that Elizabeth is "very friendly" (p. 24), she also seems very lost in this portrayal. Her mental and spiritual malaise seems to match the slowness with which she traverses the deck. Instead of socializing, she retires to a quiet spot as quickly as possible.

The church, particularly in this story, seems to be a facade behind which Elizabeth hides whatever true feelings she has. As long as she is present, and smiles sufficiently, no one can doubt that she is serious about the issue of salvation. They will also, she perhaps hopes, leave her alone. She may escape the scrutiny of the outsiders who are along on the trip, and that of her fellow saints, but she cannot escape from Gabriel; he comes to her to complain about and hold her accountable for what he considers disrespectful behavior by Johnnie. After repeatedly urging Johnnie not to get into mischief and not to be fresh—directives that should have gone to Roy—Gabriel is shocked when Johnnie declares: "Don't worry about me, Daddy. Roy'll see to it that I behave" (p. 26). His effort to use the public setting to humiliate

Johnnie having failed, Gabriel can only nurture his hatred for Elizabeth's son by threatening to whip him once they return home and by taking his rage to Elizabeth. He fails to have any power of introspection about his own behavior and its influence upon Johnnie.

Because it is not made clear in "The Outing" that Johnnie is illegitimate, there is no internal evidence to inform Gabriel's hatred of Elizabeth's son. The closest indication we get of Johnnie not being Gabriel's son is his reference to Elizabeth in response to Johnnie's behavior: "He's your son, alright" (p. 31). Although "your" is not emphasized, the remark nevertheless aligns Johnnie's parentage more closely to Elizabeth than to Gabriel. Yet without the illegitimacy as a clear-cut motivation, or something comparable to it, we can only judge Deacon Gabriel Grimes as an intolerant example of Christianity, who, like Sister McCandless and Sister Daniels, would like to strap the young people into the harness of blind subservience to God. His conversation with his wife illustrates his own hatred and lack of Christian behavior as well as her inadequate shelter in the church.

> "I want you to talk to Johnnie," Gabriel said to his wife.
> "What about?"
> "That boy's pride is running away with him. Ask him to tell you what he said to me this morning soon as he got in front of his friends. He's your son, alright."
> "What did he say?"
> He looked darkly across the river. "You ask him to tell you about it tonight. I wanted to knock him down."
> She had watched the scene and knew this. She looked at her husband briefly, feeling a sudden, outraged anger, barely conscious; sighed and turned to look at her youngest child. . . .
> "I'll talk to him," she said at last. "He'll be alright." She wondered what on earth she would say to him; and what he would say to her. She looked covertly about the boat, but he was nowhere to be seen.
> "The proud demon's just eating him up," he said bitterly. He watched the river hurtle past. "Be the best thing in the world if the Lord would take his soul." He had meant to say "save" his soul.　(p. 31)

Gabriel, representative of both parental and church authority, evokes echoes of the theme of freedom from oppression that Baldwin developed in *Go Tell It on the Mountain*. Youth, again reflected in the Johnnie character, is repressed not only by age, but also by authority that is supposed to come from God. Unfortunately, this authority, because it has been so tremendously perverted, is a direct threat to youth. Baldwin's indictment of the church, then, centers upon its ability to stifle youth and suppress creativity in all age groups; it also substitutes fear for love and power for faith.

Because it leaves no room for the expression of "unacceptable" emotions, the church connection forces Elizabeth to hide her anger with Gabriel. Their private history is still at the center of their interaction, however. If we tie this scene to the other stories and assume that Johnnie is illegitimate, the conversation shows that Gabriel can never forgive Johnnie for being Elizabeth's first born or Elizabeth for having had the child. Her resignation to Gabriel's ways is personified in her "barely conscious" anger, which is sighed away before it can be realized, and in the way she looks about the boat "covertly." Elizabeth seems to have accepted the tensions in her life—that her first-born son will never be loved by her husband, that Gabriel may provide shelter, but never affection, and that she is almost powerless to do anything to change the intensity of her husband's disapproval of Johnnie. So she goes back to comforting her children when she can and to being silent as much as she can. The final image we have of her is walking beside Gabriel back to the boat when the picnic is over. Gabriel strides beside her carrying the baby, and Elizabeth tries to support Lois, "who stumbled perpetually and held tightly to her mother's hand" (p. 47).

Lois's stumbling is a metaphor for the Grimes family as well as for the saints. Those who consider themselves the elect of God, but who are hypocrites in reality, are literally stumbling. Because they are blinded in that fundamental part of their lives, they are also blinded to dealing with human beings in familial and other relationships. Gabriel is a prime example, but some of the women among the saints do not escape Baldwin's ironic treatments of their faith and sometimes of them as human beings. Sister McCandless and Sister Daniels, who is mother to the young lady to whom the boys want to present the birthday gift, are a continuation in a long line of staunch church sisters who will be criticized more openly in *If Beale Street Could Talk* and *Just Above My Head*. In "The Outing," the two women are presented as humorless fanatics who wear their religion like medals.

Sister McCandless makes her debut with Praying Mother Washington in *Go Tell It on the Mountain* in The Temple of the Fire Baptized; both women tower over their fellow saints in their degree of commitment to church work. Praying Mother Washington is painted most vividly on the Sunday that her granddaughter, Ella Mae, stands before the minister with Elisha to be lectured for "walking disorderly."

> Her grandmother, who had raised her, sat watching quietly, with folded hands. She was one of the pillars of the church, a powerful evangelist and very widely known. She said nothing in Ella Mae's defense, for she must have felt, as the congregation felt, that Father James was only exercising his clear and painful duty; he was responsible, after all, for Elisha, as Praying Mother Washington was responsible for Ella Mae.   (pp. 16–17)

Responsibility to youthful charges is one of the major attributes of these churchwomen, who appear often as minor characters in Baldwin's works. Instead of having their own guilt portrayed, these women try to impress upon the youngsters that they should feel guilty about their very existence and that they should pray to God for forgiveness, for the mere state of being human is one of uncleanness, one that needs to be cleansed by God. Being ever vigilant against the possibility of sin presupposes that there are things that one can do that will elicit pangs of guilt strong enough to send one howling before the altar of the Lord; being brought low, as Florence is in *Go Tell It on the Mountain*, can be prevented if one follows the teachings of the elders and gives one's life to Christ at an early age. Promoters of unworthiness before the eyes of the Lord, keepers of conscience, these women are swirling, frequently negative forces in the tempestuous seas of youth in which their charges find themselves.

In her own exemplary, unblemished example, Praying Mother Washington finds the model for her exacting expectations of the young folks. Sister McCandless is no less exacting; her power comes not only from her religious example, but also her physical stature, which is almost stereotypical in its dimensions. She is described in *Go Tell It on the Mountain* as "an enormous woman, one of the biggest and blackest God had ever made, and He had blessed her with a mighty voice with which to sing and preach, and she was going out soon into the field" (p. 57). That description is given more graphic proportions in "The Rockpile"; the "bigger, calmer" Sister McCandless takes the injured Roy from the man who is carrying him and throws him "over her shoulder as she once might have handled a sack of cotton" (p. 13). The exaggerated image serves to undercut Sister McCandless' strength at the same time as it underscores it. It does not take an overly large woman to carry a child, yet this is the feature Baldwin emphasizes. Comparing her effort to lifting a sack of cotton evokes connotations of an outsized woman beyond claims to femininity. And since most of Baldwin's references to the South are negative, the reference to cotton evokes further unpleasant connotations about the woman's strength.

Sister McCandless, then, can tower over sinners and suspected sinners both physically and spiritually. Her size, which can bring to mind the comforting bosom of Jesus or the soothing mammy, can also be used to intimidate the less strong-willed into religious services they would perhaps prefer not to participate in. Sister McCandless arrives at the tarry service in *Go Tell It on the Mountain* predicting that God will work with John in a "mighty way" and espousing the need for "a revival among our young folks" (p. 58). She is sure in her faith, confident that there is "no halfway with God," and unsympathetic when John maintains that Elizabeth may not come because "she mighty tired." Sister McCandless staunchly retorts: "She ain't so tired she can't come out and pray a *little* while" (p. 59), which angers John into staring at her "fat, black profile." John may feel anger toward her, but he recognizes her influence upon his fourteen-year-old mind. When Sister McCandless and Sister Price begin the service with Elisha, "just to warm things up" (p. 59), John voluntarily joins in the singing, "because otherwise they would force him to sing" (p. 60); however, he does not rejoice.

Women like Sister McCandless have a difficult time remembering when they were young, and especially when they were young girls— or perhaps they remember too well the sinful thoughts they had then; they would prefer to claim, as Sister Moore does in *The Amen Corner*, that they "ain't never been sweet on no man but Jesus" (p. 34). Memory does not serve them to be tolerant of their children, their grandchildren, or their neighbors' children. Sister Daniels, Sylvia's mother in "The Outing," is a terror to Roy, Johnnie, and David. "They were all frightened of the great, rawboned, outspoken Sister Daniels" (p. 21), and none of them would think of approaching her and asking her permission to present Sylvia with the birthday gift. Instead, they plot and scheme until the too-holy woman goes off to the bathroom; they then rush to Sylvia with their present. Sister Daniels can see no innocence in youth, and especially not in "unsaved" youth. Those whom she cannot drive into the church she can corral her daughter away from. Roy has professed religion, and is therefore "safer" than Johnnie and David, but they are all suspect; and the boys are no less suspicious of the saints, for Roy maintains of his "religion": "I got a Daddy-made salvation. I'm saved when I'm with Daddy" (p. 27). The boys' first encounter with Sister Daniels on the boat makes her position clear:

> "I ain't never seen none of these young men Shout," said Sister Daniels, regarding them with distrust. She looked at David and Johnnie. "Don't believe I've ever even heard you testify."
> "We're not saved yet, sister," David told her gently.
> "That's alright," Sister Daniels said. "You *could* get up and praise the Lord for your life, health and strength. Praise Him for what you got, He'll give you something more." (p. 28)

She also "grumbles" that she would like to see Sylvia do some shouting, too, and Elisha gently suggests to her that "can't *all* make as much noise as you make . . . we all ain't got your energy" (p. 29). "Sister Daniels smiled and frowned at this reference to her size and passion and said, 'Don't care, brother, when the Lord moves inside you, you bound to do something. I've seen that girl Shout all night and come back the next night and Shout some more. I don't believe in no dead religion, no sir. The saints of God need a revival'" (p. 29).

Sister Daniels' blushing and her insistence upon a revival highlight the discrepancies in Christian behavior and Christian action. The woman is flattered that her zealous shouting has been noted; that potential to be seen, and to show off, can be capsulized in a revival. Many times throughout "The Outing," mention is made of Sister Daniels' desire for a revival and many times, parallel to that, the narrator comments upon how the saints like to make their godliness known to the world. In this "Christian" church, public display becomes more important than the true saving of souls. Ostentatious example is believed to serve as effectively as sincere, charitable invitation in getting outsiders to become members of the church.

Until the boys have experienced a revival and a commitment or a recommitment, Sister Daniels prefers that they keep a distance from Sylvia. The short conversation between Sylvia and Sister Daniels in which the point is made about distance illustrates the heavy-handed nature of the religion the saints practice and of their uncompromising attitude toward youth.

Sister Daniels threw a paper bag over the side and wiped her mouth with her large handkerchief. "Sylvia, you be careful how you speak to these unsaved boys," she said.

"Yes, I am, Mama."

"Don't like the way that little Jackson boy looks at you. That child's got a demon. You be careful."

"Yes, Mama."

"You got plenty of time to be thinking about boys. Now's the time for you to be thinking about the Lord."

"Yes'm."

"You *mind* now," her mother said.   (p. 32)

The littering and the detail of the large handkerchief suggest again an unfeminine portrayal that borders on buffoonery and ridicule. Any mother can be concerned about her daughter's sexual awareness, but Sister Daniels puts the subject in the context of evil and uses the threat of the church to reinforce her advice to Sylvia. Sylvia is powerless against the unbending nature of her elders, therefore, within both the church and the family. Religion practiced by the saints is ultimately oppressive to all who encounter it.

We wonder, nonetheless, if the youth do not sometimes seek approval of their elders even within the repressive strictures outlined. Shortly after the conversation Sylvia has with her mother, the saints have service on board the boat. Sylvia, almost as if she has directly heeded the earlier commands, is among the first to start Shouting. Sylvia, though, has some choice in the matter; when nine-year-old Lois begins to Shout, we exchange glances with Roy and Johnnie and are "obscurely troubled" as Elizabeth is. The child is clearly unhappy in all her human encounters; is she old enough to suspect that the only release for her may be in the church? Her isolation had been remarked upon during the boarding: "Johnnie's nine year old sister, Lois, since she professed salvation, could not very well behave as the other children did; yet no degree of salvation could have equipped her to enter into the conversation of the grown-ups; and she was very violently disliked among the adolescents and could not join them either" (p. 23). Is she now becoming fanatical in the only life she sees available to her at the present time? Will she continue in this youthful denial of her humanity to the point where she will arrive at a state similar to that of the elder sisters?

Sister McCandless has anticipated the service as another showing of the elect quality of the saints; she came aboard planning for and commenting upon it. She demands that Johnnie, Roy, and David come to the service and predicts again that God will work in a special way, that He is "going to touch everyone of these young men one day and bring them on their knees to the altar" (p. 29). She almost Shouts before the service begins, which points back to Baldwin's earlier comment that the "saints of God were together and very conscious this morning of their being together and of their sainthood" (p. 22). After all, through their example, they could possibly bring the word to the nonbelievers on board. While Sister Daniels at least has Sylvia, it is clear that Sister McCandless' religion is her whole life; no mention is made in any of the works of relatives or charges assigned to her, other than those who go along with the church territory that she has earned through long years of dedicated service.

The church service aboard the picnic boat represents the greatest ironic treatment of the saints that Baldwin offers in the story. There is a clash, first of all, of secular and sacred concerns. Certainly the Bible teaches that one should be consistent in one's religious beliefs, that one should have religion on Wednesday as well as on Sunday, but it does not teach that professed Christians should show off their piety simply for the sake of showing off. The service therefore seems peculiarly incongruous in the context of the picnic, almost reminiscent, in fact, of the near slapstick treatment of religion in *The Green Pastures.* Ironic treatment is further enhanced by the use of the boat as the setting for the service in a gesture reminiscent of many songs from black folk tradition that emphasize getting on the "gospel ship." In polite blasphemy of that well-known image, Baldwin has transformed a picnic boat into a gospel ship. The connection is underscored when Father James bellows out that he wants the congregation to "make this old boat *rock*" (p. 36). The rocking imagery combines the sacred reference from the gospel ship with the literal rocking of the picnic boat and other connotations of rocking that are used in connection with swaying, dancing, and having a good time.[4] Designed with all the elements of buffoonery, the service is made even more ridiculous by the intensity of the Shouting and the feverous pitch of the worshipers, which contrast so sharply with the setting in which it is held.

The roles those staunch churchwomen play can also provide speculative commentary on some of the other women. What we may be seeing in Sister Daniels and Sister McCandless is what Florence may become and what Elizabeth Grimes *could* grow into in "The Outing."

As wife of an ordained, though nonpracticing, minister and the wife of a deacon, her actions in church service cannot be lukewarm; nor can she be halfheartedly committed. If her life with Gabriel increasingly brings fewer happy moments, she may find herself permanently on the altar of her Holy Master. Her troubled look at Lois' Shouting may be one that understands too well that lost position of women and girl/women who turn to the church when they feel they have no other source of spiritual sustenance or comfort. Whatever future there is for Elizabeth is in the church. She values her children too much to leave them without physical shelter, and Gabriel's disapproving eyes indicate more with each encounter that spiritual shelter is beyond him. Elizabeth's future, if not utterly bleak, is at least predetermined.

In contrast to the rather closed future we can speculate upon for Elizabeth is the much happier attitude of Mrs. Jackson and her daughter, Lorraine. These two women, completely out of the church in the story, are the most spiritually healthy of the adult females portrayed. How they are viewed by the young boys is important to how Baldwin's narrator ultimately views them in the scheme of criticism of the church. Roy, David, and Johnnie all feel comfortable around the Jackson women (to be sure, they are David's mother and sister, but Roy and Johnnie never feel a comfort around Elizabeth similar to that which David feels with his mother and sister). It is Lorraine who gives the boys advice about the kind of present they should buy for Sylvia. The fact that they have trusted her enough to ask her advice gives her a favored position in the story. As the group stands together before the boat leaves the dock, how the boys feel about both women is also apparent in their joking interaction with them.

We are only provided with a brief glimpse at these women who would be considered "unsaved" by the saints of Gabriel's church. Yet the physical placement of them on the boat and the placing of their sympathies combine to make them positive images in our minds. They are aligned with youth and growth against age and stiflement. They share a smiling reaction to Gabriel's admonitions along with the boys, and we sense that their tone and their smiles are "correct." More casual and carefree in attitude, more capable of enjoying life instead of passing judgment upon those who try, these women are the beginning of the inversion of assumed goodness that Baldwin would return to and culminate in *If Beale Street Could Talk*. Because they are not of the church, they may be thought by the saints to be ungodly, but we know from their behavior, from their reaction to the saints, and from our own knowledge of the saints that the outsiders are perhaps more in the spirit of Jesus than are those who most profess to be so.

Sister McCandless and Sister Daniels, in their stereotypical physiques, show those staunch churchwomen in the religious realm. Four black women in "Sonny's Blues" allow glimpses of these women in the sacred and the secular realms.[5] [The narrator's mother in "Sonny's Blues" is a God-fearing woman who survives tragedy and who tries to teach her narrator son to be prepared to deal with trouble, which will surely touch him in this world.] Treated in a straightforward manner through actions that evoke intrinsic respect, this woman is perhaps one of the most positive images we have of the women who have defined their roles in relation to the church. There is nothing in her portrayal to suggest that there is a gap between how she acts and what she believes, as there was in the Elizabeth of *Go Tell It on the Mountain*; still, the woman finds her reason for being in the self-effacing relationships with her husband and children, which tie her to other of Baldwin's women. She gives her life to making the lives of her family tolerable, and she pushes self into the background in order to save her husband from his own hatred so that he may yet receive the reward of Heaven.

This mother, like Elizabeth in the stories and in part of *Go Tell It on the Mountain*, is related through the eyes of her son; but here, a first-person limited point of view is used in contrast to the third-person limited point of view Baldwin uses in *Go Tell It on the Mountain* and in the other stories. Impressions of the mother are therefore more clearly filtered through her son, but they nevertheless coincide with some of the previous impressions we have of black women in Baldwin's works. [Sonny's mother is a long-suffering black woman who has been the hold on society and sanity for her husband, who witnessed the cruel murder of his brother at the hands of whites and who has carried that image to his own death.] Although no physical description is given of her, the mother is tied to the other women in the *tone* of the story she relates, which makes her a witness to suffering and places her in the company of those who hope for deliverance. She *sounds* as workworn in the vineyard of the world as Florence, and as knowledgeable of God's grace as Sister McCandless.

Her life has been dedicated to saving her husband's humanity and to providing him with a bit of relief from his hatred of whites. After her husband's death, her objective is to save her male children. The narrator, the elder of her two sons, seems secure and stable; the mother's attention therefore focuses on Sonny and on the sense of responsibility Sonny's brother should feel for him once she is dead. She tries to instill that sense of responsibility by recounting the story of their uncle, who had been killed one night when a group of drunken white men "aimed" their car "straight at him," quickly reducing him to "blood and pulp" (p. 100). The father, who witnessed the death and who had felt the kind of responsibility for his brother that the mother wants the narrator to feel for Sonny, "was like a crazy man that night and for many a night thereafter" (p. 100). The mother has been her husband's anchor and has encouraged him through life after the loss of his brother. Never did she allow him to tell his sons of his brother's death. Now, the mother tells the narrator: "I ain't telling you all this . . . to make you scared or bitter or to make you hate nobody. I'm telling you this because you got a brother. And the world ain't changed" (p. 101). When the narrator shows that he does not want to believe in that harsh vision, the mother continues: "But I praise my Redeemer . . . that He called your Daddy home before me. I ain't saying it to throw no flowers at myself, but, I declare, it keeps me from feeling too cast down to know I helped your father get safely through this world. Your father always acted like he was the roughest, strongest man on earth. And everybody took him to be like that. But if he hadn't had *me* there—to see his tears!" (p. 101). She has had no life—and seemingly has not desired any—beyond caring for her husband and children. She has become the universal bosom of comfort in this world until her troubled husband could reach the world beyond. No background information on her allows us to see how she has come to be where she is, but she has uncomplainingly fallen into the role of WOMAN: saving her man, keeping his suffering private so that he could remain respectable in the public eye, planning for her children as she sees her own death approaching.

Roles she has played have been traditional ones of wife, companion, and comforter. As her husband's helpmeet, she brought to him the only comfort she knew how—that of the church and God. She has kept her husband in touch with the "church folks" the narrator mentions visiting at their house, and she has tried to turn her husband to God to prevent him from being consumed by bitterness. She has borne her husband's burden and forced him to bear it in order to protect her children. She insinuates her greater capacity to consume suffering in the statement that she is proud to have helped her husband through the world; perhaps she feels that if she had died first, her husband would have been utterly lost and embittered. Her bosom of comfort has ensured a peaceful death for him.

Now that her own death is imminent, she passes the role she has played for the father, and that the father has played for the uncle, on to the narrator. "You got to hold on to your brother," she warns, "and don't let him fall, no matter what it looks like is happening to him and no matter how evil you gets with him. You going to be evil with him many a time. But don't you forget what I told you, you hear?" (p. 101). The schoolteacher narrator must try to bridge the gap between himself and Sonny, who inclines toward a bohemian life-style and drugs. Understanding of Sonny's trouble and, through it, the validity of the mother's advice, is what the story is about. The mother has known suffering; she and her husband have lived the blues. Sonny's drug life, his living the blues, is reflected in his piano playing, but the narrator has managed to a large extent to escape the pain and unpleasantness in life. Through showing Sonny that he is *there* through his pain, the narrator comes to an understanding of suffering and of the blues, which are an essential part of transcending that suffering.

The other black women in the story expound upon the thesis that Sonny's mother develops about suffering and provide the narrator with an opportunity to understand more about his brother. Through the role they play, these women establish a link of continuity between their roles as women and the mother's role as woman; they all provide something the males need but seem unable to acquire on their own. Participants in "an old-fashioned revival meeting" (p. 110) on the street, the other three women sing and testify for the gathering crowd. Their rendition of the "*old ship of Zion*," which "*has rescued many a thousand*" (p. 111), forces the narrator, who is observing from his apartment window, to suspect that there is much human misery behind their singing. They have experienced the downs of life and have been outside the morality about which they sing so convincingly. The narrator can see the effect of the singers upon the curious bystanders: "As the singing filled the air the watching, listening faces underwent a change, the eyes focusing on something within; the music seemed to soothe a poison out of them; and time seemed, nearly, to fall away from the sullen, belligerent, battered faces, as though they were fleeing back to their first condition, while dreaming of their last" (pp. 111–12). These people have not been protected as the narrator has, so he stands drawn to and repelled by the exposure of pain he sees reflected in their eyes and in their postures. The epiphanic revelation the women provide for the narrator continues as he sees Sonny poised at the edge of the crowd, "faintly smiling, standing very still." The lead singer passes a tambourine among the crowd and "Sonny dropped some change in the plate, looking directly at the woman with a little smile" (p. 112). Vicariously, through his drug habit, Sonny knows the singer's possible tales of woe, the pain that the singing manifests. Religion and music are as much a release for the woman and her fellow singers from the heroin of the world as piano playing for Sonny is a relief from the literal heroin. Thus the narrator witnesses what he does not yet consciously understand: that people deal with suffering as best they can, whether they escape into the church or into drugs. The shock of recognition he sees passing between Sonny and the suffering woman is what must also pass between himself and Sonny. With the woman's behavior as guide, the narrator moves one step closer to the key to communication he must unlock with Sonny.

The woman's experience becomes the analogy for Sonny to articulate to the narrator what using drugs is like. "'When she was singing before,' said Sonny, abruptly, 'her voice reminded me for a minute of what heroin feels like sometimes—when it's in your veins. It makes you feel sort of warm and cool at the same time. And distant. And—and sure.' He sipped his beer, very deliberately not looking at me. I watched his face. 'It makes you feel—in control. Sometimes you've got to have that feeling'" (p. 113). Sonny has invited his brother to come with him to a club that evening where he is scheduled to play, and he emphasizes that some guys need that feeling to play. The narrator persists in trying to force Sonny to separate himself from that kind of self-inflicted suffering; in other words, to deny his need for heroin, to overcome the hell of living in some other way. The narrator finally asks Sonny if he "wants" to continue using heroin; there is a pause and a response: "While I was downstairs before, on my way here, listening to that woman sing, it struck me all of a sudden how much suffering she must have had to go through—to sing like that. It's *repulsive* to think you have to suffer that much" (p. 114). Sonny agrees that there is no way "not to suffer," but maintains that people "try all kinds of ways to keep from drowning in it, to keep on top of it, and to make it seem—well, like *you*. Like you did something, all right, and now you're suffering for it. . . . But nobody just takes it. . . . *Everybody* tries not to. You're just hung up on the *way* some people try—it's not *your* way!" (p. 115). Still revealing a sheltered attitude, the brother at least has reached a point of being able to discuss the drug addiction openly with Sonny, and his knowledge of his mother's suffering perhaps gives additional validity to the experience of the singer.

Part of Sonny's psychology of blaming the victim, even when the victim is oneself, is reminiscent of the rape case with Deborah in *Go Tell It on the Mountain*. To blame circumstances and the general condition of human beings and society would be to suggest that suffering is perpetually, unrelentingly, with us. To blame the self justifies the bleak view at the same time that it suggests that if the individual somehow improves, the suffering *may* be alleviated.

It will take listening to the jazz set a few hours later for the narrator to understand fully what Sonny is suggesting about suffering and for him, through listening to the music, to understand his own pain in the loss of his daughter and his isolation from Sonny.[6] Meanwhile, those church sisters who resemble ones we have seen before serve as the impetus for the narrator's initial awareness and for the sharing conversation he has with Sonny. Through the example of the women, who have probably experienced more suffering than the narrator can begin to imagine, he begins to see into a world from which he has sometimes deliberately locked himself away.

As functional characters, then, these women touch without touching and influence without knowing that they are doing so. Their singing is perhaps as revelatory to Sonny and, through Sonny, to the narrator, as, later and more intimately, Julia's position is to Hall Montana in *Just Above My Head*. Through singing and guiding, the women in "Sonny's Blues" perform some of the most acceptable roles that can be performed by black women in Baldwin's fiction: they help without hindering; they give spiritual understanding to Sonny and the narrator and only take small collections in return; and they disappear before their influence turns sour or dissolves.

Ruth Bowman in "Come Out the Wilderness"[7] is the most developed example of Baldwin's treatment of black women in *Going to Meet the Man*. Here is a woman who believes that no amount of cleansing will be able to wash her whiter than snow, and she, of all the women in

Baldwin's early fiction, is the one who has most internalized the guilt that other black women feel. With Ruth, however, the guilt begins initially in an assumed act of sin, the assumption that she has gone outside the strictures of the church and therefore jeopardized her soul, and goes from there to association with her skin color. The assumed sin of premarital sex, which has caused her to be rejected by her father and brother, becomes equated with the blackness that her brother points to as being as "dirty" as the sin he thinks she has committed. To be purified, therefore, to be made as white as snow, can never be an option for Ruth, because she locates her guilt in her blackness; like Rosie Fleming in Kristin Hunter's *God Bless the Child*, she can never be redeemed because she can never turn white. Guilty therefore from the point at which she recognized she was black and unacceptable, Ruth will try to find a secular source of redemption to erase her church-centered sin—a mission doomed to failure, because she will never be able to escape herself.

Ruth's search for redemption takes the form of her trying to find a man, a secular "savior" who will somehow negate her identification of blackness with dirtiness (guilt). She is in many ways a pathetic woman who finds her identity only in unfulfilling romantic relation-ships from which she has difficulty extricating herself even when such relationships become emotionally and financially destructive to her. The story of Ruth's plight begins a move away from the church- and religion-centered stories in which black women have appeared previ-ously in Baldwin's fiction. Ruth grew up in a church environment in the South, but has moved beyond that when the conflict of the story develops. Her life is nonetheless complicated by the fact that the good and evil frame of reference from the church is her only measure for evaluating her life even after she is no longer an active part of the church. The guilt she feels may just as easily have the fear of hell as its source as any other chimeric representation of one having strayed from a straight and narrow path.

Her dilemma is capsulized in the situation in which she currently finds herself. She shares an apartment in Greenwich Village with Paul, her white lover, who seems to be a pause after many interludes with black and white men. She has moved from a background that stressed the sinfulness of sex before marriage to open indulgence in that very sin. She literally lives in the wilderness of the sin and guilt of the unsaved to which the title of the story refers. Her very exis-tence is in conflict with what she has been taught; her attempt to escape that previous environment is ironic in that it has merely intensified it. The day we see into Ruth's current life and the brief flashbacks into her past are a journey into frustration and the ambivalence she feels toward herself and her lover. Ruth is presumably in love with Paul, but hates his lack of commitment to their relationship; she wants to make demands upon him, but cannot do so because of her own inhibitions; she wants to be with him, but hates the tension created when they are together; and she wants honesty and openness in a relationship that can only survive through lies and superficialities.

Twenty-six-year-old Ruth, a few years and many relationships out of the South, has given up much to become involved in the relationship with Paul. She has given up family, both in terms of blood and cultural kinship, by refusing to live in the South or in Harlem. Ruth is afloat not only in terms of her mental attitude toward Paul, but also in her cultural position. She is in pain, but not in an environment where blues could make her pain endurable. She is in despair, but she is severed from the communal supports that could lift her troubled burdens at least temporarily. She does not attend church, is not a member of any social club, does not socialize in Harlem, knows no black women (all of her secretarial colleagues are white), and apparently has little contact with black men (one works in her office, but she does not meet him on a personal basis until late in the story). Perhaps, to her confused mind, even casual association with other blacks would increase her burden of guilt, would reflect back to her the rejected position she feels herself in by virtue of her color. Considering her peculiar circumstances, then, it is no wonder that this anomaly is so confused in her relationship with Paul.

Ruth is the personification of a black person in Baldwin's fiction whose guilt causes her to hate herself. Her own devaluation of herself has dulled her to insults from others, thereby severing her from the political history that would give her the sensitivity to respond to insults and degradation. She has no noticeable reaction when Paul calls her "girl" (as in "You're a nice girl" [p. 174] and "You're one of the nicest girls I ever met" [p. 175]), although it is made clear that her mother works as a maid down South, and it is clear on other occasions that Ruth sees things in terms of black and white. Surely she would have been aware of the implications of the use of that word. Or perhaps, in her desperate effort to seek salvation through Paul's whiteness, she considers the derogatory term much less detrimental than the larger burdens of sin and guilt that she carries with her. Whatever the reason, she does not respond negatively when Paul calls her "girl"; on one occasion, she even repeats his "girlish" description of her.

Ruth's and Baldwin's attitude toward the use of the word "girl" also extends to Mr. Davis, the black man in the office who asks Ruth to become his secretary and who also calls her "girl." He wants Ruth for the job, in contrast to "the girls out there" because she is "the most *sensible* girl available" (p. 184). Ruth's lack of political history, therefore, merges with the general chauvinistic attitude Baldwin allows his male characters to exhibit toward his female characters; her limitations in perception are Baldwin's limitations in characterization (conception). The evaluation is supported by another stereotypical comment Paul makes to Ruth: "'You're sweet, funnyface,' he sometimes said, 'but, you know, you aren't really very bright.' She was scarcely at all mollified by his adding. 'Thank heaven. I hate bright women'" (p. 173).[8] Rather than fight with Paul about the place he has assigned to her, Ruth instead uses the comment to think back to her life with Arthur, a black man and musician, and "how stupid she had felt about music" (pp. 173–74) when she lived with him. Ruth accepts the fault as her own, without considering that it is not necessary for every human being to know about painting (the context of Paul's comment) or about music. Although Ruth thinks of some of her lovers as boys, in a seeming counterpart to Paul's description of her, she never actually calls one so in conversation with him. Besides, her general insecurity would not give the word the same power or connotation in her mouth as the word "girl" has with Paul and with Mr. Davis.

The involvement with Paul has also caused Ruth to lose pride in self and to become insecure in her worth as a woman; in contrast to the other black women in Baldwin's fiction, for whom pride is often the source of guilt, Ruth has allowed guilt to dissolve all traces of pride. She knows Paul is living from her resources, and will probably be happy with the raise she will get by becoming Davis' secretary, but she cannot bring herself to change their relationship. She has lost that basic right that one lover has with the other in demanding honesty and sharing. Consistently, she "dares" not push toward a confrontation with Paul. She senses that he has lost interest, and she knows he is biding his time, trying to find a way to make a graceful exit, yet she lingers in limbo, unable to hold him and unable to face the reality of his departure. Her inability to act is just as destructive as Elizabeth's and Florence's inability to confront Gabriel.

Ruth's actions and attitudes toward Paul are those of the anxious seventeen-year-old who awaits an invitation to the prom from the captain of the football team; they are not the seasoned responses of a woman who has been involved with many men, including a four-year live-in arrangement with Arthur, a man twenty years her senior. Her indecisiveness, that paradoxical mixture of love and hatred, of approach and avoidance, haunts Ruth from the first scene in the story. She awakes wondering what time Paul has come home and whether he has a hangover, but she dares not ask him directly. When she once questioned him about his comings and goings, he had pointed out that "they were not married" (p. 171), a statement that effectively denied her right to wonder about him at all—at least directly to him. So she wages the battle in her mind. The usual pattern is that he is out and she goes to work, desperately waiting for a phone call from him, and she handles her approach/avoidance in this manner: "She would have had several stiff drinks at lunch and so could be very offhand over the phone, pretending that she had only supposed him to have gotten up a little earlier than herself that morning. But the moment she put the receiver down she hated him. She made herself sick with fantasies of how she would be revenged. Then she hated herself; thinking into what an iron maiden of love and hatred he had placed her, she hated him even more" (p. 171). The woman presents no self that Paul can respect and has little that she herself can respect. The offhandedness covers her bleeding heart and undoubtedly conveys to Paul that all is as well as it can be under the peculiar circumstances of their relationship.

But the mixture of delight and venom, of love and hate, returns daily, as does her inability to act to extricate herself from the situation: "She knew that he was going to leave her. It was in his walk, his talk, his eyes. He wanted to go. He had already moved back, crouching to leap. And she had no rival. He was not going to another woman. He simply wanted to go. It would happen today, tomorrow, three weeks from today; it was over, she could do nothing about it; neither could she save herself by jumping first. She had no place to go, she only wanted him" (p. 172). The mixture sometimes takes the form of outrageous sarcasm. When she discovers Paul has spent the evening with Cosmo, who "did not think women were worth much" (p. 173), her venom comes out when she feels Paul change his mind about terminating their relationship, his expected breaking off turning into "It's about time I got started on that portrait of you," to which Ruth's reaction is: "His decision, now, to do a portrait of her was a means of moving far away enough from her to be able to tell her the truth. . . . She had always been flattered by his desire to paint her but now she hoped that he would suddenly go blind" (p. 174). Her venom turns to nervous anticipation as she waits in the office for Paul's call; she fidgets, "debating whether she should telephone Paul or wait for Paul to telephone her. . . . She thought of Paul sleeping while she typed and became outraged, then thought of his painting and became maternal; thought of his arms and paused to light a cigarette, throwing the most pitying of glances toward the girl who shared her office, who still had a crush on Frank Sinatra" (pp. 177, 178).

When Paul finally calls and tells her he is going to an art gallery with Cosmo and that the gallery owner has a daughter, she thinks: "I hope to God she marries you. . . . I hope she marries you and takes you off to Istanbul forever, where I will never have to hear you again, so I can get a breath of air, so I can get out from under" (p. 185). Her outward show of cool (they both laugh playfully during the conversation) belies her inner turmoil, which is surely turning her into an alcoholic. Her correct evaluation of Paul's "openness" with her about the gallery owner's daughter only increases her turmoil: "To tell everything is a very effective means of keeping secrets. Secrets hidden at the heart of midnight are simply waiting to be dragged to the light, as, on some unlucky high noon, they always are. But secrets shrouded in the glare of candor are bound to defeat even the most determined and agile inspector for the light is always changing and proves that the eye cannot be trusted" (pp. 186–87).

Ruth's actions are especially problematic when they are stacked against what she claims she wants most: peace. Her tumultuous relationship with Paul makes her consider psychiatric help, which she imagines will accomplish great things for her, particularly to make her at peace with the world and with her blackness. Yet she hates herself too much to seek actively the separation from Paul that could lead to her peace, or at least the beginnings of a peaceful state. Tied to her hatred is possibly a fear that breaking away will not bring about the desired peace, that it will simply increase the turmoil she feels. She imagines that she would have found that peace if she had never left home, and that it is now available only in either Paul's death or her own.

Caught in a psychological trap to which peace is the virtual antithesis, Ruth shares with other black women in Baldwin's fiction the subordination of her very soul to the man in her life. She is just as dominated sexually by him as other of Baldwin's women are and will be by the men in their lives, for the sexual pleasure to be derived with Paul overshadows the fact that Ruth is sacrificing her money, health, and life to a man who is only using her (she may wish to use him for purposes of salvation, but his use of her is much more psychologically damaging). Still, most of her dissatisfactions with him dissolve, momentarily, in the face of his lovemaking. It is here that she grants to him that ability to save; she becomes the "dark continent" surrendering to "a mortal as bright as the morning, as white as milk" (p. 175). Their lovemaking anticipates that between Mrs. Hunt and Frank in *If Beale Street Could Talk*, in that Paul assumes the role of a god. He has the ability to make Ruth "tremble and cry" beneath "the rude thrusting that was her master and her life" (p. 180). Related in connection with Ruth's mother, the comment nevertheless defines Ruth, for she has made Paul her "master" and her "life," and she remembers when their lovemaking has been very good.

Ruth's transference of expectations of salvation from the sacred to the secular is reiterated in a brief occurrence as she sits waiting for Paul to call her office. She stares irritably at a chapel across the street, which has an "ugly neon cross" proclaiming "Jesus Saves" (p. 177). And indeed, her irritation is just, for in this story, Jesus does not save; men do. Ruth has come to Paul with that subtle expectation in mind that he will bring her out of the wilderness of confusion in which she finds herself upon meeting him. She had left Arthur when she "got over feeling that she was black and unattractive" (Arthur's part of saving her), had gone to the Village and waited tables where, "after a year or so, and several increasingly disastrous and desperate liaisons, she met Paul" (p. 182). Arthur partly saves her from her own evaluation of herself, and Paul saves her from other unspeakable horrors.

Understanding and believing where Ruth is at twenty-six can be accomplished only if we accept where she was at seventeen. If we accept the circumstances of her life in the South and those surrounding the one incident that has caused her to run away, then it is easy to believe that she willingly stagnates in the relationship with Paul. Ruth's problems with men began when her older brother "had surprised her alone in a barn with a boy. Nothing had taken place between herself and this boy, though there was no saying what might not have happened if her brother had not come in. She, guilty though she was in everything but the act, could scarcely believe and had not, until today, ever quite forgiven his immediate leap to the obvious conclusion" (p. 181). The brother hits her and beats the boy unmercifully. When no one believes her innocence, she screams:

> "Goddamit, I wish I had, I wish I had, I might as well of done it!" Her father slapped her. Her brother gave her a look and said: "You dirty . . . you dirty . . . you black and dirty——" Then her mother had had to step between her father and her brother. She turned and ran and sat down for a long time in the darkness, on a hillside, by herself, shivering. And she felt dirty, she felt that nothing would ever make her clean. (p. 181)

Ruth condemns herself just as her brother has. She has thought earlier when she gets news from home of her brother's irreputable habits that she "had shamed him and embittered him, she was one of the reasons he drank" (p. 179). Only an individual who hates herself as much as Ruth does would even attempt to assume responsibility for her brother's degeneration. Would he not have resorted to drink if she had stayed in the South? It is a weakness in Ruth's character that she fails to think logically about the situation. She perhaps thinks that she has such a profound effect upon her brother's life because she recognizes how profoundly people can affect her own life. Failing to see that her brother, like herself, must take responsibility for his own success or failure, Ruth gives in to the flaw of guilt in her character that consistently makes her believe that she has a broader sphere of negative influence than she in fact has. How she views her brother, consequently, becomes another measure of the limitations in Ruth's character—her paranoia, her self-imposed inadequacies, her self-hatred. The load of guilt with which she weighs herself down is too much for any healthy human being to carry.

Her brother's and her father's dissatisfactions with Ruth lead indirectly to the degenerate life she leads and directly to her severing connections with the church. More important, they lead to Ruth thoroughly internalizing many whorish stereotypes about herself. Her brother yells, "you black and dirty . . ." (p. 181) and the space can be filled in with whore, strumpet, slut, or whatever. The two traits are forever mingled in Ruth's mind. To be black is to be dirty, whorish, unclean, and guilty. She begins to live the "black and unattractive" existence from which Arthur "saves" her and for which her father and brother have thoroughly prepared her. After the incident in the barn, "she and her brother scarcely spoke" (p. 181). Her father "dragged her to church to make her cry repentance but she was as stubborn as her father, she told him she had nothing to repent" (p. 181). To the brother and the father, the sister and daughter whom they have known for over seventeen years is, in a matter of minutes, dirtied beyond cleansing. They have accepted the myth of the lewd, lascivious black woman who loves the pleasure of the body more than anything else. They reject her and condemn her to the psychological isolation that will be joined with the physical isolation in Greenwich Village.

Another fact relevant to the brother's reaction to his sister, and one that will be more relevant with brothers and sisters in later Baldwin works, is the brief and subtle undertone of incest that pervades the scene surrounding the brother's discovery of Ruth in the barn: "His own sexual coming of age had disturbed his peace with her—he would, in good faith, have denied this, which did not make it less true" (p. 181). Just as the brother would deny that he sees his sister in a sexual context, so would Ruth deny it, and perhaps that knowledge she will not face is a part of the psychological confusion that is her daily constant. To her, she must be guilty and sinful if there is something in her that could possibly inspire her brother to remotely consider a flesh-and-blood union with his sister, which would make him consider that most forbidden of sins. So Ruth runs away from that possibility, and away from her father's notion of church.

If her father believes she is unredeemable, and her brother shares that opinion, it is not surprising that, after the barn incident, Ruth feels that "nothing would ever make her clean" (p. 181). First of all, from her father's point of view, she has sinned, then compounded the sin by refusing to ask for forgiveness in the church that he values so much. She adds to both of these sins for years by refusing to go to church and by refusing to associate with her relatives in Harlem who follow her father in attending church. Their religion, reduced to "vindictiveness" and an inability to deal with "concrete" realities, drives Ruth even further out of the fold. Still, she is not without the influence that her father's brand of religion has upon her. She remarks to Paul, when he says what a "nice girl" she is, that her father "wouldn't think so" (p. 174).

Without the safety of the church, and without a savior, Ruth turns to the men who most approximate that image with which she has grown up. She runs away to them to seek shelter from the place from which she has already been cast out, and she believes subconsciously what her father and her brother have insinuated about her, for she lowers herself to depths they could never have imagined. Her life becomes a perpetual state of atonement; she says at one point that she is "punishing herself." Her affairs before Paul are "disastrous and desperate liaisons" in which she voluntarily stays involved, and she calls her affair with Paul a form of punishment that reinforces her guilt:

> He had power over her not because she was free but because she was guilty. To enforce his power over her he had only to keep her guilt awake. This did not demand malice on his part, it scarcely demanded perception—it only demanded that he have, as, in fact, he overwhelmingly did have, an instinct for his own convenience. His touch, which should have raised her, lifted her roughly only to throw her down hard; whenever he touched her, she became blacker and dirtier than ever; the loneliest place under heaven was in Paul's arms. (p. 187)

Ruth's state of guilt—ever present, sometimes vague, but intense—is an exaggeration of what most of the black women in Baldwin's fiction to this point perhaps have felt. By virtue of being a woman, and especially a black woman, Ruth feels as if there is something for which she must apologize. From her own point of view, she can never be right with anyone else because she is not right with herself, that is, she is not acceptable to herself. Perhaps her discomfort with blackness is an intensification of what many critics have hinted is the case with Florence in *Go Tell It on the Mountain*. Because we see less of Florence, we must surmise the extent of her feelings; with Ruth, we see that she will perhaps always act and react in direct proportion to her own indictment of herself for being black and dirty. Instead of asking the question the Invisible Man does— What did I do to be so black and blue?—she assumes that blackness and blueness are inherently her own fault and her own disease, and she believes that they will always make others respond to her just as negatively as she responds to herself. She is a classic example of the black woman in Baldwin's fiction who condemns herself and acts throughout as if she is condemned. She cannot be free of her guilt until she finds a source other than males in which to seek salvation, and she can never find such a different source until she is free of her guilt; such is her permanent dilemma and the cause of her continued stressful, frustrating, paradoxical existence.

This lost woman, floundering in the wilderness of serial affairs, is lightly hopeful that yet another man may be able to save her. That man is Mr. Davis, who requests that she become his secretary. Davis is what the father and the brother are not: a relaxed, sensitive black man. Unaccustomed to good treatment by men, Ruth is uncomfortable with Davis. She dares not hope that he will like her, because her affair with Paul will come out, yet she hopes he will like her, provide a chance for her to come back into the fold, to come out of the wilderness. Invited to share lunch with Davis, she notes his dress and concludes how well he fits into his environment. "There were no flies on Mr. Davis" (p. 188), she thinks, so his blackness cannot be dirty in the ways hers is. It is that cleanness, undefined at this point, but clearly felt, that makes her hope against hope for a possible involvement with Davis; he makes her feel "safe," which underscores the savior role. The man is secure, quietly confident with women and still in touch with his black roots. "She was responding to him with parts of herself that had been buried so long she had forgotten they existed. In his office that morning, when he shook her hand, she had suddenly felt a warmth of affection, of nostalgia, of gratitude even—and again in the lobby—he had somehow made her feel safe. It was his friendliness that was so unsettling. She had grown used to unfriendly people" (p. 191).

Davis represents the possibility for salvation, not the reality, and his positive influence is undermined by the tense afternoon Ruth spends waiting to hear from Paul. Forced to leave work without hearing from him, increasingly tense as she imagines him with the gallery owner's daughter, she begins to barhop in between calling the apartment to see if he has returned. An hour and four drinks later, with her agitation at a peak, she is at last able to realize that Paul can no longer save her, but she cannot let go. Finally, in tearful frustration, she rushes into the street, where "she walked briskly through the crowds to hide from them and from herself the fact that she did not know where she was going" (p. 197). The story ends on this note of indecision.

Her thoughts near the end of the story, though, have returned to the color imagery of her "sinful" youth and that which has been relevant to her blackness and to Paul's whiteness. Her color, the tangible manifestation of her dirt and guilt, can presumably be overpowered by Paul's purity, his whiteness. Unfortunately, in some things, she is "whiter" than Paul and he is "blacker" than she. She at least feels some commitment to their relationship; he has no respect for it. Since he has not accepted the cleansing role she has assigned to him (or cannot, or has been unaware of it), she has terrible thoughts now that the end is in sight. Of Paul's face, which used to be "the light that lighted up her world" (this light imagery goes along with the "lifting" imagery she has used earlier), she concludes: "Now it was all gone, it would never come again, and that face which was like the heavens [master and god] was darkening against her" (p. 194). Now that Paul can no longer save, is indeed becoming the darkness she has dreaded and which she has identified with the awesomeness of her lonely nights, she laments:

> She wished that she had never met him. She wished that he, or she, or both of them were dead. And for a moment she really wished it, with a violence that frightened her. Perhaps there was always murder at the very heart of love: the strong desire to murder the beloved, so that one could at last be assured of privacy and peace and be as safe and unchanging as the grave. Perhaps this was why disasters, thicker and more malevolent than bees, circled Paul's head whenever he was out of her sight. Perhaps in those moments when she had believed herself willing to lay down her life for him she had only been presenting herself with a metaphor for her peace, his death; death, which would be an inadequate revenge for the color of his skin, for his failure, by not loving her, to release her from the prison of her own. (pp. 194–95)

For how can the god save if he does not die? And what could cause him to die but his concern, like Jesus, his love for the people for whom he chooses to lay down his life? Since Paul does not love her, he cannot save her. Ruth sees, but she is unwilling to comprehend.

Other reflections upon color and the white lovers Ruth has had reveal that her problems are compounded by a strange mothering instinct. She wants to be saved, but she also wants to nurture. She thinks of a young man (boy, she calls him) and the confrontation about plantation history that occasioned their breakup. A man standing at the bar evokes these memories in her because he reminds her of the boy and of Paul. Ruth concludes that he, like the boy and Paul, is "lost." They turn to black women like herself in an effort to find themselves, and some of these women, like Ruth, need that seeking even as they realize they cannot ultimately provide what the "boys" need: "The sons of the masters were roaming the world, looking for arms to hold them. And the arms that might have held them—could not forgive" (pp. 196–97).

With this comment, which precedes by a few sentences Ruth's dash out into the night, Baldwin changes the thematic focus of the story. It shifts the burden of guilt completely to Paul for something inherent in his racial history instead of keeping attention on how Ruth has tried to use color to her own advantage (for healing purposes). As a member of a powerful race, Paul may be guilty of any number of things, but it is the power and purity Ruth sees represented in Paul's color that have driven her to him for salvation. For Baldwin now to suggest that it is Paul who is really seeking salvation is fine, but that is not where we expect to be led and left. For what does such knowledge do for Ruth? It does not really free her from Paul, and it certainly does not make her think better of herself. If this epiphanic revelation is truly to be taken as such, then Ruth should recognize that she has been the source of sustenance and power, and she, not Paul, bears the gift of salvation. That revelation should give her strength and inspire her with a specific direction, not to wandering the streets in a physical symbol of the mental confusion which, if the last scene is to accomplish its purpose, should be resolved by now. For Ruth not to know where she is going leaves a possibility that she will return to Paul in a denial of what she has presumably just learned. Such an action would ensure her continued wallowing in the wilderness of guilt, doubt, and confusion instead of her emergence as a healthy, or potentially healthy, black woman.

Ruth is left as a black woman who has been set adrift culturally and racially and has not found supports viable enough to provide what she has lost. She knows the path of the church is too restricting for her, but what she has found thus far is equally restricting. She cannot conceptualize an existence for herself beyond that of someone judging her and holding her accountable for her actions, which perpetuates her sense of guilt. She hates the situation with Paul, but it at least keeps her consistently engaged. When she is confronted with the prospect of Paul's permanent absence, she wanders out into the night in an utter state of confusion. Because she has not yet totally assumed responsibility for herself and for her own happiness, she does not know where to turn. She has grown up seeking comfort, support, approval, and criticism from sources outside herself; that they have all failed her has not lessened her enthusiasm for searching. With Paul's departure, she is finally confronted with a do-or-die situation; the story ends with her dilemma unresolved. Out of the church, but not outside the pull of its morality; out of the black community, but not free of the implications of blackness; Ruth is a lost woman who cannot find within herself the power to make a life for herself. In her weakness she has ties with Elizabeth, and in her outsider status she anticipates Ida in *Another Country*—with the exception that Ida will find the strength to move into another realm of self-definition and will attempt to make her way outside the black community and outside the church.

CHAPTER THREE

THE EXORCISING MEDIUM

Another Country

Guilt and suffering are paramount in *Another Country* (1962), where Baldwin again treats the relationship between a black woman and a white man. Less directly tied to the church, but still no less harsh in evaluating herself, Ida Scott is a paradox of stricture and freedom. She is unmarried and living away from home, so there is no relative or other authoritarian figure looking over her shoulder to keep her on the straight and narrow path. She can therefore act, and, minus the unrelenting conscience of a mother or an aunt, she can act more freely than an Elizabeth or a Florence can. At one of the final important scenes in the novel, however, we discover that she has been almost as strict in judging her own actions as a Sister McCandless would have been. Like Ruth Bowman in "Come Out the Wilderness," Ida may be out of the church, but she is not completely shed of the conscience that a church upbringing has bequeathed to her.

Baldwin has set up the novel in such a way that we can measure Ida's guilt only in direct proportion to the guilt she forces others around her to feel. Upon the death of her brother, Rufus, she moves into the circle of whites who have been closest to him and tries to make them assume responsibility for his suicide. She accomplishes her goal almost too well, for she suffers in direct proportion to her ability to inflict suffering upon them. She is guilty, her actions unconsciously show, of the same things of which she accuses Rufus' friends—having failed to see that Rufus was suffering, or if she saw, having failed to do something about it. Her assertions in the novel are often contrary to this evaluation, but her actions suggest otherwise. Since a major premise of the novel is the need to experience other people's suffering in order to know one's own, and since Ida works so hard to make other people suffer, their suffering becomes a measure of her own. She has no narrative voice assigned to her in the story; therefore, the white characters and the narrative voices following them become mirror images for the pain and guilt she feels for having literally failed to be her brother's keeper. Indeed, her nearly fanatical perpetuation of Rufus' memory hints at the incestuous connection between brother and sister that Baldwin will develop symbolically in *If Beale Street Could Talk* and explicitly in *Just Above My Head*. Rufus' and Ida's case provides the psychological antecedent for what becomes a major theme in Baldwin's later fiction.

Ida's notion that she should have felt responsibility for Rufus has grown in part from the church-centered family of which her mother is head. Both she and Rufus have grown up in the church and both can attribute the earliest expressions of their musical talents to opportunities provided for them by that church environment. For Ida, therefore, there is the double guilt associated with the fact that she has moved from sacred to secular expressions of her talent and, within that secular environment, she has failed to be honest in her singing; she has used her body to try to further her career as a singer. There is a more pervasive guilt, therefore, in having failed her mother and her brother by turning from their good little sister and daughter to "the biggest whore around." All of the places where Ida finds herself as an adult are a contrast to the safety of the church in which she found herself as a child and as a teenager.

Ida becomes the burden bearer for Baldwin's major theme in the novel, a function that allows her character to develop—within severely compressed space—but that also places her at the center of Baldwin's overall purpose for the novel. That purpose can be capsulized in a comment about one of the other characters in the novel. Vivaldo, Ida's white lover, roams the streets one night wondering where she is and rehearsing the excuses she will present to him when she does arrive. He is distraught, unable to face Ida with his fears about their rapidly deteriorating relationship and equally unable to understand Ida's vengeful approach to their affair. Baldwin says of

Vivaldo at this point: "Love was a country he knew nothing about." [1] That sentence serves as a metaphor not only for what happens to Vivaldo and Ida, but for all of the sexual love relationships in the novel. In a world where numerous copulations and infidelities occur, [2] and in which people are forever trying to commune with their bodies but are limited by them, Baldwin suggests that each individual is more than an island: he or she is a country apart from everyone else around him or her. This is true in love, and it is especially true when one experiences suffering and pain.

Baldwin's metaphor suggests that human beings are isolated from each other by sex, race, culture, and nationality as well as by some existential loneliness of the human spirit. For any human being to reach out to another, therefore, great effort is necessary. The effort intensifies in direct proportion to the level of involvement. Little is needed for impersonal cocktail party conversation; more is needed for casual sexual involvement, the passing fulfillment of physical need; but the greatest effort must be exerted between people who would truly love, care for, and commit themselves to each other. When Rufus (black) meets Leona (white) at a jazz set, for example, he is smugly confident that she is attracted to him. When she accompanies him to the party afterward and he sees her as a possible sexual outlet, she becomes slightly more individualized for him, and he must concentrate on his "line" to the extent necessary to seduce her. After the seduction and beginning with the growth of the affair, Rufus is forced to see Leona as a person, not merely as an outlet. To love her would be to exert the greatest effort possible toward going into her country and in turn allowing her into his. Race and culture make such openness impossible for Rufus. Instead of opening up and sharing with Leona, he becomes closed to such an extent that he drives her insane and destroys himself. [3] The negative example with Rufus and Leona will be replayed with Ida and Vivaldo as we watch to see if Ida will be more giving and forgiving than her brother.

To Baldwin, love relationships mean responsibility and, more important, exposing one's self: vulnerability. At the heart of vulnerability is a trust that the loved one will understand whatever is revealed to him or her and will not use that knowledge as a weapon. The lover, in turn, has the responsibility to keep the weapon of his or her knowledge sheathed. These are lessons that Ida and Vivaldo must learn. Because human beings instinctively seek their own survival and usually prefer pleasure to responsibility, the distance from one country to another is often too great a leap for them to undertake. Thus, they use each other as receptacles of their passion, or to advance careers, or to play the roles of wives and husbands—for marriage does not dissolve the distance between the countries.

This basic tendency in human beings to protect themselves from each other is complicated by several things, but especially by race. Though Baldwin's novel treats the distance between white males and white females, between Americans and Frenchmen, and between heterosexuals and homosexuals, the greatest distance he explores is that between blacks and whites. That engulfing distance informs Rufus' suicide a few pages into the novel and his sister Ida's vengeful reaction to the whites she accuses of having passively watched her brother die. Rufus kills himself because of his physical, moral, and mental degeneration, because he watches himself become an animal in his relationship with Leona. Except for a few scenes with Leona, his racial dilemma is full blown at the novel's opening rather than dramatized in it, but we quickly realize that the differences between blacks and whites form the basis of his problem. He has already "received the blow from which he never would recover" (p. 14), and his memory of racial incidents clearly shows that his depression is beyond alleviation. Has Ida received the same blow?

Ida enters the novel after Rufus' death to accuse Vivaldo, Cass, and Richard, Rufus' long-standing friends, of having failed to understand him well enough to save him. It is because he was black that he died, Ida maintains, and they, downtown in his presence, could not see about Rufus what she, uptown in Harlem, had no problem in seeing. They were too concerned about themselves (Vivaldo and Richard are writers and Cass is Richard's wife) to make that trip into Rufus' troubled country. Although they shared a bohemian or near bohemian life-style with Rufus, they never really made the effort to understand him. Later, Eric, a former lover of Rufus who was in Paris at the time of the suicide, will also be drawn into the circle of implied guilt.

For all its actions, the novel is really more of a treatise on the ideas of isolation, communication, and understanding that the actions are designed to dramatize. Ida, as black woman in a bohemian, sometimes middle-class, white world, becomes one of the focuses of the distance human beings must cross to *know* each other truly and thoroughly. Few critics have considered Ida worthy of extensive commentary *in her own right*; they usually comment on her only passingly in relation to other characters' development and fulfillment.

George Kent, though, considers her one of "the more adequately developed characters" in *Another Country*—along with Rufus and Eric—but his short article does not allow for extensive commentary. Colin MacInnes maintains that Rufus and Ida "redeem the book," and Fred L. Standley asserts that "the narrative strand of Vivaldo and Ida is central to the novel's movement; it is, after all, the presence of these two characters which runs through all three sections."[4] Ida certainly has individuality in the novel, but she serves too as a way for the white characters, especially Vivaldo and Cass, to learn more about themselves and more about Ida and Rufus, and thereby about blacks in general.

Ida comes into the novel with a purpose, then; she wants vengeance for Rufus' death. She wants to induce guilt in the whites at the same time she wants to use them, especially Ellis, a white television producer, to further her career as an aspiring singer. She makes constant references to the need for whites to pay dues, but the nature of the dues paying is more often surmised than articulated. Certainly she wants Vivaldo to feel guilt, to experience mental suffering, but she has little idea of the ultimate purpose of her vengeance. Is guilt enough, or is the guilt designed to alter consciousness? Does she simply want to make Vivaldo uncomfortable by wielding sexual and racial power over him, or does she really want to effect some essential change in him? And she does not appear to have thought out where the relationship with Ellis will take her if and after she becomes a singer.

Ida grows into personhood as the novel progresses; she is, Eckman maintains, "the figure with whom Baldwin was most concerned."[5] Initially, she is Rufus' little sister who sets out to taunt, and if possible punish, those she considers responsible for his death. She becomes, as Stanley Macebuh concludes, "the personification of Baldwin's rage."[6] Therefore, though she has a recognizable presence, she is more a medium, a vehicle for the memory of Rufus and the medium through which the whites can exorcise their guilt for having somehow failed Rufus. Her relationship to Rufus points back to the earlier Baldwin fiction and forward to the later fiction; it resembles the brother/sister relationship Baldwin implied would be ideal in *Go Tell It on the Mountain*—if Florence would submit to expectations—and that he develops as such in *If Beale Street Could Talk* and *Just Above My Head*. To Ida, Rufus is the most important male image in her life; in fact, it could safely be advanced that Ida, unlike Florence, worships her brother. To Ida, Rufus is the quintessential big brother. The fact that Rufus is older and the assumed protector, unlike Gabriel, may be relevant. Rufus becomes a godlike figure to Ida personally and symbolically in that he dies in order that she may live, grow, and blossom into her full potential. Rufus as brother takes on dimensions of the Polyneices role; like Antigone, Ida ensures a peaceful death for her brother by forcing those who have had most intimate contact with him to remember him well even if they have not buried him properly. As a sacrificed Christ figure, Rufus is a constant reminder of the need to live fully, but to keep one's life in order for that final reckoning. Rufus is central; Ida is an extension of that centrality after his early disappearance from the novel: thus, a major problem from the beginning is how much of Ida is Ida and how much of Ida is Rufus. She becomes a priestess keeping vigil at the altar of her brother, a servant to his memory. Of secondary importance in comparison to Rufus, she is nonetheless the major focus for the themes of guilt and redemption that are worked out in the novel.

The earliest scene we have to support the notion that Rufus is more legend than flesh and blood to Ida occurred when she was still a teenager in pigtails. This scene is apparently one of many in which Ida cherished the occasions on which her big brother appeared from his romantic life downtown to rescue her from her parents' apartment. On those outings, she was a princess and Rufus the wand carrier who made her wishes come true.

The scene under consideration occurred the one time Vivaldo accompanied Rufus to visit his parents and Ida, and her glorification of Rufus is apparent. She is delighted to see her brother and gives Vivaldo the aura of a "glamorous stranger" (p. 120) because he is in Rufus' presence. Mrs. Scott explains that when Ida and Rufus were younger, "Rufus just couldn't do no wrong, far as Ida was concerned" (p. 121), that Ida had crawled into bed with him on nights when she felt afraid because "she just felt *safe* with him." To the young Ida, Rufus was her ticket away from the physical ugliness of her neighborhood as well as from the many traps it held for young people, away from "cans, bottles, papers, filth" (p. 118), away from the likes of Willie Mae, a former girlfriend of Rufus, who has had "some cat turn . . . her on, and then he split" (p. 122). Ida clearly disapproves of Willie Mae, but who can say that the fourteen-year-old girl will not be a Willie Mae in two or three years? Those are the kinds of things from which, perhaps unconsciously, she expected Rufus to remove her. She says later: "I'd counted on Rufus to get me out of there—I knew he'd do anything in the world for me, just like I would for him. It hadn't occurred to me that it wouldn't happen. I *knew* it would happen" (p. 349). And when Rufus killed himself, that expectation was shattered. "I felt that I'd been robbed," Ida says, "and I *had* been robbed—of the only hope I had" (p. 350).

Presented as one of Vivaldo's reminiscences after Rufus' death, the scene of the visit to the Scott home serves not only to establish Ida's relationship to Rufus; it also serves to establish the guilt that Vivaldo will increasingly feel for having failed Rufus, especially after having been granted such an intimate look into Rufus' private world. The fact that Vivaldo is encouraged to recall the scene after his renewed acquaintance with Ida, and following Rufus' funeral, underscores her value as tangible penance. Vivaldo's guilt for having failed Rufus is compounded by the fact that he has helped not only to remove Rufus from his own life, but that he has also caused him to be removed from Ida, for whom he occupied such a special space.

To Ida, Rufus had represented Dream with a capital D, and his death meant a reality she was not ready to face. Near the end of the novel, when Cass asks what one should replace dreams with, Ida says with re.lity. Throughout most of her sordid adventures, however, she is unable to follow her own advice. She consciously sets out to pay those who were around Rufus back for what she thinks they have done to him. Her commitment to Rufus is shown in two emblems that she uses to remember him; both serve as talismen by which the priestess of the altar keeps the candles lit for the god she worships. If she serves him faithfully enough, perhaps she will exorcise her own guilt for the moments when she has briefly allowed the flame to die. The two emblems are metaphors for vengeance and both suggest the extent to which Ida has little life of her own. Her major objective is to live for Rufus.

The more prominent of the two emblems is a ruby-eyed snake ring Rufus brought to Ida when he returned from the navy. The most tangible sign of her desire for vengeance, it is simultaneously the symbol of her own imprisonment. As long as she wears the ring, there can be no Ida; there can only be Rufus' little sister who will not allow herself to grow into a person or a woman. The ring is first mentioned when Rufus is wandering around on the night he commits suicide. He thinks of the good times as opposed to his current circumstances, of the gifts he has brought to Ida, of the startling discovery that she is growing into a beautiful woman. He thinks of watching her twist "the ruby-eyed snake ring" (p. 12) on her long little finger as she thanked him for a shawl he had brought her, and he is glad she cannot see him now, for he is acutely aware of how his family, like John Grimes's mother Elizabeth, had been "counting" on him.

Encircling Ida's finger, the ring extends its imprisoning power to her mind and body as she uses both to make Vivaldo and others pay their dues for taking Rufus away from her. She says she has been robbed; through the memory of the ring, she expects to have her coffers replenished. The ring is a prominent adornment, a tangible memory in most of Ida's dealings with whites, and it becomes the identifying characteristic by which she is remembered. When she calls Cass asking for information about Rufus because the family has been out of touch with him for so long, it is Ida's ring that Cass recalls most vividly: "She remembered a very young, striking, dark girl who wore a ruby-eyed snake ring" (p. 79). Combining both higher and baser qualities in its precious stone and the venomous snake image, the ring will increasingly become a symbol of Ida's tortured relationship with whites, of the mixture of goodness she attaches to her brother and the destruction she attaches to whites. But even as she herself is in many ways a precious rarity, she allows the memory of her brother to poison all of her relationships. Only when she is able to separate her life from her brother's, her desire for vengeance from her need for love, is she able to take off the ring.

Meanwhile, it binds her to Rufus, and it keeps her voluntarily isolated within her own country. Her arrival at Cass and Richard Silenski's house on the afternoon following Rufus' suicide (but before his death has been discovered) shows her clinging to the ring because she cannot cling to her absent brother. Since Cass, Richard, and Vivaldo, who is also present, have seen Rufus last, Ida comes seeking more information about him. Her concern about where he is and how he looked is tied to the ring. "He's the only big brother I got," she explains, after she has spent some time haunting the streets trying to find Rufus. "She sipped her drink, then put it on the floor beside her chair. She played with the ruby-eyed snake ring on her long little finger" (p. 88). Rufus is always present, sometimes subconsciously, in Ida's memory. Even at the gayest of times, or so it would seem to others, Ida twists, plays with, or strokes the ring on her finger.

Cass remembered it immediately, and it is what Vivaldo sees most vividly after he first makes love to Ida. Ida sleeps restlessly and stirs, "as though she had been frightened. The scarlet eye on her little finger flashed" (p. 148). Even in giving her body to Vivaldo, she does not give of herself; she shuts him farther away from her even at those moments she is presumably most private with him. The essential gulf she sees between them, what will continue to make them two countries instead of one, is that she is black and he is white.

The ring is no less striking when Eric meets Ida for the first time. His attention goes from the ring to features in Ida that remind him painfully of his affair with Rufus. "On the little finger of one hand, she wore a ruby-eyed snake ring. . . . She was far more beautiful than Rufus and, except for a beautifully sorrowful, quicksilver tension around the mouth, she might not have reminded him of Rufus. But this detail, which he knew so well, caught him at once" (p. 211). Eric can see Ida's resemblance to Rufus, but she is also a walking monument to his memory. She is wearing the shawl he has given her, and the ring; both point to her desire for vengeance.

In difficult moments, when she is unsure or when she is in the process of making a decision, Ida uses the ring as a touchstone to reinforce her determination. On the night that she and Vivaldo watch a movie with Cass and Eric, who has a bit part in it, Ida is anxious to get rid of the men so she can go to Harlem to meet Ellis. She persuades Cass to go with her: "I wish you'd come up and have one drink with me up there," she says to Cass, and "she kept twisting the ring on her little finger" (p. 291). Because Cass is having an affair with Eric and Ida knows it, Cass feels Ida uses that knowledge to force an outing that might otherwise have been considered casual. Ida may twist her ring, as if undecided, but she is resolved to use Cass to cover her own assignation. As they talk in the cab on the way to Harlem, Ida emphasizes to Cass the distance between herself and Vivaldo: "'I'll never marry Vivaldo, and'—she tapped her ring again—'it's hard to see what's coming, up the road. But I don't seem to see a bridegroom'" (p. 292). She will continue to shut herself out in part because she does not believe either Vivaldo or Cass is capable of understanding her and in part because there is something in her that does not desire exposure even if she were capable of opening up to someone; her fondling of the ring heightens her separateness.

Twin symbol of vengeance and isolation, the ring can only lose its significance when Ida ventures into someone else's country and allows that someone to enter hers. That someone is Vivaldo. Only when Ida stops punishing Vivaldo and allows him to become spiritually intimate with her can she take off the ring. That growth and progression occurs near the end of the novel. In a scene with Vivaldo in which she decides to tell all, Ida slowly begins to distance herself from the destructive side of Rufus' memory. She reveals her affair with Ellis, explains what Rufus has meant to her, and analyzes why she has been driven to hurt Vivaldo. She must reexamine her actions because, unexpectedly, she has fallen in love with Vivaldo. She makes that announcement, then sits "perfectly still, looking down, the fingers of one hand drumming on the table. Then she clasped her hands, the fingers of one hand playing with the ruby-eyed snake ring, slipping it half-off, slipping it on" (p. 345). Her gesture indicates the last step she must make to be truly one with Vivaldo. She recognizes her love for him, but she still clings to Rufus. Her confession of love leads to other confessions and explanations and finally to cleansing tears. Not yet able to part with the ring, Ida tells Vivaldo of still other affairs with white men, releasing heart-wrenching tears. "She covered her mouth, her tears spilled down over her hand, over the red ring" (p. 355), which is the last reference to the ring. It is still a strong enough reference to indicate future direction—that Ida will soon take it off. At least the snake-eyed reference is diminished here and, more important, Ida's tears are washing over the ring, which may suggest that the cleansing of her soul will extend to the associations she connects with the ring. Nothing has touched it before; by allowing the tears to taint it, so to speak, she simultaneously allows them to cleanse it of unpleasant connotations. Her resolve, after all, is to stay with Vivaldo and try to make their relationship work.

The second emblem that ties Ida to Rufus and that receives more than passing reference is a pair of earrings she wears. They are cufflinks made into earrings and, though Ida does not know it, were originally a gift of love from Eric to Rufus. In a way, therefore, while Ida claims to have known empirically and intuitively much more about Rufus than his friends did, there are still some things she does not know. The cufflinks are also mentioned on the night when Rufus wandered the streets before his suicide. Being picked up and fed by a homosexual on the prowl forced Rufus to remember the cruelty with which he had made Eric pay for loving him and the special things that Eric had done for him. Eric, rich white boy from Alabama who discovered it was his fate to love men, had given up the last vestige of heterosexuality for Rufus. Eric

> had had a pair of cufflinks made for Rufus, for Rufus's birthday, with the money which was to have bought his wedding rings: and this gift, this

confession, delivered him into Rufus's hands. Rufus had despised him because he came from Alabama; perhaps he had allowed Eric to make love to him in order to despise him more completely. Eric had finally understood this, and had fled from Rufus, all the way to Paris. But his stormy blue eyes, his bright red hair, his halting drawl, all returned very painfully to Rufus now.   (p. 43)

His guilt forces Rufus to give the cufflinks to Ida, and he thinks that they are "now in Harlem, in Ida's bureau drawer" (p. 44). Ida wears them proudly, thus exhibiting another tie to Rufus' past and stifling her future.

Eric notices the earrings on the night he stands at the bar waiting for Vivaldo and Ida. Ida throws back her head laughing at something one of the musicians has said and

> her heavy silver earrings caught the light. Eric felt a pounding in his chest and between his shoulderblades, as he stared at the gleaming metal and the laughing girl. He felt, suddenly, trapped in a dream from which he could not awaken. The earrings were heavy and archaic, suggesting the shape of a feathered arrow: *Rufus never really liked them.* In that time, eons ago, when they had been cufflinks, given him by Eric as a confession of his love, Rufus had hardly ever worn them. But he had kept them. And here they were, transformed, on the body of his sister.   (p. 211)

It is a painful memory for Eric and, unknowingly, Ida succeeds in making at least one of Rufus' friends remember him intensely. Later, Eric finds the courage to mention the earrings: "They're very beautiful . . . your earrings." "Do you like them?" she asks. "My brother had them made for me—just before he died" (p. 218). And she uses the occasion to perpetuate her legendary view of Rufus and her own philosophy developed as a result of what has happened to Rufus. She says to Eric:

> "He was a very beautiful man, a very great artist. But he made"—she regarded him with a curious, cool insolence—"some very bad connections. He was the kind who believed what people said. If you told Rufus you loved him, well, he believed you and he'd stick with you till death. I used to try to tell him the world wasn't like that." She smiled. "He was much nicer than I am. It doesn't pay to be too nice in this world." (p. 218)

Included in that "cool insolence" is a hint that Eric, since he has confessed to knowing Rufus, may also be guilty of having abused him in some way. Ironically, it is Eric who could testify to Rufus' abuses, because Rufus hated himself and the world too much ever to allow anyone to get close to him.

Ida's shortsightedness about Rufus' true personality and his past life shows again that she does not know him as well as she professes, for she has seen him only in the family context in Harlem, when he was decidedly on his best behavior. She never learns, for example, that it was just as important for Rufus to keep the romance going with her as it was for her to believe in that romance, even if it meant he had to borrow money from Vivaldo to play the big man with his younger sister. Too busy blaming the whites in the novel for having seen only a portion of Rufus' personality, Ida fails to see that she herself is guilty of the same failing. Rufus' trips to Harlem have probably been infrequent, even more so in the last couple of years of his life, so there are many gaps, from the earlier period as well as from the latter one, when Ida really did not know her brother's true status and frame of mind. Her need to implicate others forestalls her confrontation with her own guilt, and she gets away with so much precisely because she is black. The whites are uncomfortable with her and don't really know what to do with her anger; their own guilt, compounded by Ida's accusations and insinuations, enables Ida to get away with a lot that she might not otherwise. It is partly a breakdown of Baldwin's thesis about guilty, blind, insensitive whites and innocent, knowledgeable, suffering blacks in that Ida is one of the blacks who is not so very innocent or knowledgeable about some things (though the corollary to this would suggest that her whoring activities are in part due to the system perpetuated by whites).

In many ways a personification of Rufus' anger and in other ways a distortion of what he actually was, Ida serves to tweak everybody's conscience or at least to dredge up their unpleasant memories. The function Ida serves coincides with the way in which her character is revealed in the novel. The story is Ida's story only in as much as she comes into contact with Cass, Vivaldo, and Eric, for point of view is theirs, not hers. We must learn of her affair with Ellis through others; we do not follow her to those meetings. What we learn of her early in the novel is reflected in Vivaldo's memory of his visit to Rufus' home and in the gathering at Cass's when Ida comes seeking information about Rufus. The only time Ida is revealed to us directly is when she speaks; otherwise, she is seen through someone else's vision and in someone else's space. This technique of presenting Ida ties her to Rufus as well. She, like Rufus, is outside the circle of whites who know them both, yet she touches all of them. To know themselves, they have to learn more of Ida, and she does not make it easy for them. She is just as elusive narrationally as she is personally to the white protagonists in the novel.

To give Ida a point of view would be comparable to giving Caddy a section of *The Sound and the Fury*. Though we learn much about Caddy through Benjy, Quentin, Jason, and Dilsey, she is still as far from us at times as the myth of the South that she is drawn to represent. We see her actions, we know what she looks like and what she wears, but we do not really *know* her; the outside, the form of her existence and of her being, will forever shield the essence of her personality from us. So too with Ida. We know how she looks, what kind of effect she has upon people and how they respond to her. Until the very last scenes of the novel, however, we are left to speculate upon her motives, upon what truly drives her to be what she is. The whites must work to get to know her, just as the reader must, for Baldwin lays most of the responsibility for the ugliness surrounding the racial situation in America upon whites. To give Ida a point of view would reduce blackness to a commonplace level where it could be easily dismissed. Instead, the whites, especially Vivaldo, must reach out to that other country and understand Ida and encourage her to forgive and understand them; that is the only path that will allow them to understand and save themselves.

For Vivaldo and Cass, Ida becomes a touchstone for racial understanding, and for Vivaldo she becomes the black woman through whom he learns more about himself. His sexual experiences before his liaison with Ida consisted primarily of clandestine visits to Harlem to deposit his white seed in black whores. Most black women have been whores to him, and he has not thought about the political, racial, or moral implications of his actions. In order to save his relationship with Ida, he must grow at the same time he must encourage her to grow. For Eric and Richard, Ida reveals to them the pitfalls that lie in wait for all human beings. Her affair with Ellis mirrors Cass's affair with Eric and perhaps forces Richard to see connections between his wife and a black woman that he would not otherwise have seen.

What we see of Ida, then, comes through her relationships with these four white characters. How the discussion of her character must be approached reflects again the kind of role black women usually play in Baldwin's fiction. They are subordinate to other characters, sacrificing for them, or like Ida, "sandwiched" in between them. Ida is therefore a thoroughly dependent character in terms of critical evaluation of the novel; she is always to be treated in someone else's orbit, not necessarily other people in her own. Her life choices are made in reaction to others, how she lives is dictated by others, and ultimately her pain and suffering are as much external as they are internal. Primarily reactive, the little portion of Ida's personality that is not can almost be overlooked.

From her entry into the novel, Ida reacts to the whites and makes them react to her. She may force them to see herself (and Rufus retrospectively) in a different light, but she almost loses her soul in the process. She represses her emotion to control others, then finds herself trapped by an equally powerful emotion, that of love. The fine line she has walked between love and hate is represented on one level by men and women and on a more important level by blacks and whites. In order for love and understanding to triumph, each character, and Ida most of all, must be baptized in suffering. Since they could not or would not witness Rufus' suffering, they must witness their own, and some of them must witness Ida's. Those who survive and grow do so because they pay the dues of cathartic identification with other suffering human beings. By immersing themselves in those other countries of suffering, they accept the vulnerability and the responsibility inherent in unselfish love.

To Cass, Ida is initially a beautiful black girl concerned about her brother, and, to us, Cass is initially the mothering center of the certified middle-class white American family. Both impressions change. When Ida arrives at Cass's door, Cass sees her as a beautiful young woman whose eyes remind her of Rufus (different characters will recognize different features of Rufus in Ida). She comments on Ida's beauty and "realized, for the first time, that a Negro girl could blush" (p. 86). That single, revisionist approach to Ida is only the first of many things Cass will discover about her and, through her, about herself. During the conversation about Rufus' whereabouts, Cass realizes "that something in Ida was enjoying this—the attention, the power she held for this moment. This made Cass angry, but then she thought: Good. It means that whatever's coming, she'll be able to get through it" (p. 90). The manipulative hardness Cass sees in Ida will take her not only through Rufus' suicide and funeral, but through the affair with Ellis and her bid to be a singer. Ida is a mixture of the kitten and the tigress; just as she combined a solemn occasion with a sense of detachment, a sense of enjoyment, she will also waver between destroying Vivaldo and loving him. She works as hard to induce guilt in him as she works to manipulate Ellis, through the pleasure of her body, to further her singing career.

Cass is willing to admit Ida into her circle of companions as a friendly gesture. She sees no harm in being generous to Rufus' little sister because Ida has no real meaning for her, except perhaps that Vivaldo is interested in Ida and that fact briefly raises the question about how Cass feels about interracial affairs. But Cass goes on with her neat little life, and the parties and gatherings with Ida and Vivaldo, until she discovers one day that Richard has compromised his writing talent and published a second-rate novel, and that she no longer believes in his ability or respects what he has accomplished. She finds herself safe, secure, the mother of two growing boys, and terribly unfulfilled and unhappy. In an effort to salvage something of her self, she engages in an affair with Eric, often using Vivaldo and Ida as the smokescreen to get away from Richard. Her stepping out of safety enables her to see Ida's situation more clearly, just as Tod Clifton's stepping out of a kind of security enables him to see in *Invisible Man.* Because Cass has risked her reputation, her children, and her husband, she begins to see a bit of the predicament in which most black women find themselves quite frequently.

These revelations come to Cass on the night that she and Eric go to the movie with Vivaldo and Ida. The men and women separate afterwards, Cass agreeing to go to Harlem for one drink with Ida, then home to Richard:

> As she said this, both she and Ida laughed. It was almost the first time they had ever laughed together; and this laughter revealed to Cass that Ida's attitude toward her had been modified by Ida's knowledge of her adultery. Perhaps Ida felt that Cass was more to be trusted and more of a woman, now that her virtue, and her safety, were gone. And there was also, in that sudden and spontaneous laughter, the very faintest hint of blackmail. Ida could be freer with Cass now, since the world's judgment, should it ever be necessary to face it, would condemn Cass yet more cruelly than Ida. For Ida was not white, not married, nor a mother. The world assumed Ida's sins to be natural, whereas those of Cass were perverse. (p. 291)

A closed chapter of female history is now opening up to Cass as she is forced to see a black woman in a specific, more than superficial way.

Her descent from her middle-class pedestal opens her eyes to what women experience who have never had the pedestal available to them. As the moment of enlightenment continues, Ida and Cass respond to each other more as women, not as females connected through their men, and Cass begins to see into another country.

Through this conversation, which takes place in the cab on the way to Harlem, Baldwin explores what Jacqueline Orsagh calls "the polarity of whore and virgin" with Ida and Cass. This part of Orsagh's discussion is revealing, but it is still somewhat limited by her extremes of interpretation. Neither Ida nor Cass is ultimately as destructive to her man as Orsagh suggests, and Ida's negative side does not need to be exaggerated to the extent Orsagh does for her point about whores and virgins to be made. It is striking to observe, too, that Orsagh sees black women in Baldwin's fiction only as they are relevant to her comments on the white females. Thus, only Ida receives any special treatment—because of her relationship to Cass.[7]

The polarity in the two women develops in the way they see themselves and the world. Ida, at twenty-two, finds it "hard to imagine" that Cass, at thirty-four, has "dealt with—two men" in her "whole life" (p. 291). Cass readily admits that she has been sheltered, while we will later learn from Ida that she has slept with many men, several of them white. Cass thinks Ida can marry Vivaldo just because she loves him, but Ida recognizes that love can be "a goddamn pain in the ass" (p. 292). The romantic vision of shelter gives way to the reality of life. To Cass's comment that Ida does not know what it is like to have a baby, Ida responds that such knowledge is easily available to her, but babies are not her "kick." What Cass sees as a part of her shelter, Ida sees in a different light:

> "*You* don't know, and there's no way in the world for you to find out, what it's like to be a black girl in this world, and the way white men, and black men, too, baby, treat you. You've never decided that the whole world was just one big whorehouse and so the only way for you to make it was to decide to be the biggest, coolest, hardest whore around, and make the world pay you back that way. . . . I bet you think we're in a goddamn park. You don't know we're in one of the world's great jungles. You don't know that behind all them damn dainty trees and shit, people are screwing and sucking and fixing and dying." (p. 293)

Cass, aware of her perceptual and visual limitations, "looked out at the park, trying to see what Ida saw; but, of course, she saw only the

trees and the lights and the grass and the twisting road and the shape
of the buildings beyond the park" (p. 293).

The safety not available to Ida and that Cass has put in jeopardy
forces them to continue their discussion—not in anger, but in a kind
of revelation that would be impossible under other circumstances.
Ida bluntly tells Cass she will not marry Eric because she is not "*that
crazy*" (p. 294), and Cass is forced to admit that the best she can hope
for in five years is that she and Eric will be friends. As it turns out, she
tells Richard about the affair later that night, and the connection with
Eric dissolves very shortly. Perhaps it has been in part as a result of
the conversation with Ida that Cass decides to tell the truth to
Richard. She willingly submits to the suffering Ida has predicted for
her. When they were getting out of the taxi, Cass had insisted on
paying the driver; "'Let me. . . . It's just about the only thing that a
poor white woman can still do.' Ida looked at her, and smiled. 'Now,
don't you be like that,' she said, 'because you *can* suffer, and you've
got some suffering to do, believe me'" (p. 296). Even though Cass has
shared a spiritual intimacy with Ida, she still relies on her economic
advantage, which has been presented as the way of escaping some of
the poverty and ugliness Ida has been talking about. From love and
life, however, there is no shelter, no safety. Eventually, the soul must
be bared to the loved one, as Cass does with Richard, and that
vulnerable baring can only bring suffering.

Yet their conversation has drawn them close enough for Cass to
defend Ida against insinuations by a member of Ellis' party. When the
woman wonders "if his wife knows where he is" as Ida and Ellis are
dancing, Cass retorts: "Mrs. Ellis and Miss Scott have known each
other for quite a long time, long before Mrs. Ellis's marriage" (p. 302),
and when the woman continues by observing "how strange that is,"
Cass responds with "Not at all . . . they both worked in the same
factory." Cass is being deliberately reckless, but she understands
enough by this point to be daring in Ida's defense. What Cass does
may be admirable, but her one trip down from the pedestal has not
enabled her to see all that goes on in Ida's world. She fails to see that
Ellis and Ida are having an affair. That knowledge is revealed to her
later that evening by Richard, when he tells her to quit using Ida and
Vivaldo as excuses for her absences because he knows Ida has been
meeting Ellis. Though Cass senses, at one point in the conversation
in the Harlem barroom when Ida and Ellis are present, "the knowledge that black people had of white people" (p. 301), her perception

does not apply uniformly to all areas of life. As Ida has said of Vivaldo earlier, in connection with Rufus, there are some things one does not want to know about a friend. Cass does not see Ida's affair with Ellis because she does not want to see it. Knowledge would bring conscience, which in turn would demand action; she would have to think of her friend Vivaldo and whether or not he should be told. So she prefers to think that Ida has met Ellis only for business purposes; she is genuinely surprised when Richard tells her the truth.

Although she does not know of the affair, she does understand that, as she had used Ida and Vivaldo as "smoke screens to cover her affair with Eric," Ida has used her to cover her meeting with Ellis:

> Why should not Ida use *her*, then, to cover from Vivaldo her assignation with Ellis? She had silenced *them*, in relation to Richard—now she was silenced, in relation to Vivaldo. She smiled, but the smoke she inhaled was bitter. When she had been safe and respectable, so had the world been safe and respectable; now the entire world was bitter with deceit and danger and loss; and which was the greater illusion?   (p. 304)

Reflecting as she is riding home in a taxi with a young driver to whom she is very much attracted, she is forced again to realize the exposure stepping off her pedestal has brought to her: "Richard had been her protection, not only against the evil in the world, but also against the wilderness of herself. And now she would never be protected again" (p. 305). It was necessary to step off the pedestal, however, in order to grow, to learn more about herself, about Ida, and about others.

The measure of her growth is her confrontation with Richard about her affair with Eric. She begins to see some of the absence of safety that has been Ida's lot every day of her life. She willingly submits, from her point of view, to the ultimate potential destruction, which would be complete loss of the pedestal and everything that goes along with it. But she makes that journey and survives. She and Richard are not completely reconciled by the end of the novel, but indications are that they will be, and they will both be stronger. Just as Cass tells Richard the truth, and causes him to suffer, she must also face an additional truth of her own: that she is partly responsible for Richard's failures because she has encouraged him to attempt things he was incapable of accomplishing.

Perhaps it is too late for Richard to change the kind of work he does, but it is not too late for reconciliation. Cass's final words to Eric that it's "too late now" (p. 341) for Richard's and her marriage are really less fatalistic than they seem, for although she denies hope in one breath, in the next she talks of weathering things out with Richard. The safety of the pedestal has been shattered, but the reality with which it has been replaced is not ultimately destructive, and that reality has been shaped in part by Cass's contact with Ida.

To Richard, Ida is also Rufus' little sister, someone who must be accepted because of circumstances. Since Richard's point of view, like Ida's, is submerged to those of Cass, Vivaldo, and Eric, he provides little more knowledge about her other than being on the scene at many of the gatherings Ida attends. His attitude toward blacks, and therefore perhaps toward Ida, is revealed in two incidents related in the novel—Rufus' treatment of Leona and the beating up of Richard's sons by a group of black boys; the baser side of black people has been revealed to him, so he does not find it at all surprising that Ida engages in the affair with Ellis.

During the scene in which Richard announces Rufus' death to Cass and in the conversation following it, he says:

> "I don't love Rufus, not the way you did, the way all of you did. I couldn't help feeling, anyway, that one of the reasons all of you made such a kind of—*fuss*—over him was partly just because he was colored. Which is a hell of a reason to love anybody. I just had to look on him as another guy. And I couldn't forgive him for what he did to Leona. You once said you couldn't, either." (p. 93)

On the one hand, his honesty about not loving Rufus is commendable, but on the other hand, he is lying when he says he does not associate the lack of love or the violence with Rufus' color. Consider his reaction when his two sons come in from a fight. He pretends to be calm and explains, when one of his sons asks if the fight has occurred because"they're colored and we're white," that "the world is full of all kinds of people, and sometimes they do terrible things to each other, but—that's not why" (p. 206), yet when his sons are settled and he returns to the living room with Eric, he mutters: "Little black bastards . . . they could have killed the kid. Why the hell can't they take it out on each other, for Christ's sake!" (p. 207). Parental anger is certainly justified in the situation, but Richard's anger focuses on violence done by blacks, not simply on violence. His comment about the boys taking it out on someone reveals, too, his subconscious admission that there is something amiss in race relations that blacks *should* take out on someone.

Richard's revelation of Ida's affair with Ellis is more functional than perceptive. It shows how far Cass has been away from people with whom she has spent a great deal of time. Ida, Richard tells Cass after the excursion to Harlem, has been with Ellis the many nights Cass has maintained she was with Vivaldo and Ida. "And it's been going on a long time," Richard concludes. When Cass asks how he knows, his question is penetrating: "How do *you—not* know it?" (p. 311), and adds that Cass and Vivaldo are "the only two in town" who do not know about the affair. What Cass and Vivaldo have failed to see with Ida and Ellis is another incident comparable to what all of his friends have failed to see with Rufus, or what they have refused to see. Vivaldo deliberately blinds himself to Ida's affair with Ellis, and Cass has similarly blinded herself subconsciously. She has not been suspicious the many times Ellis has been out without his wife and apparently enjoying the company of Ida. And she has not been suspicious earlier that evening in Harlem, even when the woman in the group made such unpleasant insinuations. Cass's desire to defend Ida has been admirable, but it has also been flawed by the fact that Cass is so willfully blind and selectively supportive. Richard can see the truth, and Ellis has confirmed it, because he has no personal, human interest in Ida that would conclude that her actions should be otherwise. For him, even though she is Rufus' little sister, and perhaps because of that fact, Ida is still a member of the nameless black mob capable of any violence or any whorish manipulation.

Eric, too, is forced to see Ida initially as Rufus' younger sister. Through her, he is forced to realize that the suffering he has gone to Paris to escape is only a miniscule portion of the pain of life, from which there is no escape. Initially, the cufflinks/earrings evoke painful memories for him of his affair with Rufus. Later, also through Ida, he is forced to come into contact with other blacks, and he is forced to witness the painful triangular development of the relationship between Ida, Vivaldo, and Ellis. His reaction to the other blacks perhaps illustrates what has happened to his relationship with Rufus. Rufus certainly made Eric suffer, but instead of understanding the agonies in Rufus that caused him to inflict suffering, Eric ran away from his pain as well as from that of Rufus. On the night he meets Ida and Vivaldo at a bar to hear Ida sing, he must sit and listen to the blues that have personified Rufus' suffering; it is something he cannot do, so he "did not really listen to the music, he could not; it remained entirely outside him, like some minor agitation of the air" (p. 214).

The musicians can be ignored because they are not the best, but Ida's stronger rendition of a bluesy song "made Eric look up" (p. 215). Eric has literally gone to another country in order to escape the painful suffering Ida sings about, and to which he must now listen and witness, thus emphasizing again the lack of protection for anyone who would truly love another.

Eric at least knows the potential for suffering, even if he has tried to escape it, and he sees that potential in Ida's treatment of Vivaldo and in Vivaldo's reaction to how other men respond to Ida. Eric sees that Ida's smiles at Vivaldo hold "some hint of the vindictive" and her lips curl sardonically at the same time he sees "how desperately one could love" Ida, "how desperately Vivaldo was in love with her" (p. 215). That desperation causes a jealousy in Vivaldo in the way Eric observes him stormily looking at a young man who watches Ida being lifted onto the stand with the musicians. Eric sees, too, that Ida clings to Vivaldo, but "there was something in it which was meant for Ellis. And Vivaldo seemed to feel this, too. He moved slightly away from Ida and picked up her handbag from the table—to give his hands something to do?" (p. 219). Eric can feel in Ida's careless maneuvers some of what Rufus has done to him, and he can see in Vivaldo's helplessness one similar to his own. That tension Eric has noticed curling around Ida's lips when he first met her personifies the tension that existed in his relationship to Rufus.

The memory of that tension continues as they walk from one bar to another. Eric is further forced to see the ugliness in the relationship between Ida and Vivaldo as they, walking ahead, engage in a conversation which drifts backward to Eric.

> He heard Ida. "—sweetie, don't *be* like that."
> "Will you stop calling me *sweetie*? That's what you call every miserable cock sucker who comes sniffing around your ass."
> "*Must* you talk that way?"
> "Look, don't you pull any of that *lady* bullshit on me."
> "—you talk. I'll never understand white people, never, never, never! How *can* you talk that way? How can you expect anyone else to respect you if you don't respect yourselves?"
> "*Oh*. Why the fuck did I ever get tied up with a *house* nigger? And I am not *white people!*"
> "—I warn you, I warn you!"
> "—*you're* the one who starts it! You *always* start it!"
> "—I knew you would be *jealous*. *That's* why!"
> "You picked a fine way to keep me from being—jealous, baby."

"Can't we talk about it *later*? Why do you always have to spoil everything?"

"Oh, sure, sure, I'm the one who spoils everything, all right!" (p. 222)

In a determined effort to blot out what he would rather not hear, Eric turns to talk with Ellis, whom he has earlier maintained that "he had no desire to talk to" (p. 221). His conscious mind may not yet have registered it, but, through Ida, he is constantly made to confront the unpleasantnesses of life. Of course, we can say that Eric's determination not to hear the conversation is a matter of politeness, of not wanting to intrude upon someone else's privacy. But it is also a function of his approach to life; he prefers the peaceful, the idyllic, to disturbances, even minor ones. Earlier, he has been pictured in an Edenic setting in his farmhouse in the South of France with Yves, his lover. Basking, swimming, drinking, and loving were the order of the day, and that is the kind of life Eric has come to appreciate following his affair with Rufus. Now he is forced to see another black person suffer and induce suffering, a black person who is tied to Rufus not only racially, but biologically.

Ever-vengeful Ida also questions Eric's relationship with Rufus, thus forcing him further back into the past he does not want to remember. At a table in another bar, Ida asks Eric if he had found it hard to be Rufus' friend, and his response in the negative causes "sweat in his armpits, on his forehead, between his legs." Intuitively sensing something more, Ida will not let the matter rest:

> "You may have wanted more from him than he could give. Many people did, men *and* women." She allowed this to hang between them for an instant. Then, "He was terribly attractive, wasn't he? I always think that that was the reason he died, that he was too attractive and didn't know how—how to keep people away." She sipped her drink. "People don't have any mercy. They tear you limb from limb, in the name of love. Then, when you're dead, when they've killed you by what they made you go through, they say you didn't have any character. They weep big, bitter tears—not for *you*. For themselves, because they've lost their toy." (pp. 224–25)

Her racial politics are harshly uncompromising, and they apply to all aspects of life. She has said earlier, of the attack upon Cass's and Richard's children: "I imagine . . . that it was in some kind of retaliation—for something some other boys had done to them" (p. 221), and Eric, for the sake of peace, had agreed. With Ida's "grim" view of love, though, he is forced to disagree by maintaining that he loved Rufus, that they "really *were* very good friends," and that it was an "awful shock" (p. 225) to him in Paris when he heard of Rufus' death. Subconsciously, Eric uses the physical distance he had hoped would diminish his own pain as the excuse for not knowing Rufus was suffering. Eric's defense comes, too, because Ida's view of Leona, Rufus' known lover, is so dismal. To Ida, Leona is "a terrible little whore of a nymphomaniac, from Georgia" and a "filthy white slut" (p. 225), images from which the sensitive Eric, who is from Alabama, would like to dissociate himself. Eric may be, as Donald Gibson suggests, "the most understanding, best adjusted character" in the novel, but Ida is still able to make him feel uncomfortable.[8]

Eric's ability to suppress things also comes out when he gets confirmation of Ida's affair with Ellis. Eric and Vivaldo become lovers on the same night Cass and Ida go to Harlem. Cass goes home, confronts Richard about her affair, learns of Ida's, then calls Eric the next morning with both pieces of news. The beautiful sexual experience Vivaldo and Eric have just shared, in which Eric discovered the surprising depth of feeling he has for Vivaldo, will not allow him to hurt Vivaldo further by telling him of Ida's long-standing infidelity, for Vivaldo has spent a great part of the evening discussing the punishing things Ida has done to him. So Eric ignores what Cass tells him about Ida and Ellis; only after Ida tells Vivaldo of her affair does Eric admit to Vivaldo that he has been told about it. At least concern for Vivaldo would make Eric's silence altruistic. Otherwise, he might seem more callous than he is, since he is more passive than active, more acted upon than doing, more the pleasure seeker than the willing sufferer. Even when things are presented from his point of view, he serves more as a medium, a reflector; he is not very reflective. What he learns from Ida's conversations can be surmised more than concluded definitively, and what he says serves as a measure of the reflection that must be going on in his mind.

To Vivaldo, the character most touched by her, Ida is the black woman with whom he falls in love and to whom he submits to be punished for the guilt he feels about all of his previous interracial relationships and for his negligence of Rufus. Before he becomes involved with Ida, his primary sexual preference had been for black whores in Harlem. To go to Harlem is to "screw" without commitment, to possess a body without being the least bit touched in return.

It is the ultimate in islandized isolation that Ida's presence will destroy, and his guilt about the lack of commitment to the bodies he uses is what makes him defenseless against her. "In Harlem," Baldwin writes, Vivaldo "had merely dropped his load and marked the spot with silver" (p. 115). The pleasure soon backfires, however, and he begins to encounter girls he wishes he had met elsewhere, or he despises the ones he meets. Ambivalence Vivaldo feels toward the girls and toward his desire and need for them is intensified because he is Rufus' friend and must see, from Rufus' point of view, the day-to-day oppression of blacks. It is when he goes to rescue Leona from a beating by Rufus that he remembers being conned in Harlem, and it is when he is trying to come to grips with the sexual habits of his neighbors that he thinks of other whores; their plight in turn directs his thoughts toward Rufus. The whores and Rufus are one in that they have both been screwed by the world at large.

Such connections, however, do not go far in informing Vivaldo's reaction to Ida. He is very much attracted to her, and says he loves her, but he has difficulty separating her from other whores he has known. His own insecurity causes him to believe almost anything of Ida, primarily because whoring black women are what he has been most exposed to. At a party at Cass's, Vivaldo insinuates that Ida is willing to use Ellis to further her singing career. She tearfully responds that he thinks she is "nothing but a whore" (p. 145). Maybe Ida has not yet considered using her body to get what she wants from Ellis, but Vivaldo's insinuation that she is capable of such an action is perhaps more devastating, in the freshness of their romance, than anything else could possibly be. Vivaldo still has in the back of his mind the mental trash that suggests that black women are unconsciously free with their bodies.

After Ida has told Vivaldo of her affair with Ellis, he reacts in a familiar way: to him, Ida is the ultimate whore who has conned him not only out of his money, but out of his affection. While he is trying to absorb all Ida tells him about Ellis, he "looked over at her, and a wilderness of anger, pity, love, and contempt and lust all raged together in him. She, too, was a whore; how bitterly he had been betrayed!" (p. 361). Sadly, Ida has not betrayed Vivaldo; he has betrayed himself. He has done so by refusing to face up to problems he and Ida have had, by choosing to believe the lies he knows she has told him about her absences, and by refusing to suffer openly what he has painfully suffered in private.

Vivaldo's guilt about having failed Rufus and about having used black women allows him to give Ida an unbridled license to cause him pain. His guilt is apparent as he and Cass are on their way to Rufus' funeral. He had earlier gone to Rufus' house, and he describes to Cass how he wanted to take Ida into his arms and kiss the accusatory look off her face; he wanted her and her family to know that, though they are black and he is white, "the same things have happened, really the *same* things" (p. 99). Cass correctly points out that the same things have not happened to Vivaldo *because* he is white. That is the essential difference between him and Rufus. So Vivaldo sits crying, feeling inadequate, wanting to protect and soothe Ida. Shortly after the service, he comments to Cass that he would like to "prove" to Ida one day "that the world's not as black as she thinks it is," and Cass adds, "or as white" (p. 108). Color consciousness, therefore, informs Vivaldo's sense of guilt. He will present himself to Ida as a fledgling Christ from whom she can exact the blood of dues paying she believes that white people owe to blacks.

When Vivaldo goes into the relationship with Ida, therefore, she easily takes advantage of his compromised position. Her vengeance is easily effected. Vivaldo understands what she is doing to him, but he lacks the power or the will to stop her. At one point, he asks Ida: "You're never going to forgive me, are you? for your brother's death" (p. 273), and her answer is silence. He says to Eric on the night they spend together: "She never lets me forget I'm white, she never lets me forget she's colored. And I don't care, I don't care—did Rufus do that to you? Did he try to make you pay?" (p. 287). He says to Ida during their final, revealing conversation: "What I've never understood . . . is that you always accuse me of making a thing about your color, of penalizing you. But you do the same thing. You always make me feel white. Don't you think that hurts me? You lock me out. And all I want is for you to be a part of me, for me to be a part of you. I wouldn't give a damn if you were striped like a zebra" (p. 348). And when he finally knows she is going to open herself up to him, he admits he is afraid, but asks her to tell him all because, he says, "I can't take any more of your revenge" (p. 351). The body he has presented to be crucified has suffered beyond death; his only hope of restoration is to bring it back to the realm of the living.

Vivaldo's submission to silent suffering has been infinitely more destructive to his psyche than anything he could have suffered openly. He has paralyzed himself with thoughts of Ida alone with

Ellis and has flagellated himself with the excuses Ida could make to him for her absences. All of her imagined excuses are an insult to his intelligence; still, he prefers those to facing the truth of Ida's affair with Ellis. He imagines her not going home from work because she has gone to see her family or is otherwise engaged in innocent activity, and "even though he knew that she was using him against himself, hope rose up hard in him, his throat became tight with pain, he willed away all his doubts" (p. 250). He torments himself, wandering the streets one night waiting for Ida to come home, only to discover when she does that "he lacked the courage to mention the name of Steve Ellis" (p. 270).

Vivaldo is unable to effect the protection he sought for Ida or that he desperately needs for himself. As Ida has accused him of doing earlier with his response to Rufus, Vivaldo has blocked out information he does not wish to know, but those things, "like demons in the dark," "reveal themselves" when least expected (p. 331). Those demons rise to chase Vivaldo into that other country he has been trying so desperately to avoid. As Ida tells her story, he can no longer escape commitment and responsibility; nor is he invulnerable to the final, crashing pain Ida heaps upon him.

Two incidents are relevant to the baring of herself Ida undergoes before Vivaldo and the reaction he has to it. First of all, Vivaldo has made love with Eric. He has been attracted to men before and sensed on one occasion that Rufus needed him to make love to him, or at least to hold him,[9] yet it is only when he tells Eric of the pain Ida has caused him is he able to love Eric. Pain, suffering, and removal of safety, Baldwin suggests, enable one to begin the opening-up process. By immersing oneself in "sins" uglier than those one is already guilty of, a certain kind of enlightenment emerges. As he embraces Eric, Vivaldo becomes "involved in another mystery, at once blacker and more pure" (p. 324). The choice of color imagery would be unfortunate but for its relevance to the blacks and whites in the novel. Vivaldo, who has been so pedestalized in his manliness and heterosexuality, is initiated into understanding Ida's sexual promiscuity by engaging in his own "perversion." Homosexuality can be considered more degenerate, "blacker" to some, and it is by going into this unknown territory that Vivaldo is better prepared to understand where Ida has been as a black person also maligned and outside the mainstream of acceptability. By being unfaithful to Ida with Eric, Vivaldo can also no longer stand in a position of absolute morality and judge her. His action with Eric is therefore purer because it is an act of love, free of using and taking, free of domination and exploitation.[10] Because he and Eric trust each other enough to be open and honest, there can be no negative evaluation attached to what they do, at least not by themselves. Vivaldo's anger with Ida is understandable, but we are presented with it against the backdrop of Vivaldo's and Eric's liaison, and that mitigates his anger and his judgment.[11]

The other incident relevant to Ida's and Vivaldo's final conversation is the discovery of Eric's and Cass's affair. Cass calls to tell Eric of her discussion with Richard just as he and Vivaldo finish making love, and the two men discuss Richard's position in the mess that Cass and Eric have created. Eric emphasizes that Richard *has* been wounded and that no one has to be admirable to feel pain, and Vivaldo responds with a comment that is relevant to his own situation with Ida: "But I think that perhaps you can begin to *become* admirable if, when you're hurt, you don't try to pay back. . . . Do you know what I mean? Perhaps if you can accept the pain that almost kills you, you can use it, you can become better" (p. 329). Armed with these two signs of wisdom and growth, Vivaldo goes home and walks into the pain that Ida uses to almost kill him. He stays with her, as Richard stays with Cass, but his trial by cross is acutely exacting.

Ida's growth in the novel is important, but it continues to be subordinated to what happens to the white characters. The final confession she makes to Vivaldo is still put in his territory, in the context of how he will respond to her. It is important that she understand what she has done and what it has cost her, but Baldwin sets up the scene so that Ida's revelation of her suffering is still done in mirror image. We measure how much she has suffered on the basis of Vivaldo's response to her suffering. Her subordination is revealed in her posture and in the fact that she begs for forgiveness; Vivaldo is not similarly driven to do so. In this connection, Donald Gibson raises some provocative questions about the racial logic of the novel, especially in its requirement that Ida, black, confess her infidelity to Vivaldo, white, but does not compel Vivaldo to confess similarly.[12] Such a turn of events emphatically places the burden of guilt upon the woman, and Ida, continuing in the tradition in which she has been conceived, finally finds herself weeping at the altar in a scene comparable to that in which Florence Grimes was involved. Unlike Florence, though, Ida does not have to wait for her lord to forgive her, for she is physically in his presence.

Vivaldo's assumption of that godlike role ties into Baldwin's theme on the need to identify with someone else's suffering. The beginning of Ida's exposure of her "sins" makes Vivaldo feel that "she was not locking him out now . . . he was being locked in" (p. 349). The process has started; he is on his way to that other country. His pain is an echo of her suffering as she explains how she hated him for allowing the affair with Ellis to continue because he was afraid of the consequences if he tried to stop it; she hates him for "pretending" to believe her because he did not want to know what was happening to her. She tells him of sleeping with white men before she left Harlem, of scorning their puniness and their sexual deviancies. Finally, she tells him of the last encounter with Ellis when she realized she could no longer endure the power he had over her. She falls to the floor in spasms of weeping as Vivaldo stands in a moment of revulsion: "He was afraid to go near her, he was afraid to touch her, it was almost as though she had told him that she had been infected with the plague" (p. 358).

Where he has been and what he has done recently force his moment of indecision resolutely into the other country.

> And yet, at the same time, as he stood helpless and stupid in the kitchen which had abruptly become immortal, or which, in any case, would surely live as long as he lived, and follow him everywhere, his heart began to beat with a newer, stonier anguish, which destroyed the distance called pity and placed him, *very nearly, in her body*, beside the table, on the dirty floor. (p. 358—my emphasis)

To feel, vicariously, cathartically, the ultimate suffering of another human being, to put oneself in that person's place, is the final stage toward closing the gap between those isolated countries. Vivaldo makes that leap; he still has a few unpleasantnesses to digest, but he at least makes that important leap. It is a sign that things will be all right when a detail Vivaldo has been seeking for his novel "fell, neatly and vividly, like the tumblers of a lock, into place in his mind" (p. 359).

With Ida and Vivaldo, as with Richard and Cass, there is still a question about what one does *after* arriving in the other country. Certainly commitment and responsibility are there, but for Ida and Vivaldo, so is reality. They are still a black woman and a white man living together in a semiartist community way ahead of permissible mores of the society. Their triumph does not end in sounding brass, but in work for Vivaldo and sleep for Ida. Their ending is much like that of the Younger family in *A Raisin in the Sun*: there are no conclusions; there is only commitment to new levels of personal and public struggle.

Ida, this mixture of love, hate, and vengeance who has been revealed to us through many characters as well as through her own presence, is not so unlike other black women in Baldwin's fiction as her spitfire personality would suggest. We have seen defiance brought low in the person of Florence, and no less is Ida's fiery spirit dampened. She had set out to hate everyone and to punish everyone, only to find herself helplessly in love with Vivaldo, or so she maintains; how she can reconcile her hatred with her professed love is questionable. She had also set out to use Ellis, only to discover, in an ironic reversal, that she, like all of Baldwin's black heroines, is really at the mercy of the men in her life, from Vivaldo to Ellis. She deluded herself into thinking that she, at twenty-two, could manipulate a veteran of sexual politics like Steve Ellis. He has been in the television and producing business long enough to have seen many little Idas who thought their talent commanded attention. And perhaps he has helped them, but he has assuredly used them as well.

Ellis' power over Ida may be in terms of prestige and influence, but it manifests itself at a sexual level. Ida tries to use the weapon of her sex against Ellis, as Rufus has earlier used his against Leona (p. 24), only to discover that Ellis manipulates and controls her more thoroughly than she ever imagined controlling him. The climactic revelation comes on the night Cass accompanies her to Harlem. Ellis wants Ida to sing with the group, but the musicians do not; they reject her because they see her as Ellis' whore, a good sister turned bad who has spoiled her brother's memory. Ellis has the power to command acquiescence from both parties, but the musicians punish Ida by not backing her up properly. It is their distaste, Ellis' ruthless power, and her realization that she has indeed defiled Rufus' memory that drive her to the decision to break with him and to share her secrets with Vivaldo.

The role she plays in relation to Ellis and to Vivaldo has its seeds in the esteem in which Ida has held Rufus. He was big brother who could rescue, and she was little sister who needed rescuing. That presupposed a kind of passivity on her part, or at least a recognition that she could not save herself without someone's aid, and that someone, Rufus, was identified with romance and power; he has the power to remove her from the pitfalls that she may encounter in Harlem. By attributing such power to him, Ida places him in the mythic role of Big Brother that Baldwin explores at length in *Just Above My Head*. With this basic attitude toward Rufus' power, it is easy for Ida to transfer such beliefs to Ellis, who has the economic counterparts attached to Rufus' romantic power. It is understandable that she sees herself, sometimes unconsciously, as a servant before the male lords and masters in her life and that she, like Ruth, punishes herself through involvement with them. She humorously refers to Vivaldo on one occasion as "the lord and master" (p. 226), but her humor backfires when it turns out that he is indeed her lord and master. Even the reference serves to echo the plight of the women in *Go Tell It on the Mountain*. And Vivaldo is no less aware of the mastering image that has both religious and sexual connotations. He thinks of his making love to Ida: "When he entered that marvelous wound in her, *rending and tearing! rending and tearing!* was she surrendering, in joy, to the Bridegroom, Lord, and Savior? or was he entering a fallen and humiliated city, entering an ambush, watched from secret places by hostile eyes?" (p. 260). The lower case in Ida's comment gives way to the upper case in Vivaldo's, for finally Ida does submit to be soothed, cleansed, renewed, and saved through the sharing encounter with Vivaldo. She becomes completely powerless before him, and it is he who must decide to be generous, grant forgiveness, and reincorporate her into the union she has violated.[13]

For all her resolve, Ida is as much victim as she is victimizing. Stanley Macebuh shares the evaluation of the peculiar position into which Ida is placed in the novel:

> Ironically, one is confronted with a curious situation in which Ida's and Rufus' anger directly elicits the regeneration of the other characters in the novel while at the same time leading to their own demoralisation. Rufus commits suicide apparently because he is consumed by fury and self-pity, and Ida herself degenerates towards the end of the novel into a whining, self-conscious adolescent unduly intent on explaining away the moral compromises she is compelled to make in order to survive.[14]

I would add as a further commentary that Ida's need for confession ties her to the Florences and Elizabeths of Baldwin's fictive world. She has certainly progressed beyond them in her ability to act, but

she is no less exacting in her measure of her own guilt, no less willing
to indict herself for clearly tangible sins than are these earlier women
for indicting themselves for imaginary sins. They have the same basis
of creation, and they ultimately fall into the same pattern of passing
judgment upon themselves, though their notions of the measure-
ment of their punishment may differ slightly.

Just as Elizabeth and Florence have been subordinate to other
characters, so has Ida. Baldwin allows his characters to find parts of
themselves by coming into contact with Ida, and she serves well in
developing his thesis about isolation of blacks and whites. In fact, she
serves almost too well, because the flesh-and-blood Ida must be
deciphered through so many mediums. She is Black Woman at the
same time that she is more individualized than that burden. She
inflicts pain, but she is ultimately more suffering than avenging. As a
representative of the blacks Baldwin believes his whites should understand in order to live with themselves and with blacks, Ida gets
saddled with too much responsibility. As an individual black woman,
it is precisely that responsibility that keeps us from seeing Ida, except
through several cloudy lenses.[15]

By focusing his thesis on Ida, Baldwin can deal with her less as
a black woman than as *the* black woman that exists in Cass's mind,
or Eric's, or Vivaldo's, or the reader's. Ida grows, certainly, and we
learn more about her, but she is still an elusive entity. At times she is
a mysterious, larger-than-life personage, much like Nella Larsen's
Helga Crane in *Quicksand*; she becomes a peacock paraded before
the white characters' notions of black womanhood. Once she leaves
Harlem, she is cut adrift from the black community except in brief
excursions to the bars in which she sings. Her family becomes irrelevant; even the memory of Rufus becomes diffused and loses force
without Ida growing in direct proportion to that loss. Though Ida
sings the blues, and even lives them, she is still not wholly at home in
that tradition. Like Ruth Bowman in "Come Out the Wilderness,"
she has no black friends, and the only time she attends church as an
adult is for Rufus' funeral. Ida's character is developed solely in the
small white community in which she assumes a part. Though their
influence may still be felt, her ties to the black community and to her
own familial heritage are short-circuited.[16] And Baldwin never really
explains how a black woman from those beginnings could so thoroughly sever connections with all the bases of support contained
there. Certainly Ida's desire to better her condition is understand-

able, but not *everything* in her past was so ugly as to be rejected completely, and she fast discovers that economic and spiritual poverty, ugliness, violence, and abuse are not limited to Harlem. Ida becomes, then, a black woman who exists, to a large extent, in a cultural vacuum, who is misguided by the economic glitter of the American Dream, but who is sensitized, nonetheless, through her integrationist contact with other suffering human beings.

We leave Ida in a peaceful sleep at the end of the novel. She has been cleansed through tears, which evokes comparison to baptism, but the question can be asked, Baptism to what? Her severed connections to the black community do not suggest that she will return there. Her baptism suggests that she has been permanently incorporated into the problematic relationship with Vivaldo. We are left wondering if Ida has really been cleansed of her tendency to guilt and to involving herself in situations for which she will feel guilty. We are left at the pinnacle of her resolution, before it has been tested by the fire of everyday existence. We may feel good about the change, but we cannot judge its depth beyond the moment. Therefore, Ida becomes a transitional figure in terms of the development of the progression away from the church. She is out physically, but questions still arise about her mental resolution in terms of ridding herself of the vestiges of the church-based ties that lead her to confession and remorse about her actions. Her ambivalent state provides a natural transition to the women in *If Beale Street Could Talk*, several of whom are not only out of the church, but who have no church-based consciences.

CHAPTER FOUR

BEARING THE BURDEN OF THE BLUES

If Beale Street Could Talk

In *If Beale Street Could Talk* (1974), Baldwin completes the inversion he hinted at in "The Outing." The novel moves its focus away from characters who are inside the church, or who have grown up in it, to characters who have consistently rejected its influence on their lives. In the dichotomy that Baldwin has set up with insiders and outsiders, with church members being insiders, the symbolism is now reversed; those within the church are "outside" the realm of human caring. The church has degenerated into a haven for people who do not wish to deal with their family problems or face the realistic pressures of the world. Tolerance, the ability to forgive, charitable sacrifice, self-effacing love—virtues traditionally associated with the church—are assigned to characters who have no history of commitment to the church. Earlier characters, such as Gabriel, might have laid claim to these virtues, but rarely did they show them; now Baldwin has stripped away the facade. People who remain in the church are publicly and privately intolerant, selfish, destructively fanatical; especially the women, who, in previous works, had retained some of the attributes of goodness even when they were repressed within the church.

Baldwin's progression away from the church is due in part to his witnessing of the many failures it has produced over the years; his characters in early works are living monuments to those failures. He concluded at one point that "there was no love in the church. It was a mask for hatred and self-hatred and despair."[1] The church has especially failed in its ability to support characters in the secular realm of their existence beyond the home—as far as Baldwin is concerned, it has provided no way of dealing with the political and social environments. Many of the tenets it has espoused have been so perverted by the Gabriels of the world that the very concept of religion needs to be redefined. *If Beale Street Could Talk* is an effort at such redefinition. Those in the novel who are inside the church, like Mrs. Hunt, are no longer saved, or even waging serious soul-searching battles; they are buffoons. In Baldwin's scheme of redefinition, those outside the church are the individuals who truly espouse the tenets of Christianity as exemplified by Christ. To an extent, therefore, Baldwin's vision has become paradoxically more secular even as it becomes more religious; the most positive characters are those Christlike ones who exist outside the church.

In contrast to *Go Tell It on the Mountain*, where the nuclear family and security were centered upon having a strong connection to the church, in *If Beale Street Could Talk*, being outside the church means having a nuclear family and potential security. It also means having the will to fight problems that arise instead of simply praying to God that those problems might be removed. Being inside the church means waiting for that pie in the sky and refusing to get involved with the police and jails, even for the sake of saving a loved one. Consequently, being inside the church means destruction of the family in fundamental ways. Certainly we can say that Gabriel had a detrimental effect upon his family, but we were left to imagine the specifics of those futuristic consequences; in *If Beale Street Could Talk*, we see the fanatical church sister Mrs. Hunt ignoring her jailed son, and we get testimony of his beatings and of his constant degradation. We do not have to speculate on what will happen to him; therefore, a harsher judgment is passed upon Mrs. Hunt and her clinging to the destructive church connection she has.

Initially, then, Baldwin moves the positive black women characters in *If Beale Street Could Talk* beyond active participation in the church. Second, he redefines the tenets of Christianity as practiced by his characters (or at least reclaims what previous characters have perverted), and he thereby releases Christianity from the storefront and post office buildings with which it has been associated previously.

This reversal in order to recapture the basic tenets of morality is a
literary manifestation of an idea that Baldwin presented many years
earlier in *The Fire Next Time*:

> It is not too much to say that whoever wishes to become a truly moral
> human being (and let us not ask whether or not this is possible; I think we
> must *believe* that it is possible) must first divorce himself from all the
> prohibitions, crimes, and hypocrisies of the Christian church. If the con-
> cept of God has any validity or any use, it can only be to make us larger,
> freer, and more loving. If God cannot do this, then it is time we got rid of
> Him.   (p. 67)

The characters in *Beale Street* have progressed to that divorce and to
the reclamation of the true love of God.

This progression certainly provides another level of discussion of
the treatment of black women in Baldwin's works. Still, the images
have not been completely changed; they have only been reworked.
Those very positive characters—Tish, her mother, and her sister—
must still be judged as either good or bad primarily in relation to how
far they are removed from the negative image of the church as represented by Mrs. Hunt. The discussion of the women can move to new
levels, but only because Baldwin has been willing to recast his approach to an image that has appeared throughout his fiction.

The majority of the black female characters in *If Beale Street
Could Talk* are women who are not tied down by their own notions of
guilt about their actions. They are women for whom morality is a
much more flexible concept than it has been in any of the previous
works. If John had been jailed in *Go Tell It on the Mountain*, for
example, Elizabeth would not conceivably have condoned stealing
from a warehouse to raise the money for his bail; but that is precisely
what some of the women in *Beale Street* accept as a natural part of
their existence. Questions of morality are no longer simplistically
two-sided; for these women, more complexity develops, and there is
ample room for extenuating circumstances. By rejecting the morality
of the fundamentalist black church, they represent characters who no
longer believe themselves guilty beyond redemption. Theirs is a
morality of action, which demands that the individual do what he or
she can to further the case of a loved one and to see the will of God
manifested on earth; there is no philosophy of sitting around waiting
for the Lord's will to be done. These women have no time to wallow in
guilt over imaginary crimes; they act and judge their actions only

in terms of effectiveness for accomplishing their purposes. They do not assume that they are forever in the position of praying to be excused for their mere existence on earth; their self-conceptions are larger than that of the Elizabeths of the world, and their consciences are more lenient than that of the Florences.

The neatness with which the black women characters in the novel fit into Baldwin's schema has not been matched by any more detailed treatment of their place in his fiction. Critics have been divided in their response to the novel, those who damn it being especially vigorous. William Edward Farrison is dismissing, even condescending in his commentary; he complains about everything from the title to the way in which the novel is told. He offers further: "Neither in numbers nor in kinds do the characters in *If Beale Street Could Talk* command the reader's highest regards. None of them are especially admirable for either good or bad qualities, except perhaps a wealth of amorality and the aplomb with which most of them revel in four-letter vulgarities and their derivatives." John Aldridge is saddened "to see a writer of Baldwin's large gifts producing, in all seriousness, such junk." On the other hand, John McCluskey finds the supportive father image attractive, especially since so many of Baldwin's earlier works revolve around destructive relationships between fathers and sons. He also applauds the general mood of optimism that pervades the novel. Finally, he maintains that the characters are realistic, not "super-folk" (a position I disagree with later in this chapter).[2] None of these critics focuses particularly on the role of the women in the novel.

The women, clearly presented and sharply drawn in opposition to each other, range from Mrs. Hunt, a sanctified, aloof, pitiful excuse for a mother, to Sharon Rivers, a glorified, long-suffering one, and to her daughter Tish (Clementine), Fonny's devoted lover and narrator of the story. Images of Sharon and Mrs. Hunt are shaped by their reactions to their children, Tish and Fonny (Alonzo), during the crisis when Fonny is wrongly jailed for rape and when nineteen-year-old Tish, pregnant with Fonny's child, works to get her baby's father out of jail. Ernestine, Tish's sister, is equally committed to saving Fonny; she provides a pleasant contrast to Adrienne and Sheila, who are Fonny's noncaring sisters. The black women are drawn at two poles: good and bad, the bad ones truly villainous in their negligence and apathy and the good ones altruistic and Christlike in their dedication and commitment. The best women in the novel are the most

Christlike because they truly understand New Testament teachings about love. The worst women, such as Mrs. Hunt, have little or no understanding of the loving sacrifices of Jesus; they are more interested in the church in its secular connotations—as ritual, show, and performance. They are different from Elizabeth in *Go Tell It on the Mountain* in that they believe the very act of going to church constitutes righteousness; Elizabeth, who goes to church frequently, nevertheless recognizes her own shortcomings. To the women outside the church, God, as He is traditionally conceived by churchgoers, is out of New York. They work, therefore, to put into practice for themselves the miracles of love and sacrifice of the New Testament; they do not wait to be lifted by invisible hands or buoyed up by the clouds of faith. Tish, her mother, and her sister, the representatives of this more-religious-than-church category of religion, are the most attractive female characters in the novel.[3]

Tish, who narrates the story, succeeds fairly early in getting us to sympathize with her position even if, later, we might not be inclined to trust completely her evaluations of scenes at which she is not physically present. It is important initially, though, that we do believe in her and sympathize with her predicament as a nineteen-year-old, unmarried, pregnant black woman who may never get married if her lover is kept in jail (for a rape he did not commit). Tish's plight offers the necessary verisimilitude to capture our attention and for us to follow willingly where she leads us as narrator. Where she leads us is to a disturbing family relationship with the Hunts, Fonny's family, and to a supportive, idealized family relationship with the Riverses, her own family. Dialogue interspersed with the narration reinforces Tish's evaluation that the Hunt women do not care for their son and brother, and that the father, Frank, will be the only familial help the Riverses can expect in their efforts to get Fonny out of jail. The Riverses, Sharon, Ernestine, and Joseph, are ideally supportive of Tish and Fonny, and provide a fortress of warmth in which Tish finds the strength to keep on keeping on. Her family is easily a foil for the Hunts, and the women in her family are the models against whom the Hunt women look like social monsters.

Mrs. Hunt, whose separation from her family and from reality is indicated by the fact that she is seldom referred to by her first name (comparable to Mrs. Breedlove in Toni Morrison's *The Bluest Eye*), is a woman who cannot be forgiven because she hates her boychild,

Fonny.[4] Any mother may have a preference for one child over another for a variety of reasons, but Mrs. Hunt has rejected Fonny, her youngest child, because he is not light-skinned and does not have good hair (Adrienne and Sheila are and do); nor has he come into the bosom of the church she values so deeply. The rejection puts Mrs. Hunt and her daughters outside the range of sympathy within the black community that would have characterized the aftermath of the sixties decade of black awareness. Blacks who were still praising mulattoes in 1974, after such an intense problack fervor, could be dismissed from racial and cultural sympathy more readily than their counterparts of decades earlier. We are not inclined, therefore, to suffer Mrs. Hunt gladly, and we see her more as a buffoon than as a serious mother image.

First of all, she is a hypocrite. She pretends that she loves Jesus and the church and that she is concerned about her family coming into the religious fold, but she is reluctant to take the time to get young Fonny ready for Sunday school and to ensure that he actually arrives at church when she sends him in that direction. The tone of Tish's evaluation of these traits is condemnatory, especially when she maintains the truth is that Mrs. Hunt is "lazy and didn't really like getting up that early" because "there wasn't anybody to admire her" in Sunday school.[5] Still, "sighing deeply and praising the Lord," she would get up, dress Fonny, and send him off, never certain that he would be in church when she arrived. "And, many times," Tish adds, "that woman fell out happy in church without knowing the whereabouts of her only son: 'Whatever Alice don't feel like being bothered with,' Frank was to say to me, much later, 'she leaves in the hands of the Lord'" (p. 26). What truly religious mother could possibly have such an irreligious attitude toward her son? And what husband, if his wife is truly converted, could possibly have such a sarcastic attitude toward her actions? Frank's comment, therefore, reinforces the portrait of Mrs. Hunt's character and solidifies the negative evaluation of her as mother and as professing Christian.

This scene, although early in the novel, is not the first glimpse we get of Mrs. Hunt. That view also shows her hypocrisy, but paints her too as somewhat of a sexual deviate. The scene is made even uglier because Fonny playfully relates it to Tish. What should be one of the most private occurrences between two people is shared with a third party, and it is that sharing that intensifies its deviancy. The tale, set against Tish's comment that Fonny *had* to go to church because Mrs.

Hunt was determined to save him when she couldn't save Frank, is evoked by Tish's questions concerning the Hunts' sex life. Fonny describes what passes for making love between his parents:

"Yeah. But not like you and me. I used to hear them. She'd come home from church, wringing wet and funky. She'd act like she was so tired she could hardly move and she'd just fall across the bed with her clothes on— she'd maybe had enough strength to take off her shoes. And her hat. And she'd always lay her handbag down someplace. I can still hear that sound, like something heavy, with silver inside it, dropping heavy wherever she laid it down. I'd hear her say, The Lord sure blessed my soul this evening. Honey, when you going to give your life to the Lord? And, baby, he'd say, and I swear to you he was lying there with his dick getting hard, and, excuse me, baby, but her condition weren't no better, because this, you dig? was like the game you hear two alley cats playing in the alley. Shit. She going to whelp and *mee-e-ow* till times get better, she going to get that cat, she going to run him all *over* the alley, she going run him till he bite her by the neck—by this time he just want to get some sleep really, but she got her chorus going, he's going to stop the music and ain't but one way to do it—he going to bite her by the neck and then she got him. So, my Daddy just lay there, didn't have no clothes on, with his dick getting harder and harder, and my Daddy would say, About the time, I reckon, that the Lord gives *his* life to *me*. And she'd say, Oh, Frank, let me bring you to the Lord. And he'd say, Shit, woman, I'm going to bring the Lord to *you*. *I'm* the Lord. And she'd start to crying, and she'd moan, Lord, help me help this man. You give him to me. I can't do nothing about it. Oh, Lord, help me. And he'd say, The Lord's going to help you, sugar, just as soon as you get to be a little child again, naked, like a little child. Come on, come to the Lord. And she'd start to crying and calling on Jesus while he started taking all her clothes off—I could hear them kind of rustling and whistling and tearing and falling to the floor and sometimes I'd get my foot caught in one of them things when I was coming through their room in the morning on my way to school—and when he got her naked and got on top of her and she was still crying, Jesus! help me, Lord! my Daddy would say, You got the Lord now, right here. Where you want your blessing? Where do it hurt? Where you want the Lord's hands to touch you? here? here? or here? Where you want his tongue? Where you want the Lord to enter you, you dirty, dumb black bitch? You bitch. You bitch. You bitch. And he'd slap her, hard, loud. And she'd say, Oh, Lord, help me to bear my burden. And he'd say, Here it is, baby, you going to bear it all right, I know it. You got a friend in Jesus, and I'm going to tell you when he comes. The first time. We don't know nothing about the second coming. Yet. And the bed would shake and she would moan and moan and moan. And, in the morning, was just like nothing never happened. She was just like she had been. She still belonged to Jesus and he went off down the street, to the shop."   (pp. 18–21)

Presumably, Tish is merely recording Fonny's story, and it should be
looked upon as his evaluation, not hers. Even so, his sharing of
unpleasantness about his mother extends some of Tish's earlier impressions of Mrs. Hunt. The woman's hypocrisy ranges to physical
possessions (also exemplified later when Tish attends church with
her) as well as it is maintained in the holy facade that allows her to
cover up animal passion. The church service is her sexual inspiration.
The pure and cleansing emotion she had started to release in church
is transformed into a degrading wallowing in the dirt of the flesh. Her
holiness will not allow her to admit that, so she plays the game like
the cats Fonny uses to describe her. Her passion is made the rawer
because she cannot confront it as such; it must be made to seem as if
she is overpowered, taken against her will. That way, she can enjoy
thoroughly the sins of the flesh, a symbolic rape in terms of wish
fulfillment, and yet remain without guilt, somehow suspended above
the baseness that is the true nature of her passion; she attributes the
baseness to someone else.

The role her husband plays as a foil for Jesus suggests again that
Alice Hunt can submit to the sexual degradation without lowering
herself. Frank takes her unto himself in the same way that Jesus takes
sinners to His bosom. Jesus washes away their troubles, as Frank
overpowers Mrs. Hunt's objections, and He makes them anew (rebirth in Christ, baptism), as the peaceful start of a new week indicates
Frank has done with Mrs. Hunt. The double entendre meanings in
burden bearing and the second coming tie the secular and the sacred
even more clearly in their perverse connection, with the effect that
what was presumed to be holy is lowered instead of the base being
elevated.

Frank calling Mrs. Hunt a black bitch also increases the lowering
effect and the drop back to the reality from which she tries to escape.
High yellow like her daughters, the once beautiful Mrs. Hunt doubt-
less believes that she has married below her station. She probably
thought she would be compensated by having the dark and thankful
Frank dotingly provide for her in one of those mythical darker-
skinned/lighter-skinned liaisons, and Frank's tailor shop business
does provide a stable life for the family until he goes out of business
(about the time Fonny is jailed). Calling the woman black forces her
from the unreality of the church to the reality of the bedroom,
where, like a bitch in heat, she enjoys the funkiness of making love as

much as the husband enjoys lowering her from her holiness. Both husband and wife have allowed their relationship to degenerate to the ugliness that Fonny makes public and that serves to show what a negative image of black womanhood Baldwin considers Mrs. Hunt to be.

That ugliness also serves as a contrast later on to the lovemaking that goes on between Fonny and Tish. Fonny tells Tish that Frank and Alice do not make love "like you and me," and that is quite true. With Frank and Alice, lovemaking represents a dismantling of religion. It is only by throwing out Jesus and replacing him with a perversion that Frank and his wife can approach each other sexually. With Fonny and Tish, who have been to church but who do not believe, their love-making is the creation of a new form of religion.[6] It represents a coming together for commitment to and preservation of their love in spite of all obstacles, especially those represented by laws and courts. For Tish and Fonny, God is out of New York, and their only salvation is through nurturing, comforting, and helping each other.

Almost parallel sexual scenes—that between Frank and Mrs. Hunt and that between Fonny and Tish—are used for drastically different purposes in the novel. Baldwin uses what happens between Frank and Mrs. Hunt as another way of rejecting the faulty, hypocritical practice of religion that is at the center of his thematic concerns in the novel. It is questionable if any sexual experience Mrs. Hunt could engage in would be considered positive. Her perversion of sex is equal to her perversion of religion; she is hypocritical about both, and both are ugly. However, as Baldwin uses the same symbolism grounded in the church to show that women connected with it no longer have to feel guilty about their connection or lack of it, so he uses sex for a dual purpose. The same symbolism is used sexually to change the meaning of what human beings can do to each other with their bodies just as the symbolism of the church can be used simultaneously to suggest that people are both inside and outside the traditional church. There is no contradiction in viewing the sexual experiences in two drastically different ways, an evaluation with which Donald Gibson concurs:

> The scenes describing sexual relations between Mr. and Mrs. Hunt contrast sharply with those describing sexual relations between Tish and Fonny. For the Hunts, sex is a grim and sadistic parody of a religious rite and as ugly as the relation between them. For Tish and Fonny the contrary

prevails. Their sexual relations are perfect, without ugliness or pain, even to the point of being highly romanticized. Although Tish is sexually innocent, a virgin, her initiation is perfectly achieved, so perfectly that the couple experience mutual orgasm.[7]

The two sexual rites parallel the distinctions in the two religious characters as best represented by Mrs. Hunt and Sharon Rivers.

Fonny's recounting of the sexual battle between his father and mother comes before the scene in which Tish recalls going to church with Mrs. Hunt and Fonny as a child. The effect is to paint the pious woman as a sanctified hypocrite not only in church, but out of it. We are prepared, therefore, for some unchristian action on Mrs. Hunt's part on that churchgoing Sunday. Fair-skinned Mrs. Hunt, who "had been a very beautiful girl down there in Atlanta" (p. 23), must escort the freshly scrubbed brown-skinned Fonny and the black Tish to church. Fonny is presented for church "looking absolutely miserable, with his hair all slicked and shining, with the part in his hair so cruel that it looked like it had been put there with a tomahawk or a razor, wearing his blue suit" (pp. 21–22). Tish, who is "dark" and has hair that is "just plain hair," and who is not attractive by most people's standards, is made to feel her unattractiveness in the tone in which Mrs. Hunt greets her. And the three parade down the street, with Mrs. Hunt cloaking herself in the expectations of Sunday morning; she guides the youngsters to their destination "like a queen making great strides into the kingdom" (p. 25). Tish will later think of walking into the church when she walks into the Tombs to visit Fonny in jail (p. 32).

Mrs. Hunt is aware of performance and show, and their parade through the streets reminds Tish of a fair. The secular context anticipates the arrival at church, where Tish points out that

> the church had been a post office. . . . They had knocked down some walls and put in some benches and put up the church signs and the church schedules; but the ceiling was that awful kind of wrinkled tin, and they had either painted it brown or they had left it unpainted. When you came in, the pulpit looked a mighty long ways off. To tell the truth, I think the people in the church were just proud that their church was so big and that they had somehow got their hands on it. (p. 27)

Size allows for show, and the secular/performance context is again emphasized over the sacred. Baldwin underscores that tendency to hypocrisy in many of his churchgoers by allowing them to worship in buildings not originally designed for church purposes. Here, the building is a post office; in *Go Tell It on the Mountain*, it had once been an abandoned store and is considered a theater by one of the characters.[8] When Baldwin was preaching, he had noted the connection between the church and the theater, and it was partly because of that recognition that he gave up preaching. He says in *The Devil Finds Work*: "When I entered the church, I ceased going to the theater. It took me awhile to realize that I was working in one."[9] The theatricality inherent in hypocritical churchgoers is what defines Mrs. Hunt.

Initially, the size of the church enables her to display her Christian responsibility by parading Tish and Fonny down the aisle and to show off her fancy dress in the process.

> We entered that church and Mrs. Hunt led us straight down the aisle which was farthest to the left, so that everybody from two aisles over had to turn and watch us. And—frankly—we were something to watch. . . . Mrs. Hunt, who, somehow, I don't know how, from the moment we walked through the church doors, became filled with a stern love for her two little heathens and marched us before her to the mercy seat. She was wearing something pink or beige, I'm not quite sure now, but in all that gloom, it showed. And she was wearing one of those awful hats women used to wear which have a veil on them which stops at about the level of the eyebrow or the nose and which always makes you look like you have some disease. And she wore high heels, too, which made a certain sound, something like pistols, and she carried her head very high and noble. She was saved the moment she entered the church, she was Sanctified holy, and I even remember until today how much she made me tremble, all of a sudden, deep inside. It was like there was nothing, nothing, nothing you could ever hope to say to her unless you wanted to pass through the hands of the living God: and He would check it out with her before He answered you. The mercy seat: she led us to the front row and sat us down before it. She made us sit but she knelt, on her knees, I mean, in front of her seat, and bowed her head and covered her eyes, making sure she didn't fuck with that veil. I stole a look at Fonny, but Fonny wouldn't look at me. Mrs. Hunt rose, she faced the entire congregation for a moment and then she, modestly, sat down.   (pp. 28–29)

The dress and the veil are important because Mrs. Hunt will shortly enter into a singing and shouting competition with a fellow worshiper, the sole purpose of which seems to be to show off their holiness and their clothing; they are "trying to outdo each other"

(p. 30). During the singing of "Blessed Quietness, Holy Quietness," the women call and respond to each other with alternating lines of the song, and the singing interlude leads to the shouting competition:

> I guess I'll remember until I die that black lady's white rose. Suddenly, it seemed to stand straight up, in that awful place, and I grabbed Fonny's hand—I didn't know I'd grabbed it; and, on either side of us, all of a sudden, the two women were dancing—shouting: the holy dance. The lady with the rose had her head forward and the rose moved like lightning around her head, our heads, and the lady with the veil had her head back: the veil which was now far above her forehead, which framed that forehead, seemed like the sprinkling of black water, baptizing us and sprinkling her. People moved around us, to give them room, and they danced into the middle aisle. Both of them held their handbags. Both of them wore high heels. (p. 32)

The details that would stick in a child's mind—the flashing rose, the swaying veil, the handbags and the high-heeled shoes—embody the contrasts in professed belief and action that drive Fonny and Tish away from the church; they never go again. Any claim Mrs. Hunt can make to being truly religious has been undercut by her performance and hypocrisy, by her refusal to separate the secular and the sacred.

Her vindictive response to Tish's pregnancy is in keeping with the personality that has been shown to us previously; her piety has already been ridiculed. She would rather "trust in God" than fight to get Fonny out of jail, and, somewhat paradoxically, she would rather believe that Tish is a slut than think her son has voluntarily made love with Tish. She calls it a "lustful action" and maintains that the Holy Ghost will cause the child to "shrivel" in Tish's womb (p. 84). In her assertion that Tish will suffer but Fonny will be forgiven, Mrs. Hunt holds the traditional sanctimonious view that pregnancy before marriage is always the girl's fault. Her rejection of the grandchild Frank has just said he would be "mighty glad" to receive provokes him beyond endurance; he knocks her down. This is another in a series of events in which his wife and daughters will refuse to offer support in family crises. Such attitudes are part of the reason Frank commits suicide later in the novel.[10] Neither her professed Christianity nor her weak heart causes Mrs. Hunt to relent when the men leave the women alone to reconcile their hard feelings. She continues to deny kinship to the child and to see her own daughters as models of behavior over Sharon's daughters: "These girls won't be bringing *me* no bastards to feed," she proclaims, "I can guarantee you that" (p. 89). She is seriously deluded about her daughters' sex lives, for, although Adrienne and Sheila are presented as self-righteously superior little snobs for whom no man would be good enough, their scandalous sexual habits (titillation, but not copulation) are known to the street-wise Ernestine. The fact that Mrs. Hunt fails to see the truth about her daughters is but another measure of her blindness about her own sexual habits and her refusal to confront the reality of Fonny's incarceration.

Mrs. Hunt disappears from the novel after this scene because she is not involved in and does not particularly care about the tangible efforts to get her son out of jail; she is content to pray. Her pernicious influence, however, is always felt when Tish talks about Frank and how Fonny's incarceration works such a destructive influence upon him. It is Frank with whom we sympathize even when he knocks his wife down, because he is on the side of life, innocence, parenthood, and reality. Mrs. Hunt sits prissily by and waits for unseen hands to work miracles.

The woman is physically and philosophically ugly to us. As Baldwin's representative of everything that is wrong with the church and with the hypocritical professors of Christianity, she serves well. In another ironic reversal, she has removed herself from the guilt earlier church women have felt by removing herself emotionally from the world around her. She has sacrificed all for her version of Christ, so there is no need for her to feel guilty about what she does on earth. She is completely one-dimensional in her philosophy, completely without participation in the secular/sacred clash that caused so many of the women in earlier works to feel guilty about their actions. Mrs. Hunt believes she is totally wedded to Christ; consequently, there is no ambiguity in her actions, at least not from her point of view. Unlike Florence, who left her mother and induced an inordinate amount of guilt for not having fulfilled her Christian duty, Mrs. Hunt is able to reject her son precisely in the name of Christianity and the idea of being dutiful ("If thy right eye offend thee, pluck it out." "One should reject father, mother, husband, and children for the sake of God.").

Mrs. Hunt's daughters have rejected their brother as surely as their mother has; they join her at the end of the spectrum of women defined by aloofness and detachment from the crisis that should bring the two families together. In their attitudes toward Fonny, in their dress, in their mutual support of their mother's position against Fonny, Adrienne and Sheila are like Siamese twins, two misplaced configurations in a world that no longer puts special value on their particular brand of virtue. The two girls could never bring their mother any bastards because they could never find any man good enough, that is, light-skinned and middle class enough, for whom they would consider having children. They are too superior to touch their "nappy-headed" brother to get him dressed for Sunday school and too condescending in their parlor room manners to make Fonny's trouble their own.

If Adrienne and Sheila had appeared in a work at the turn of the century, they would have been tragic mulattoes or members of a blue-vein society, probably the latter. They are superficially concerned about manners and clothing and education, but not about deeper questions of morality and the political nature of the society in which they live. They are willing to believe that Fonny's incarceration is his own fault, which shows the level of their perception. Their attitudes are made clear in the scene of the announcement of Tish's pregnancy, which is a central (if not *the* central) one in the novel, the only time all members of the two families get together and discuss Fonny's and Tish's situation. The girls arrive with their noses in the air, quietly superior to the "trash" they believe they have been forced to call upon. "They smiled at an invisible host of stricken lovers as they entered our living room, and Adrienne, the oldest, who was twenty-seven, and Sheila, who was twenty-four, went out of their way to be very sweet with raggedy-assed me, just like the missionaries had told them" (pp. 76–77).

Aloofness and parlor room manners allow the sisters to keep their distance from trouble and the reality of Tish's and Fonny's predicament. Tish chides Adrienne for not visiting Fonny in jail, for preferring to be out with "some half-honky chump" instead of attending the family meeting. Adrienne says nothing in response, but her silence says to Tish that Adrienne "would never again, for *any* reason, allow herself to be trapped among people so unspeakably inferior to herself" (p. 82). Silence and aloofness soon give way to the confusion when Frank strikes Mrs. Hunt. The two sisters assist their mother as the men leave, Sheila accusing the Riverses of "sneering" at her mother's faith and Adrienne referring to them as "funky niggers" who have overreacted simply because her mother asked who was going to take care of the baby.

Class consciousness clearly separates the women. Yet Tish can transcend their hatred of Fonny to feel sorry for these advocates of such a fleeting pretentiousness. She notices that Adrienne is "too old" for what she is wearing, and that Sheila is "too young" (p. 77). She sees that flashy clothing does not make Sheila secure and that the makeup Adrienne wears does not hide the fact that her "skin was rejecting the makeup by denying it any moisture" and that "the face and the body would coarsen and thicken with time" (p. 88). Though they have tried to escape Harlem by going to City College and to escape sympathy for their brother by maintaining he would not be in jail if he had stuck to reading and studying, they will forever be two black women who are basically plain in spite of their light skin.

The Hunt women leave the Riverses, whom they consider "foul-mouthed people," and step out of any further concern about Fonny. Tish, Sharon, and Ernestine have "to look squarely in the face the fact that Fonny's family didn't give a shit about him and were not going to do a thing to help him. *We* were his family now, the only family he had: and now everything was up to us" (p. 92). Alice Hunt recedes into religion; Adrienne and Sheila disappear into activities they consider suitable to the images they have of themselves. There is little substance to the sisters and little that we have to consider beyond the announcement scene. They serve to show how uncaring Fonny's family is about him, but, as individuals, they elicit very little interest from us. We do not care about them or about what may happen to them; indeed, Tish, who has little reason for being sympathetic toward them, is perhaps more so than we are. The women are cultural and racial anachronisms whose tragedy is that they do not realize how far out of time and place they really are.

The blandness and boredom surrounding Fonny's sisters is counteracted by the vivacity surrounding Tish's sister Ernestine, who represents an evolved stage of black womanhood. She has moved from the primping of early years to commitment to black community health, especially that of children; she is at this stage at the time of Fonny's and Tish's trouble. Ernestine is an activist, an untiring worker who commands attention and action of most people with whom she comes into contact. She is Tish's supporter and a source of strength. Unlike the Hunt sisters, whom we cannot imagine even walking the streets of Harlem, let alone manuevering in them, Ernestine is streetwise and politically conscious. She knows the possibilities for life-stifling activities in the legal system that Adrienne and Sheila prefer never to

encounter and that Mrs. Hunt leaves in the hands of the Lord, and
she knows how to offset some of the destructive activities. How she
arrived at this state will clarify later on how she thinks in assisting
Tish and Fonny. She has gone from being "vain," from having her
"hair curled and her dresses . . . always clean," to "wearing slacks
and tying up her hair and . . . reading books like books were going out
of style." She resolves to take "no more of the white man's lying shit"
(p. 47) and begins to work in a hospital, where one of her first experiences is to see a twelve-year-old Puerto Rican girl die from drugs.

Her appearance during the confrontation with the Hunt clan reflects her politics ("She was wearing gray slacks and an old blouse and
her hair was untidy on her head and she wore no makeup" [p. 88]).
She is not interested in the superficial outside, for her mind and heart
reflect the commitment that guides her life. She is outspoken in her
indictment of the women and in expressions of anger evoked by their
indifference and their hypocrisy. To Sheila's complaint that Sharon is
sneering at her mother's faith, Ernestine responds: "Oh, don't give me
that bullshit. . . . You so shamed you got a Holy Roller for a mother,
you don't know what to do. You don't sneer. You just say it shows she's
got 'soul,' so other people won't think it's catching—and also so they'll
see what a bright, bright girl *you* are. You make me sick" (p. 86). She
threatens to tear out Adrienne's Adam's apple with her fingers or
carve it out with a knife if she so much as touches Tish. In an atmosphere that has degenerated into insult and hatred, Ernestine can
play the role that will subdue the Hunts. Her street language and
dramatic gestures reinforce her point. Again, since sympathies have
been created in favor of the Riverses instead of the Hunts, we are
willing to tolerate the limits to which Ernestine goes. She is in pain at
witnessing the lack of caring the Hunt women show even as she is in
the process of insulting them.

For women who are so timid about sex, and who would reduce
lovemaking between Fonny and Tish to something ugly, they find
their timidity turned against them as Ernestine hurls sexual insults at
them. When Sheila says, "I knew we shouldn't have come," Ernestine
stares at her, laughs, and replies: "My. I must have a dirty mind,
Sheila. I didn't know that you could even *say* that word" (pp. 87, 88).
The women are more than ready to go, but Ernestine's insults follow
them out the door and to the elevator:

> "Ladies," she said, and moved to the elevator and pressed the button. She
> was past a certain fury now. . . . "Don't worry. We'll never tell the baby

about you. There's no way to tell a baby how obscene human beings can be!" And, in another tone of voice, a tone I'd never heard before, she said, to Mrs. Hunt, "Blessed be the next fruit of thy womb. I hope it turns out to be uterine cancer. And I mean that." And, to the sisters, "If you come anywhere near this house again in life, *I will kill you.* . . . You just cursed the child in my sister's womb. Don't you *never* let me see you again, you broken down half-white bride of Christ!" And she spat in Mrs. Hunt's face, and then let the elevator door close. And she yelled down the shaft. "That's your flesh and blood you were cursing, you sick, filthy, dried-up cunt!" (pp. 90–91)

The words are ugly in the mouth of any human being, but especially from one woman to another. Ernestine becomes the heavy in this scene in her threats of physical violence and in the intensity of the insults. Interestingly, she uses the word "cunt" in referring to Mrs. Hunt (as Tish uses it earlier referring to Adrienne). The word is not one that women frequently use to insult other women; it is a word men use to insult women. Consider the context in which Baldwin uses the word in *Another Country*. Richard and Cass argue in front of Eric about writers, and Richard implies that Cass would prefer a guy like Vivaldo to himself. "And you know why? You want to know why? . . . Because you're just like all the other American cunts. You want a guy you can feel sorry for, you love him as long as he's helpless" (p. 208). And again, in anger, several pages later, Richard calls Cass a cunt when he discovers her affair with Eric (p. 316). In the language they use, therefore, Ernestine and Tish are identified with males. Even the virtuous qualities Ernestine espouses in helping Fonny and Tish, then, are tied in some ways to the masculine qualities Baldwin prefers at times over feminine ones. Ernestine's language identifies her with such traits, as it identifies Tish with some of Baldwin's male narrators.

Ernestine's angry words heap a reality upon the Hunt women that they consistently refuse to face. Since we have already seen Mrs. Hunt in an act of what passes for lovemaking, her pristine response to Tish's pregnancy is permeated with hypocrisy. Since we have already seen her degraded in her own marital bed, we know that her hopes for her daughters are grounded in fantasy; Ernestine's words and actions could force her to reflect upon her own sexual situation. It is only because Ernestine comes back from the elevator in tears, and trembling, that we are willing to accept that her outburst has caused her perhaps as much suffering as it will cause the recently departed Hunt women.

Still, it is precisely because Ernestine is a woman of action that help will come to Fonny and Tish. It is through her work with children that Ernestine is able to locate a lawyer, Hayward, to take Fonny's case. It is Ernestine who discovers that Bell, the white cop who is behind all of Fonny's troubles, killed a twelve-year-old black boy a few years before; how that information can be used in court is not yet clear, but at least Ernestine is a person who believes in gathering all the ammunition she can, and she has a thorough file on Bell. It is Ernestine, too, who consistently forces Tish to see the ugliest possibilities in the war they have to fight so Tish will not be surprised and perhaps have a miscarriage if those things become reality later on.

Ernestine acts as a nurturer and a protector for Tish, a kind of mother image. She makes Tish see that whether or not Mrs. Rogers, the woman who has been urged by Bell to accuse Fonny of raping her, has indeed been raped is irrelevant. They must plan as if she had been and as if she believes her story about Fonny. Their course of action must be to discredit Bell and to show that he was out to get Fonny for another incident. It is Ernestine who makes Tish realize that Sharon is the only person who can follow Mrs. Rogers to Puerto Rico and try to get her to change her testimony. It is Ernestine who looks after Tish when Sharon is in Puerto Rico and who insists, with Joseph, that Tish quit her job. And it is Ernestine who cultivates the actress for whom she works in order to get enough money for Fonny's bail. Ernestine, then, combines the virtues of the Elizabeths and Florences of the world with a new trait: action uninhibited by external forces or inner doubts. She is understanding and loving, but she refuses to stand by and hope that things will get better. She takes matters into her own hands as often as she can.

The role Ernestine plays in relation to Tish offers a glimpse at another idealized bond in the Baldwin canon—that between two sisters. No sisters in any of Baldwin's works prior to this point have been old enough to have a real relationship (remember the children in *Go Tell It on the Mountain* and in the stories); Elizabeth, Florence, Deborah, Esther, and Ida have all been the only females in their families. Baldwin has created many families—in "Sonny's Blues," in *Tell Me How Long the Train's Been Gone*—in which no female siblings are present. To have two young black women who share their heartaches and hopes in *If Beale Street Could Talk* is quite a different presentation. Tish has in Ernestine the confidante and big sister that Elizabeth found in Florence and that Deborah so desperately needed. With the character of Ernestine, Tish is buttressed on all sides in her distressing time during Fonny's arrest; she has a supportive mother and father, a lover, and a caring sister. She and Ernestine form another bond in that little world Baldwin creates to withstand all outside pressures.

Ernestine and Tish join with their parents, Sharon and Joseph Rivers, in forming the idealistic, fairy-tale family structure that is the core of *If Beale Street Could Talk*. Sharon and Joseph are unmatched in parental concern, caring, duty, tolerance, responsibility, and support. Some critics, such as John McCluskey, maintain that, in the creation of this family, Baldwin was finally able to achieve in familial relationships what he had been working toward since *Go Tell It on the Mountain*. Joseph, unlike Gabriel Grimes, truly loves his offspring.[11] He resorts to stealing from the docks where he works (Frank steals from the garment center) and selling the goods to help raise money for Fonny's bail (Fonny has become the son for whom no sacrifice is too great).[12]

Just as the father image is idealized in *If Beale Street Could Talk*, so is that of the mother. Sharon is perhaps unlike any black mother, in fiction or in reality. She is equally as supportive as Joseph, but she also has qualities that sometimes stretch credibility. Still, unlike the women in *Go Tell It on the Mountain* and "Sonny's Blues," whose long-suffering Christian patience is their dominant virtue, Sharon is outside the church, the antithesis of Mrs. Hunt. In a novel that derides the form of Christianity practiced as irrelevant and stymying, Sharon's position is a plus, just as Mrs. Hunt's is a minus.

Sharon Rivers is the active culmination of all the portraits of black mothers who have appeared in Baldwin's fiction to this point, and she anticipates those who will appear in *Just Above My Head*. I emphasize *active*; the many mothers prior to Sharon may have wanted to do the same things that she does, but they were unable to. For example, Elizabeth may have wanted to help John in his battles, both silent and verbal, against Gabriel, but she lacked both the strength and the position of support for offering such active assistance. The mother in "Sonny's Blues" may have wanted to explain things to Sonny just as the mother in "Come Out the Wilderness" may have wanted to take her daughter's side against her husband, but neither woman could do more than hope for the best in their passively supportive roles. The shadowy Mrs. Scott, Rufus' and Ida's mother in *Another Country*, wended her way along passively instead of trying to assist her troubled son and her wayward daughter; indeed, this mother simply disappears from the novel in the same way that the mother is equally diminished in *Tell Me How Long the Train's Been Gone*. In both cases, the glimpses of them we do get suggest that they are further developments of the Elizabeth tradition. With Sharon Hunt, Baldwin takes that tradition out of the closet and makes it a viable, though idealized, concept again. Sharon is the quintessential mother whose very presentation evokes memories of those earlier mothers who were so ineffectual, but whose desires to assist their children may have been just as strong as hers. Sharon has the advantage of a supportive husband who is not in conflict with either of his children and who would stand by her, with them, through any crisis. She becomes MOTHER to highlight all the earlier portraits of mothers; her very idealization is the source of all the problems we have with her.

Sharon's reaction to Tish's pregnancy is perhaps the most questionable scene in which she appears, and the one in which her role as idealized mother is most clearly presented. Tish comes home, exhausted, knowing the time has come to share her news with someone. When Tish tries to tell Sharon the news, but breaks into tears instead, Sharon already knows what the problem is (as does Ernestine). In a way, then, it is Tish who is in for a surprise because the tolerant Sharon has bided her time and not pressed her to verbalize what is already known. Sharon's reaction once the news is out is calm, controlled, almost proud.

> She said, "Tish, I declare. I don't think you got nothing to cry about." She moved a little. "You tell Fonny?" . . .
>
> "What you crying about?"
>
> Then she did touch me, she took me in her arms and she rocked me and I cried.
>
> She got me a handkerchief and I blew my nose. She walked to the window and she blew hers.
>
> "Now, listen," she said, "you got enough on your mind without worrying about being a bad girl and all that jive-ass shit. I sure hope I raised you better than that. If you was a bad girl, you wouldn't be sitting on that bed, you'd long been turning tricks for the warden." . . .
>
> "Tish," she said, "when we was first brought here, the white man he didn't give us no preachers to say words over us before we had our babies. And you and Fonny be together right now, married or not, wasn't for that same damn white man. So, let me tell you what you got to do. You got to

think about that baby. You got to hold on to that baby, don't care what else happens or don't happen. *You* got to do that. Can't nobody else do that for you. And the rest of us, well, we going to hold on to you. And we going to get Fonny out. Don't you worry. I know it's hard—but don't you worry. And that baby be the best thing that ever happened to Fonny. He needs that baby. It going to give him a whole lot of courage." (pp. 40–41)

It is a wonderfully encouraging scene that borders on fantasy. First of all, Sharon has given Tish the space she needed by refusing to confront her with the suspicion of pregnancy. Second, she refuses to make an issue of marriage, which would have been the reaction of Florence's mother or Elizabeth's aunt. And she defends her daughter's action in the face of the harsh, uncompromising world around them. Fonny's incarceration is also important to Sharon's reaction, as well as the fact that Sharon, who is outside the church, is not as harsh in her judgment of presumed moral lapses as more conventional black mothers would be. Still, the tone of the scene is so extremely positive that it overshadows those considerations and suggests that the reaction is solely due to Sharon's personality as mother.

In the scene quoted, Baldwin has eradicated the tension that is usually present between parents and their children in his fiction. A different kind of tension will return in *Just Above My Head* between Julia and her father, but the majority of the siblings and their parents from this point on in Baldwin's fiction at least manage a peaceful coexistence. Here, with Tish and her mother, the peacefulness extends into a blissful, ideal relationship. The daughter, unlike Florence, has nothing to fear from her mother and nothing to feel guilty about for the actions she has committed. There is a sharing, a freedom in the relationship that never could have existed between John and Elizabeth, between Elizabeth and her aunt, or between Florence and her mother. That space to grow, which John so desperately needed from Gabriel in *Go Tell It on the Mountain*, is cheerfully granted to Tish by her mother as well as her father. The limits of parental authority have been relaxed, and the child has been endowed with a trusting confidence in the parents that enables her to consider sharing her most secret of secrets with them. Tish is four years older than John, but the comparison between them is no less valid. From the way his character is set up, one can easily imagine John being under the influence of Gabriel for a long period beyond his fourteen years. In contrast, the freedom Tish feels and the support she is given show the openness of the relationship Baldwin may have desired in the earlier work and that he can now imaginatively claim.

Sharon sees Tish's pregnancy as a cause for celebration; nothing is allowed to detract from that context.[13] Sharon considers the occasion so special that she takes out a bottle of "very old French brandy," which she has had for years, to formalize the announcement to Joseph and Ernestine: "Daddy poured and Mama gave us each a glass. She looked at Joseph, then at Ernestine, then at me—she smiled at me. 'This is a sacrament,' she said, 'and, no, I ain't gone crazy. We're drinking to a new life. Tish is going to have Fonny's baby.' She touched Joseph. 'Drink,' she said" (p. 54). Joseph is equally as encouraging and supportive as Sharon, Ernestine stands with tears in her eyes, and the sacrament is truly considered holy.[14]

This scene is perhaps one of many that led John Aldridge to consider the novel larger than life, a position I share. Aldridge complains that Baldwin "has produced another fantasy of rather large social implications, this time one in which the characters of black people living in contemporary Harlem are shown to be so noble and courageous that one is constrained to wonder how we ever imagined that conditions in the black urban ghetto are anything other than idyllic."[15] The good vibes continue to flow within the Rivers family until the mood is destroyed by the arrival of the Hunts; meanwhile, Sharon is one of the major keepers of the good vibes. The brandy is her idea; she decides to elevate Tish's pregnancy to something glorious and wonderful. That is her privilege as the idealized mother.

Her unorthodox behavior, as mentioned, can be explained partly in the nontraditional attitude she holds toward the church. It is only on holiday occasions, Tish tells us, that her family goes to church. Sharon's identity is secure in her family and work; she does not need the religious source in the way that Mrs. Hunt finds identity in it. Just as Fonny and Tish make a religion out of romantic love, Sharon makes hers out of familial love. Tish comments on her family's lack of regular religious habits: "We were Baptists. But we didn't go to church very often—maybe Christmas or Easter, days like that. Mama didn't dig the church sisters, who didn't dig her, and Sis kind of takes after Mama, and Daddy didn't see any point in running after the Lord and he didn't seem to have very much respect for him" (pp. 25–26). The comment, which is made on the occasion Tish goes to church with Fonny and Mrs. Hunt, shows the contrast between the Riverses and the Hunts. Sharon, like Ernestine, believes in

human action, not in waiting on the Lord. If God helps those who
help themselves, then that is fine, but Sharon and her family do
not believe in praying for miracles that they can bring about for
themselves.

Sharon's unorthodox behavior as mother is also partly explained by
her own unorthodox behavior as a young woman. She had been
daring enough to run away from home with a drummer to pursue a
singing career and, when they parted and the career possibility
failed, to fall in love with and marry Joseph after knowing him only a
week. She is still "young" enough, therefore, to empathize with
young love and the unpredictable circumstances it can create. She
had met Joseph at a bus station in Albany where she sat "trying to look
tough and careless" (p. 35), but conveying only her fright. Joseph had
fallen for her and pursued her to New York, where "within a week, he
had married her and gone back to sea" and Sharon, "a little stunned,
settled down to live" (p. 37). Sharon had been twenty when she
married Joseph. She had trusted him enough and believed in the love
enough to respond favorably to him, and her faith has been rewarded,
for at the time of Tish's pregnancy, she and Joseph have been married
about twenty-five years. Her personal history, therefore, could account for her tolerant behavior toward Tish and Fonny, for the young
people *would* be married if Fonny had not been jailed.

Sharon's levelheaded approach to life also serves well in the scene
with the Hunts. She controls Tish by her mere presence and prevents
her from saying things to Mrs. Hunt that would be as harsh as what
Ernestine says. She urges Mrs. Hunt to understand Frank's intense
feelings for the welfare of his son; failure to heed the admonition is
what makes Frank knock his wife down. Sharon thinks of Mrs. Hunt's
weak heart when the woman falls, insists that the men get out of the
way and allow the women to handle the situation, and explains
the seriousness of Mrs. Hunt cursing the child. In addition to Mrs.
Hunt's weak heart, Sharon maintains:

"She got a weak head. . . . The Holy Ghost done softened your brain,
child. Did you forget it was Frank's grandchild you was cursing? And of
course it's *my* grandchild, too. I know some men and some women would
have cut that weak heart out of your body and gladly gone to hell to pay for
it. You want some tea, or something? You really ought to have some brandy,
but I reckon you too holy for that." (p. 86)

And she peacefully pleads with Mrs. Hunt to accept the child: "But the child that's coming. . . is your grandchild. I don't understand you. It's your *grandchild*. What difference does it make how it gets here? The child ain't got nothing to do with that—don't none of us have nothing to do with *that!*" (p. 89). She is never vindictive toward the Hunts, but she does not attempt to prevent Ernestine from being so. Perhaps Sharon feels they deserve to be made a little uncomfortable.

Just as Sharon has been ideal in accepting Tish's pregnancy, she also has an ideal response to Fonny bringing Tish home early on the morning following the night of Tish's loss of virginity. The scene in which Fonny and Tish first make love comes immediately after the ugly scene with the Hunt women. Structurally, it serves to counteract the effect of the Hunt women's presence, if not blot it out completely, and to consecrate what has happened between Fonny and Tish. Sharon does not get excited when Fonny and Tish show up; she merely asks where they have been. In the face of Fonny mentioning marriage to explain the night out, Sharon's paltry objections quickly dissolve. Joseph enters the room and anything else to be said is between him and Fonny. "We, the women," Tish says, "were out of it now, and we knew it" (p. 106). So they wait patiently while Fonny and Joseph go into another room; they return shortly, and the entire family agrees about the marriage. Sharon is there as a silent, supportive force in the scene, but she has no large critical part to play in objecting to her daughter's decision at such an early age (Tish is eighteen), or in objecting to Fonny, or in squarely confronting what they all know has happened a few hours earlier between Fonny and Tish.

In contrast to the background role she plays in the proposal scene, Sharon is outspokenly supportive of Tish in Hayward's office when he tells them how complicated the case has become as a result of Mrs. Rogers' disappearance. Tish bursts into tears, and Sharon counters with:

"Tish . . . you a woman now. You *got* to be a woman. We are in a rough situation—but, if you really want to think about it, ain't nothing new about that. That's just exactly, daughter, when *you do not give up*. You *can't* give up. We got to get Fonny out of there. *I don't care what we have to do to do it*—you understand me, daughter? This shit has been going on long enough. Now. You start thinking about it any other way, you just going to

make yourself sick. *You* can't get sick *now*—you know that—I'd rather for
the state to kill him than for *you* to kill him. So, come on, now—we going
to get him *out*."   (p. 118)

The tone and language of Sharon's speech could very easily be in the
mouth of Joseph, or other of Baldwin's male characters, especially in
expressions like "we are in a rough situation" and "This shit has been
going on long enough." Rufus' repeated refrain before he commits
suicide in *Another Country* is "This shit has got to stop" (p. 61).
Sharon's urgent outburst convinces Tish that they must steel their
nerves and prepare for the fact that someone has to pursue Mrs.
Rogers to Puerto Rico. That someone, as Tish and Ernestine later
agree, has to be Sharon.

For a middle-aged expectant grandmother, whose traveling experiences range from Birmingham to Albany to Harlem, to undertake a
trip to Puerto Rico in pursuit of a woman whom she has never seen
requires no small stretch of the imagination. Yet it is a measure of
Sharon's idealized portrait as mother that allows her not only to
undertake the task, but actually to go and find Mrs. Rogers. This
working-class black woman, who lives in a housing project and who
has perhaps never even fantasized an island vacation, manages her
task with competency and with a finesse that, if not incredible, at
least forces us to view her in a different light. She plans for her trip
with a strategy comparable to that of Ernestine's. Of the two
snapshots Tish has of Fonny, Sharon takes the one in which he appears with his arm around Tish, smiling into the camera. The sympathetic intent is to get Mrs. Rogers to realize that such a smiling young
man, so obviously in love with Tish, could not possibly be the young
man who has raped her. Sharon also chooses clothing to portray
herself as a concerned mother, not as a forceful, inconsiderate gringo
who has come to strong-arm a change of testimony from Mrs. Rogers.
It is a testament to her ideal image as mother that Sharon, who is
afraid of flying, takes to the air to help her offspring, for indeed Fonny
is as much hers as Tish is.

Sharon's trip to Puerto Rico allows Baldwin to develop some of the
ideas he has hinted at of the political connections between American
blacks and other Third World peoples. They need to form a sympathetic bond against the forces that oppress them. Sharon's sympathetic young cab driver senses that need. He attaches himself to
her for the duration of her stay, adopting her in the best sense of that

word. He and the Spanish family who own the restaurant where Fonny and Tish have eaten frequently are the positive images of Spanish-speaking people in the novel. They join forces with the blacks and the Italians against Bell, the cop who would divide blacks and Puerto Ricans and conquer both by having them fight each other. That political implication pervades Tish's relation of Sharon's trip to Puerto Rico as well as other parts of her narration.[16] And Sharon capitalizes on that connection as well. When she meets Mrs. Rogers, she emphasizes that they must help each other because they are both black.

Too unstable to accept that argument or to believe in its ultimate truth, Mrs. Rogers screams Sharon out of her life and, two days later, collapses into a miscarriage and insanity. Pietro, the father of the child, understandably refuses to ask Mrs. Rogers to rethink the testimony she has given, and Sharon has gone to visit the woman alone. Before she resorted to the appeal to common color, she had appealed to Mrs. Rogers as a mother (Mrs. Rogers has other children) and, recognizing the vulnerability and fear the girl feels, as a daughter. But the mother image that is so idealized in New York has no appeal in Puerto Rico. Sharon must return to New York without having accomplished her goal, and the D.A. now has an additional excuse to keep Fonny in jail until the deranged Mrs. Rogers is well enough to testify against him (the potentially hopeless case Bell would love to see).

Nonetheless, Sharon's going to Puerto Rico represents the ultimate contrast to images of womanhood embodied in Mrs. Hunt and her daughters. Her commitment to family is unquestionable, and her sacrificial ability to *do* immortalizes her among black mother images in Baldwin's fiction. She recognizes no limitations that could be placed on her by church and society, and it is that freedom of thinking and action that makes her an unusual image of black woman to this point in Baldwin's fiction. Certainly Ida is a woman of activity, but she is by no means as psychologically free of external influences as Sharon is.

The most important image of black womanhood we see in *If Beale Street Could Talk* is Tish, primarily because Tish is the first black woman Baldwin allows to tell her own story. He had used a third-person limited point of view with Ruth in "Come Out the Wilderness," but he had never trusted a black woman to relate her own story, or trusted himself enough to dare adopt that pose. Sylvander comments briefly on Baldwin's ambivalence about using Tish as narrator; she quotes Baldwin: "To try to tell a story from the point of view of a pregnant woman is something of a hazard. I tried to avoid it, but she's the only one who can tell the story."[17] Baldwin's decision may reflect his sensitivity to criticism that he had not given black women a truly enviable and integrated place in his fiction.[18]

Tish's first-person narration is recognizably different in its major stylistic features from Baldwin's omniscient point of view in *Go Tell It on the Mountain* and from a male's first-person narration in, for example, *Tell Me How Long the Train's Been Gone* (1968). The typical descriptive sentence below from *Go Tell It on the Mountain* contains a wealth of metaphorical language. It is consciously designed to carry the theme of the novel in terms of the conditions of sin and guilt (the grime of life) that exist within the Grimes family. Dust and dirt pervade their apartment just as surely as they pervade the distortions Gabriel has made of religion.

> Dirt was in the walls and the floorboards, and triumphed beneath the sink where roaches spawned; was in the fine ridges of the pots and pans, scoured daily, burnt black on the bottom, hanging above the stove; was in the wall against which they hung, and revealed itself where the paint had cracked and leaned outward in stiff squares and fragments, the paper-thin underside webbed with black. (pp. 21–22)

Sin lives in the lives of the characters in the same way the dirt clings to the walls and appliances. The omniscient narration, by its very nature, is depersonalized even when it carries images of almost living things. The sentence itself is very complex, with ideas just as embedded in it as the dirt is in the walls and the floorboards. In the novel, language carries theme, and metaphor and subject are synonymous.

Omniscient narration can allow for the plays on language that Baldwin develops in *Go Tell It on the Mountain* and would account for some of the differences in narration there and in *If Beale Street Could Talk*, but there are also some differences in comparing Tish's first-person voice with that of Leo Proudhammer's in *Tell Me how Long the Train's Been Gone*. Leo's voice has overtones of the metaphorical language Baldwin uses in *Go Tell It on the Mountain*, and the sentence structure is sometimes equally as complex.

> When Caleb, my older brother, was taken from me and sent to prison, I watched, from the fire escape of our East Harlem tenement, the walls of an

old and massive building, far, far away and set on a hill, and with green vines running up and down the walls, and with windows flashing like signals in the sunlight, I watched that building, I say, with a child's helpless and stricken attention, waiting for my brother to come out of there. (p. 8)

The windows become a beacon of the bond between the two brothers, and the hilly setting emphasizes the distance between them. The sentence conveys the notion that the child Leo is just as imprisoned as is his brother Caleb.

We can see some conscious differences when we consider a descriptive sentence from *If Beale Street Could Talk*. The language operates upon a single level, with Tish stating explicitly the secondary meaning instead of leaving that to be inferred by the reader.

Her hair is turning gray, but only way down on the nape of her neck, in what her generation called the "kitchen," and in the very center of her head—so she's gray, visibly, only if she bows her head or turns her back, and God knows she doesn't often do either. (p. 33)

For sheer number of words, Tish's description of her mother's hair is an unusually long sentence for *If Beale Street Could Talk*, which is not the case with the sentences quoted from *Tell Me How Long the Train's Been Gone* and *Go Tell It on the Mountain*. Tish usually narrates in spurts of choppy sentences or choppy phrases within longer sentences. Although she and Leo Proudhammer relate experiences from about the same ages in their lives, Tish's narration is always simpler. Yet the simplicity is not merely a matter of typography; her language is consciously less metaphorical than narrators in other Baldwin works, and her diction is less abstract. Her images are invariably concrete (going to the Tombs is like crossing the Sahara, Fonny's face looks as though it is plunging into water, a piano player's hands are beating the brains out of a piano, tears are like orgasms, skin is like raw, wet potato rinds), and she works to make concrete those that are abstract by nature:

Being in trouble can have a funny effect on the mind. I don't know if I can explain this. You go through some days and you seem to be hearing people and you seem to be talking to them and you seem to be doing your work, or, at least, your work gets done; but you haven't seen or heard a soul and if someone asked you what you have done that day you'd have to think awhile before you could answer. But, at the same time, and even on the self-same day—and this is what is hard to explain—you see people like you never saw them before. They shine as bright as a razor. (pp. 8–9)

Like narrators before her, however, Tish is very critical in unveiling the "shit" of the political and legal system in America.[19]

Tish is also far more conscious of audience than the previous narrators (as Hall Montana will be in *Just Above My Head*). It is important to her that the audience know and sympathize with her social situation and use it in evaluating or responding to the legal hassles she and Fonny are having. She is careful to reveal information for its strategic advantage. She begins her narration with a visit to Fonny in jail, remarking by the way: "I hope that nobody has ever had to look at anybody they love through glass" (p. 4), a comment deliberately meant for us as readers. A few lines later, she gets more familiar by saying, "You see: I know him." Then she announces her pregnancy to Fonny, then she tells us they are not married, *then* she tells us their ages. The effect is sympathy, first of all, for separated lovers, then especially for expectant parents who are separated. When we discover that the child is illegitimate, and that the parents are little more than children, our sympathy is total. It will be many, many pages before we know why Fonny is in jail, but we *feel* at this point that whatever the reason is, it is unjust. As Tish rides home on the bus, she continues the sympathetic second-person references and draws them out to a dramatic appeal: "—Can you imagine what anybody on this bus would say to me if they knew, from my mouth, that I love somebody in jail? . . . Can you imagine what anybody on this bus would say? What would *you* say?" (p. 9). *We* would say that there is something inherently wrong with a system that creates such suffering and that causes so much pain between lovers, for, after all, *we* believe in love.

I contend that Baldwin allows Tish's femininity to make the public appeal for sympathy. Who could possibly blame this hurt young woman for bringing all her defenses to bear in helping her lover? It is like crying when all else fails; it is a permissible action for women, but not for men. It can be argued that there is an implied male audience that Tish appeals to for approval (the "you" of the narration), one that will identify with Fonny's plight *as male*. In this sense, the narrative voice itself is subservient as it appeals to the implied audience, and that subservience is grounded in femininity. Even when Hall cries out almost as loudly in *Just Above My Head*, and at times even louder, the effect is not the same. His is the inconsolable pain of one brother crying out for the loss of another in that age-old respectable union of male/male liaisons; Tish's cry is the potentially consolable lament of the individual who has been wronged and believes that wrong can and should be righted.

Tish is a new breed of narrator for Baldwin, one who can relate complex emotions and issues in the simple style that is designed to reflect her age and her predicament as well as her educational level. She is intelligent, analytical, and politically cognizant of events happening around her. Although Tish can deal with complex issues, she does not have the complex voice that is often the case with Hall Montana and some of the other Baldwin narrators; consequently, the characters she presents are idealized and one-dimensional. For her portraits of the female characters, this means that the types that lead from Elizabeth and Deborah continue through Sharon Rivers and Ernestine (they will culminate in the presentation of Ruth and Mama Montana in *Just Above My Head*). Tish's narration, even when she assumes an omniscient stance, falls short of allowing Sharon or Mrs. Hunt or any of the other women to wrestle with the kinds of questions that consumed Elizabeth. There is no other side to Mrs. Hunt, no mechanism to allow us to see if she really feels differently about her church activities than the scenes in which we find her would suggest. There is no other side to Sharon Rivers, no reflection to detract from the idealized portrait we get of her as a committed, sensitive, caring mother. With the narration in her hands, Tish keeps complexity out of the family situation and locates it in the legal and social system that is presented as the enemy of all the idealized characters who are revealed to us; it is evil, and the family, with the exception of Mrs. Hunt and her daughters, is good. A similar dichotomy is set up in *Go Tell It on the Mountain* between the saved and the sinners, but there Baldwin manages to give much more depth and substance to the either/or situation; in *If Beale Street Could Talk*, substance and shades of gray give way to celebration of goodness and its possible triumph over the forces of evil. In some ways, a fairy tale of hope has replaced a genuine effort to live in this world as realistically as possible, though certainly the issues being confronted are real ones.

The unusual features in Tish's narration do not point to a similar unusualness in her character. In her relationship to Fonny, she is a very traditional black woman character. Her raison d'être comes from her man; she is very little without him. Her attitudes toward sex, the baby, and general male/female relationships have been shaped by Fonny. It is Fonny who makes the story what it is; Tish is only as alive, as suffering, as in pain as Fonny's predicament demands that she be. From their very earliest encounters, Tish's reality is shaped by Fonny's reality.

In fighting for Fonny, in making his pain our pain, his reality our reality, Tish's role resembles the one Ida plays for Rufus in *Another Country*. Without her need to avenge Rufus' death, Ida would have a far less complex reason for appearing in *Another Country*. Without Fonny and his predicament, there would not be a story to relate in *If Beale Street Could Talk*. In this comparative sense, therefore, *If Beale Street Could Talk* is just as male oriented as *Another Country* is. Somewhat surprisingly, Tish's growth is not as measurable as Ida's, nor is there ever the final separation of the male and female psyches in *If Beale Street Could Talk* that is implied in *Another Country*. Tish and Fonny are one; or rather, Fonny is the center of the circle and Tish revolves around him.

From the time they had a childhood fight and made up, they had been the Romeo and Juliet of the neighborhood, a little island of caring and concern against the uncaring streets in which they had met. They had known, Tish maintains, long before they had any knowledge of or sexual interest in each other, that they would always be together. Their togetherness means, though, that Fonny is primary and Tish is secondary; and she willingly accepts that state of affairs. It means that Fonny's evaluation of Tish *as woman* takes precedence over her own thoughts. In fact, she almost always agrees with Fonny.

Initially, Tish accepts Fonny's evaluation that she is not very pretty. About herself, she says: "Well, I'm dark and my hair is just plain hair and there is nothing very outstanding about me and not even Fonny bothers to pretend I'm pretty, he just says that pretty girls are a terrible drag" (p. 22). She excuses Fonny's judgment by saying that he is really thinking of his mother when he makes the comment about her. Intended to show a preference based on substance rather than superficiality, the comment simultaneously conveys a chauvinism that Fonny retains on other occasions. When Daniel, an old friend of Fonny, visits the couple in Fonny's rented room, Fonny teasingly remarks: "Tish ain't very good looking, but she can sure get the pots together" (p. 129), and Tish is happy that she and her man are together and all is right with the world. And indeed there is no reason for complaint built into her character; as far as we know, she has no ambition beyond being wife to Fonny and mother to his children. She works at a perfume counter in a department store, and no mention is ever made of her wanting to go to school or otherwise change her status. While comments like Fonny's can be used to suggest that the relationship between Fonny and Tish is grounded in reality, they nevertheless suggest that that reality must judge itself by something external to it. How can someone be considered *not* pretty unless there is a standard of prettiness against which she is being judged? What Tish fails to see in herself, in her voluntary blindness, she can comment on much more analytically in another context. Of her mother, she says: "I think she's a beautiful woman. She may not be beautiful to look at—whatever the fuck *that* means, in this kingdom of the blind" (p. 33), yet she refuses to lift her own blinders when Fonny makes such references to her.

In addition, this woman who is able to relate her story with perception, humor, and imagination accepts Fonny's evaluation that she is not very bright. In explaining to Daniel why he would like to escape with Tish from New York, Fonny says that he is "scared of what might happen to both of us—without each other. Like Tish ain't got no sense at all, man—she trusts everybody. She walk down the street, swinging that little behind of hers, and she's *surprised*, man, when some cat tries to jump her. She don't see what I see" (p. 125). Later, when Tish finds herself in a situation where Fonny's evaluation seems accurate, she says: "Fonny is right about me when he says I'm not very bright" (p. 167). She has just been approached by the young hoodlum who is ultimately responsible for Fonny's trouble with Bell. She had felt a hand on her hip and thought it was Fonny until it dawned on her "that Fonny would never, never touch" her that way in public. Fonny returns, beats the guy up, and is almost arrested by Bell. The cop must relent when the shopowner testifies on Fonny's behalf, and thwarting of Bell's power causes him to stalk Fonny until he gets him in jail. And Tish partly blames her lack of gray matter in bringing about the whole situation.

In the priorities in Fonny's life, Tish fits into a comfortable second place position. She does not have to worry about competition from other women, but Fonny's art is first in his life. On the night he and Tish first make love and when he pledges his commitment to her, he explains his position:

"I live with wood and stone. I got stone in the basement and I'm working up here all the time and I'm looking for a loft where I can really work. So, all I'm trying to tell you, Tish, is I ain't offering you much. I ain't got no money and I work at odd jobs—just for bread, because I ain't about to go for none of their jive-ass okey-doke—and that means that you going to have to work, too, and when you come home most likely I'll just grunt and keep on with my chisels and shit and maybe sometimes you'll think I don't even know you're there. But don't ever think that, ever. You're with me all the time, all the time, without you I don't know if I could make it at all, baby, and when I put down the chisel, I'll always come to you. I'll always come to you. I need you. I love you. . . . Is that all right, Tish?" (pp. 95–96)

And Tish responds, "Of course it's all right with me." Later, when Fonny is talking with Daniel, he emphasizes the same point: "I got two things in my life, man—I got my wood and stone and I got Tish. If I lose them, I'm lost" (p. 125). Again, the wood and stone come first, and Tish accepts the order of things, the place and worth that Fonny has assigned to her; that role is the source of her fulfillment and underscores Tish's urgency in getting Fonny out of jail.

Tish believes that things happen between men and men, as between Frank and Fonny, Joseph and Frank, Joseph and Fonny, and Fonny and Daniel, that can never happen between women. At those times, such as the morning Fonny asks Joseph for his daughter's hand in marriage, women should recede into the background; they should simply trust their men to make everything turn out all right. Women, Tish says, "must watch and guide," but men "must lead" and they "will always appear to be giving far more of [their] real attention to [their] comrades" (pp. 72–73) than they give to women. Woman must trust that her place is secure.

The religion of love that Fonny and Tish create depends upon Fonny being in the role of Lord and Master. He guides Tish through sexual initiation, and he is responsible for the change she undergoes, the religious conversion in the creation of their love religion. He initiates the action, calms her fears, baptizes her, and brings her forth anew. He is her Lord, and he calls her by the thunder of the sexual explosion they create. Henceforth, she is his. A song they laughingly sing with Daniel is revealing in its content:

When he takes me in his arms,
The world is bright, all right.
What's the difference if I say
I'll go away
When I know I'll come back
On my knees someday

> For, whatever my man is
> I am his,
> Forevermore! (p. 129)

Being his forevermore means accepting what he has to offer, a relevant context in which to place Tish's pregnancy. She views the conception of the baby as the giving of a portion of Fonny's life to her, a
sacred trust comparable to that of God and the Virgin Mary. Tish
says: "And when he started to pull out, I would not let him, I held
on to him as tightly as I could, crying and moaning and shaking with
him, and felt life, life, his life, inundating me, entrusting itself to
me" (p. 177). She is sure that this is the moment the baby was conceived, the giving of the trust she also accepts. The many scenes in
which Sharon, Joseph, and Ernestine admonish Tish to get the baby
here safe and sound are symbolic reminders to save Fonny's life from
Bell and others in the legal system who would kill him by turning
him into a bowing and scraping "nigger." The time Tish spends waiting for the baby to be born, especially near the end of the novel, is
intricately intertwined with the time Fonny has spent in jail. The
baby waits to be born; Fonny waits to be released. Both lives must
be saved.

Tish's position in relation to Fonny represents the position of all the
women in the novel in relation to all the men. No woman in the novel
is complete without the intellectual or emotional support of a man or
a male figure, on either a real level or a symbolic one. Tish is essentially an appendage to Fonny and to Baldwin's notions of masculine
superiority. Whether it is a matter of judging beauty or being guided
through daily life, Tish believes she cannot function without Fonny.[20]
For Sharon, Joseph is the Lord and Master. His approval of Tish's
pregnancy makes everything all right, just as his approval of the
marriage proposal has done earlier. The women may make up their
minds before he does, but his stamp of approval is needed before
they can experience true peace of mind. For all her independence
and going off from Birmingham to Albany, Sharon's life is only stabi-
lized and she finds purpose only after she meets Joseph. Never once
does she find reason for complaint against him, and never once does
she disagree with a decision he makes. Remember, too, she admonishes Tish to save the baby for Fonny, for what it will mean to him; she
does not mention what it will mean to Tish.

Mrs. Hunt is as much an appendage to her masculine God as Sharon and Tish are to the men in their lives. God is suitor and Mrs. Hunt sacrifices all for Him, even her son. Frank expresses this view of his wife's perverted relationship with God in the scene in the Rivers home. He threatens to blow off some heads if his son is not soon out of jail, then says to his wife: "And if you say a word to me about that Jesus you been making it with all these years, I'll blow your head off first. You was making it with that white Jew bastard when you should have been with your son" (p. 81). Ernestine has also referred to Mrs. Hunt as a "half-white bride of Christ" (p. 91). By submitting herself totally to a spiritual master, Mrs. Hunt has deprived her family of maternal affection. In the physical realm, however, especially the sexual, Frank is her lord. She calls on the Lord during the sexual encounter Fonny describes and Frank assumes that role for her by saying things such as "*I'm* the Lord," "The Lord's going to help you, sugar," and "You got the Lord now, right here" (pp. 19, 20). Frank is her sexual master in an ugly context just as powerfully as Fonny is Tish's sexual master in what to her is a beautiful one.

Even Ernestine, in her aggressive, streetwise independence, must seek masculine advice and help in getting Fonny out of jail. She must defer to Hayward's skills in spite of her gathering information about Bell's prejudiced policing habits (no one would think of getting a female lawyer for Fonny). Though Ernestine anticipates Julia Miller in that she remains without a lover at the conclusion of the novel, she is not as healthy as that absence would suggest in a schema of progression. She spends her time serving and helping others instead of focusing on her own future; she has almost become asexual, which makes the absence of male lovers in her life less significant than it seems initially (and she still serves Fonny). Finally, Adrienne and Sheila have little identity beyond looking for light-complexioned black men to rescue them from the sordid future lives they envision in Harlem. Without their male rescuers, the sisters are in "terrible trouble" (p. 45), so they take out their frustration and anger on their "nappy-headed" brother.

More is seen of women in active, decisive positions in *If Beale Street Could Talk*, and certainly Tish's role as narrator is a new departure. Those who are active are clear in their denial of any church influence over their actions. Their characters are consistently free of the guilt earlier black women would have felt for their actions. The only possible feelings of guilt Tish or Sharon or Ernestine could have can only result from failure in their attempts to get Fonny out of jail, and even if that possibility should develop, it would not have a church-based morality as its source. Though free of guilt, the women are not free of the basic position of woman in Baldwin's works as inferior to and in need of man. Though most are free of the masculine God, they are ultimately not truly free of domination, because their happiness and fulfillment are tied to their lives with male figures. It is a limitation in their conception that they seek for no more and ask no questions about the way things are. Good they do and good feelings they inspire are short-circuited by the fact that they have never heard of freedom from men and never desired to know of it.

CHAPTER FIVE

PERVERSION IN PARADISE—OR SALVATION?

Just Above My Head

Julia Miller, the central black female character in *Just Above My Head* (1979), reenacts the process of extrication from church influence that the women in Baldwin's fiction have undergone as a group since 1953.[1] The characters had reached the point of Ida and Tish in that they were not shown to be as actively involved in the church as Elizabeth and Deborah were. Now, with *Just Above My Head* and Julia, Baldwin starts off with his character solidly within the fundamentalist church again. And not only is she in the church, she is almost fanatically involved; she is the spiritual leader to whom others turn for consolation and salvation. The process of her progression beyond the church, therefore, is especially intriguing, for Julia does make the trip beyond the church; in fact, she is almost as extreme in the secular life she lives as she was in the fervor of her religious ministry.

While she is active within the church, Julia shares some traits with the earlier black women characters. Like Sister Margaret Alexander, she is the leader of her church, and she, similarly, leaves the church. Whereas Sister Margaret's departure marks the ending of *The Amen Corner* and we do not witness the effects of her decision, most of what we see of Julia is shaped by her life outside the church. As with Florence and Elizabeth, there is a period during which Julia feels acute guilt for how she has treated her mother; her guilt is based upon her feeling that she has committed a sin, specifically the sin of pride. But her character, and her relationship to the church, are much more complex and complicated than the earlier women's. In an extension of what has been suggested in *If Beale Street Could Talk*, Julia begins a destruction within her own family as long as she is associated with the church; it is only when she gives up the church—and tries to redefine religion in terms of secular commitment to family and friends—that she is able to grow in ways that win approval from the male narrator (and presumably from Baldwin).

The complexity represented by Julia's ability to free herself from the church signifies that more options are available to her; her life can no longer be measured in simple terms of good and bad, black and white. The increased complexity that Hall, the narrator, sees in her is thus tied to the secular world in which she can operate without being ultimately condemned for doing so and, significantly, without condemning herself. Florence was condemned and believed herself to be condemned for making a decision for independence; Julia, on the other hand, makes decisions that become the source of Hall's fascination with her. As a churchgoer, she is a powerful but understandable brat, easily categorized from Hall's point of view. As a woman out of the church, who prostitutes herself in an effort to get herself and her brother out of New Orleans, she becomes for Hall the most provocative, interesting, and unfamiliar woman he has ever known. Her new source of power and interest for him derives from the fact that she has severed herself from the strictures of the church, has survived that severing, and has defined a life for herself that goes beyond almost everything she has known in her earlier life. With Julia, there are more possibilities for good and evil, more possibilities for extenuating circumstances, more possibilities for decisions to be made out of individuality and necessity, not out of expectations and church rules and regulations.

Baldwin has also moved his earlier progression of the treatment of black women characters back beyond *If Beale Street Could Talk* in that he allows a male narrator to reveal Julia's character and story to us instead of allowing her to reveal them for herself. Hall's treatment of Julia serves not only to reveal character, but to extend many of the themes and concerns about family, community, and church that Baldwin had touched on repeatedly in his earlier works. Julia is as much, if not more, the center of *Just Above My Head* as Ida is the

center of *Another Country.* The difference is that we see much more
of Julia and, because she is one of the male narrator's primary concerns, he lets us in much more on the many parts of her personality,
which allow us to shape a response to her. Hall's central position in the
novel continues the critical problem of trying to see the black female
characters in the absence of male characters, but it simultaneously
undercuts that problem somewhat. We leave the novel believing that
Julia has somehow transcended the structural limitations and that her
roles as daughter, sister, and friend have overshadowed the comple-
mentary roles that Hall plays for the people around him.

   Just Above My Head synthesizes Baldwin's ideas on sexual and
familial relationships. Lines of demarcation between erotic and platonic love disappear. Fathers and daughters engage in incestuous
relationships; sisters and brothers in extended families are equally
"incestuous." Incest here is being defined not only as sexual contact
between persons who are related by biological ties, but sexual contact between individuals who have lived closely enough together to
form extended families that are often bonded together more solidly
than families with biological ties. Incest here can also mean the
desire for sexual contact among the members of those closely knit
extended families; it also refers to the hidden desires of members
within biologically related families to engage in sex with each other.

   In a violation of the traditional attitude of black writers in passively
evading a subject like incest, Baldwin consciously reveals the taboo
and declares it, if not usual and common, at least quietly pervasive.
Baldwin's stance in blatantly treating incest between biologically related individuals is very bold. Prior to his treatment of the topic,
Ralph Ellison, Toni Morrison, and Alice Walker were among the few
black American writers who had been so brave.[2] Baldwin's thematic
concern makes Julia's portrayal even more provocative; in the incestuous situation that usually makes the offspring the victim, Julia is
presented simultaneously as a victim and as a consenter to what her
father does to her. On the one hand, therefore, the incest theme
clouds the presentation of the black woman's character. On the other,
the fact that Julia is finally able to move beyond even that ugliness to
become an independent, thriving woman makes her character all the
more provocative and complex within the schema of Baldwin's treatment of black women. Julia is certainly a victim of incest, but the
larger issue is Hall's preoccupation with it and his filtering of Julia's
character through the implications of suppression and submission

inherent in participation in incest. What fascinates Hall forces us to be conscious of how he uses those fascinations to disclose character or to disguise it, as well as of what he is disclosing or disguising about himself.

Julia, presented to us through the eyes of Hall Montana and his account of the involved relationships between the Millers, Julia's family, and the Montanas, his own family, shares with Hall the role of older sibling in their respective families. Julia feels as responsible for Jimmy, her younger brother, as Hall feels for Arthur, his younger brother. It is in part because of their shared anxiety, responsibility, and love that Hall wraps Julia's life so intimately with his own. But he is also interested in her in less platonic, less objective ways. To Hall, Julia is the tainted goddess, the elevated whore. As a person who is bound by his own limited imagination to keeping rules, Hall is fascinated by Julia's ability to break rules and to survive nonetheless. She, like Arthur, lives the life she sings about in her song, while Hall can only stand, like Keats's drooling little boy, with his nose pressed firmly against the sweet-shop window of life, gazing at the life he really wishes to live. He certainly lives and loves, but the living and loving he actually engages in are merely the surface coverings for what he would really prefer to do. Julia in her incest and Arthur in his homosexuality are sources of fascination for Hall. They are the movies; he is the moviegoer.

We should not assume, however, that Hall's recognition of similar roles he and Julia share in any way suggests to him that they are equal. He does not think in such terms. He reflects upon Julia for what she has meant to Jimmy as well as for what she evokes in him concerning his own masculinity. Julia enters the novel clothed in power, and she retains some kind of power throughout. For Hall, who would like to think that his masculinity is reasonably intact, Julia represents the elusive quality of womanhood that can somehow ensnare him in spite of himself, and thereby reduce his power as male. He is therefore simultaneously drawn toward her and cautious about her. She is the most complex woman he comes into contact with during the course of the novel and, as such, she inspires him to reflect longer and more thoroughly upon her than upon any of the other women characters he encounters.

Hall is our only source for viewing Julia's actions and for trying to understand them. As the mediating voice between how he views Julia and what she actually is, he presents the obvious problem of the narrator biased by his own beliefs and expectations. Therefore, we must constantly evaluate him even as he is commenting upon and evaluating Julia and what happens to her. What he says and does in reaction to Julia must be weighed against what other characters in the book do and say. While these other characters are also seen through Hall's eyes, the relationships they hold in respect to him influence the degree to which he presents them ironically or not, and the degree to which he values their place in his life validates or negates their trustworthiness. His mother, Florence, for example, is unquestioningly presented as a good, respectable human being who has a clear view on the world and the people around her. What she has to say about Julia and her father, Joel, would carry more weight than anything Joel himself could say. Similarly, anything Paul has to say would be equally valuable because Hall respects his father so much. Since Baldwin has set up the novel, then, so that it is impossible to see the women without considering the men, how the men are considered is as much an evaluation of the women as any purely objective evaluation could be.

An involved and circuitously narrated story inspired by the death of Arthur, who has risen to become an internationally acclaimed gospel singer, the novel is no less about women and attitudes toward them. The center of Arthur's life, after all, is homosexuality; the questions it raises about masculinity and sexuality in general in turn involve questions concerning male/female relationships. Therefore, two years after Arthur's death of a heart attack in a pub in London, Hall looks back over the thirty-nine years of his brother's life in an effort to understand the pain, anguish, and love that defined it. To remember Arthur is to remember Jimmy, Arthur's lover, and the initial insecurity Arthur felt in loving men rather than women. And to remember Jimmy is to contemplate Julia, his child prodigy preacher older sister, who has made life miserable for him, her parents, and her extended family, but who has also provided a source of redemption. Arthur's relationship to Jimmy mirrors in many ways Hall's relationship to Julia. Both raise questions about what individuals need in terms of spiritual and physical sustenance in this world and about the damage they do to themselves and others in the process of fulfilling those needs. For Baldwin, as for his narrator Hall, "life is the toughest motherfucker going" (p. 364); it involves situations that one cannot predict and from which one cannot easily extricate oneself. It involves value judgments that can only be made by those who have suffered through their private hells, and it involves violations of mental and physical space that can only be fully understood by those who have been so victimized. Hall's and Julia's roles as older brother and older sister force them to live vicariously whatever pain is heaped upon their younger brothers. Hall sees his role at times as more intensely demanding than Julia's, but their positions in their respective families force him to pay increasing attention to Julia as a serious, hurting, used and abused girl/woman. The notion of family ties them all together.

Julia, Jimmy, Arthur, and Hall are tied together in explicit sexual connections, and other members of their families share some of the same perversion in familial relationships. Two days after her mother is buried, her father, Joel, violates fourteen-year-old Julia. Jimmy, four years younger, will, at twenty-one, enter into a homosexual relationship with Arthur and continue it until Arthur's death fourteen years later. Hall, narrator and exorcist in the novel, has an intense sexual relationship with Julia for a short while when he is thirty and Julia is twenty-one. Indirectly, Baldwin poses the themes of brotherhood, sisterhood, fatherhood, blood relations, and general kinship that underlie the incest theme in the novel. Incestuous contact is sometimes a way for characters to try to "save" themselves, almost in a religious context, from other unpleasant circumstances in which they may be involved. Awash in sexual baptisms and rebaptisms reminiscent of the encounters in *Another Country* and *If Beale Street Could Talk*, few of the characters save themselves or each other; yet they are all as necessary to each other as breath.

In many ways, Julia is the center of Baldwin's spiritual, sexual, and familial confusion in the novel. Called to preach at the age of seven, Julia offers a look at how a black woman in Baldwin's novels will evolve; we had glimpses of Florence and Elizabeth as young women, but we did not see their childhood and adolescent years in scenes that are as sharply focused as those with Julia. Unlike Tish, who tells her own story, Julia has no narrative voice; her life and passions are revealed through the male psyche of Hall Montana. By restrumming the instrument of pain and suffering that Julia has had to play—by revealing her blues—Hall hopes to transcend his own blues about his brother's death. Since Julia is a living example of transcendence of the most excruciating kind of physical and emotional pain, that of incest, her suffering can help Hall understand his grief. Indeed, there are shades here of Baldwin's earlier story, "Sonny's Blues," where one

brother tries to understand the physical and spiritual suffering of
the other by wrapping himself, through the pain of a woman, in the
brother's pain. Just as Sonny's brother was able to understand Sonny's
suffering only when he heard the women sing about the troubles of
the world, so too is Hall able to see more clearly the pain and suffering in Arthur's homosexual life by understanding Julia's suffering
through incest.

Julia, then, is a new high (her ultimate peace and contentment) and
a new low (her incest and prostitution) for Baldwin in his treatment
of black women. Even the confusion of Hall's rambling narrative
technique does not overshadow her vibrant, pathetic, and surviving
complexity. In a novel of nearly six hundred pages, marked by extra-
neousnesses, Julia is provocative, engaging, and disgusting. Ultimately, she is tolerable because she at least has managed to find
peace. Hall relates her story and Arthur's life as if he is putting
together a thousand piece puzzle. He starts in the lower righthand
corner, finds something recognizable and easily assembled in the
center and moves to that, then moves to the upper righthand corner
before returning to his point of departure. The novel is saturated
with the flashback technique that has become Baldwin's trademark.
When Hall reveals what of those many, many years he and Julia have
known each other therefore influences our reaction to him as well as
our knowledge of and response to her.

How we perceive Julia in the first few scenes in which she appears
in the novel is affected, first of all, by the fact that Hall himself is
seeing her from a distance. She is not yet someone with whom he
holds conversations, and she is not yet someone with whom he assumes the omniscient role in revealing her thoughts to us. In the
mysterious aura of her youthful ministry, therefore, Julia is presented as an object for our speculation about her actions and motives.
Because Hall knows so little about her at this point, he can sug-
gestively attribute feelings to her; unfortunately, what he believes he
sees in Julia is all we have to go on as well. We are led to uncover Julia's
reaction to and reflections upon her pain at the same time Hall
uncovers them. Because she, like Ida in *Another Country*, has no
initial voice in our perception of her, she is made more mysterious
and mythical to us. Her painful reduction from the mysterious to the
very real world of flesh and blood in her incestuous relationship with
her father is still not enough to make Hall see her completely without
blinders. Initially, he sees Julia from the outside, looking in upon the

effect she has had upon other people and they upon her. When he is finally allowed on the inside, when she finally has those long conversations with him, and when she finally becomes his lover, there is nonetheless an elusive quality about her, something he will never be able to understand. The recognition of her complexity, and his own inability to reduce her to the level of the microscope, is partially what ties Hall so permanently to her. He may give up trying to penetrate her private depths, but he will never give up seeing her as that unconquerable essence of femininity, which has brought him to compromise, not to victory.

Most of the novel is a flashback set against a Sunday afternoon barbecue at Julia's house when Hall is forty-eight and she is thirtynine; their ages let us know that both have survived physically. Hall will recount their suffering. Superficially prompted by questions from his son Tony to end his two-year silent grieving for Arthur, Hall reflects upon the past, providing us with an image of Julia that both evokes thoughts of previous Baldwin women characters and moves beyond them.

Julia is comparable to Florence in her jealousy of her brother Jimmy, although that jealousy is not as warranted as is Florence's of Gabriel. Also, Julia eventually arrives at a state of guilt also comparable to that of Baldwin women we have seen earlier. Julia's position within her family and her community is tied to her ministry, and she uses that ministry to make sure she remains the center of attention instead of having that role relinquished to Jimmy. Although Jimmy is younger and seemingly no threat, and Julia is clearly the center of attention, there is something in her that will allow no detraction from herself as the chosen center. Her ministry is couched in terms of the tension naturally created between males and females and intensified because of Julia's personality.

Hall's flashbacks reveal, first of all, that the seven-year-old Julia was a unique brat, a luxury none of the other Baldwin women have been allowed. Her mother, Amy, whose New Orleans background has encouraged her belief in the supernatural, supports Julia's claim to the ministry as revealing her precocity. Joel quickly realizes what a gold mine his daughter is. Certainly Julia believed that some force larger than herself had touched her mind and heart, and there is no denying that she knows the Bible and can preach some hellfire sermons. In her early years, however, she reaps more destruction than salvation.

Amy's account of how Julia announced early one morning that the Lord had called her to preach is a prelude to Hall hearing her first sermon and to the scene in which male/female tensions surrounding Julia are made clear. Amy's need to believe causes her not to doubt Julia at all, but to conclude: "There she was, my daughter, who didn't belong to me no more" (p. 80), and they immediately pray for a sign that the call is indeed genuine. The sign, which thoroughly convinces Amy, comes in the laughing peacefulness of Joel's arrival from work. She begins to treat her daughter like a grounded angel; Joel adopts the roles of devoted father, stage manager, and holy witness to Julia's sermons. Two years later, when Julia is nine, Hall hears her preach when the Montana and Miller families go to church together. Julia's sermon on David is frighteningly effective and Hall's heart "thunder[s]" with the rest of the congregation. Surprisingly, Julia is aloof after the storm she has caused:

> The floor beneath my feet shook, the very walls seemed to rock, the storm burst in a thunder of hands and feet and the wrath of the piano, the racing—like horses!—of the tambourines, and the people started to shout. Julia stood there, above it, watching, like a high priestess. She had caused this storm, or it had come through her, but she was neither singing nor shouting, and her eyes might have been fixed on Egypt.   (p. 73)

That detachment, the personal blindness that accompanies Julia's belief in her chosen status, leads to Jimmy's emotional stress and to Amy's death. But there is also in Julia an awareness of the power she has, and it is that power that almost destroys Jimmy and that so irritates Hall. At the Montana home later, Julia's emotional distance is seen further. In response to a childish disagreement with Jimmy, Julia calmly affirms: "I'm in the Lord's hands" (p. 77). Her calling quickly becomes a source of pride, sensed if not clarified in her nine-year-old mind. To be anointed, to be called, is to be chosen beyond the average human creature, and it brings a power that demands quiet tolerance from others. To her parents, therefore, Julia is beauty and Jimmy is beast. Hall has concluded as they walked home from church that Julia "frightened" him and, indeed, the inscrutable nature of her anointment is frightening. She had simply announced to her mother that she could not attend school because God had called her; such an overwhelming announcement from a seven-year-old must have had an otherworldiness about it.

Julia wields power over Jimmy's fate and her parents' actions in two other scenes in the Montana home on that fateful Sunday. Jimmy could not be forgiven for not revering his sister as almost everyone else does. After all, for a four-year-old he is excusably normal. Yet he is punished; his mother slaps him "hard, twice, across the face" (p. 77) and admonishes him to be good. Without response, Julia simply runs and puts her head in her father's lap. Later, Hall's parents try to explain to the Millers that Jimmy is "just a little boy," that "it ain't the Holy Ghost that's raising him, it's you" (p. 81) and that Julia is still their child in spite of the anointment. When Paul, Hall's father, says, "But I also *might* know something about the Lord's anointed," Julia responds with, "That may be why you're not among them" (p. 81).

Her anointed status saves Julia from her violation of the assumed distance between adults and children, and her taking power directly away from a male figure of authority. Amy mutters "*Speak, Lord Jesus!*" (p. 81) at Julia's passing judgment on Paul, but Julia is unwilling to let the matter rest. She takes center stage: "'My father,' said Julia and left his lap and stood in the center of the room, 'my father'— in that really terrifying voice, one could not imagine where it came from—'I am to deliver the Word tonight, and we must not break bread in this house.' Tears rolled down her face. 'You have mocked the Lord's anointed,' she said, 'and I—I am about My Father's business,' and she walked out of the room" (pp. 81–82). In the "dreadful silence" that follows, Amy tremblingly pursues her daughter, drawing her silent husband after her.

Until her tearful announcement, Julia has been dispassionately detached from the scene. Then, in a few words and a reliable emotional reaction, she wills her parents away from what she judges to be an unpleasant situation. Amy and Joel do not question her passing judgment on Paul or listen to Florence's comment that Julia is tired, should be put to bed, and should be restrained from preaching that night. They leave, solidifying in Julia's mind the extent of the power she has over them. The father, the signified listener, becomes even more important since he acutely recognizes the tangible rewards of Julia's preaching. He will very crudely encourage her to continue preaching when she wants to quit. Since Hall does not take Julia's perspective here—as he will later with her and with several other characters—her motives are unclear. Perhaps she genuinely believes she does the Lord's will; but she also recognizes her power. *Knowing* her parents will follow, she leaves the room. The scene manifests sinful pride that will bring her low at the age of fourteen and that will cause the guilt she feels following her mother's death.

No one questions Julia's handling of the scriptures, the New Testament demands for tolerance and forgiveness of others. Still, Julia takes Paul's comment as a personal insult, and reacts as a child who has lost its favorite toy, not as an anointed minister of God. Julia's position and power, therefore, stretch credibility; so does her status as a black child within a black community. By cloaking herself in the mantle of God, she isolates herself from others. In ironic blasphemy, the parent whom she has intoned as the heavenly father rapes her five years later.

Underneath the actions described in the walkout scene, there is a larger dynamic at work. There is an inversion, first of all, of the usual roles of authority. Instead of the parents, the assumed authorities, giving the orders, Julia does; she uses her God-given status for control, to establish clearly that she has the power to make her parents do her bidding. That inversion of youth and age, of childhood and adulthood, draws initial attention away from the fact that the males in the scene have also had their roles usurped. The larger issue of who holds power, in terms of male and female roles, of who can give orders and have them executed, provides the meatier context in which to view Hall's evaluation of and reaction to Julia. It will become increasingly clear as the novel goes on that Joel has no power over his daughter as long as she is in the ministry and what little power Amy may have had initially is pushed into the background by her illness. What Hall sees, therefore, is that three males, all of them older and presumably possessing more authority than Julia, have been forced into inferior, powerless positions because of her. Paul is first to be humiliated by Julia's questioning of his relationship to God, then Joel is humiliated because he has no control over what the women in his life do. Although Hall finds Joel a questionable character, he is not lacking in respect for Paul. To have Paul humiliated by a nine-year-old pint-sized imitation of female humanity assaults everything Hall values in terms of the roles men should play in the lives of women. For Hall, who has his manhood fresh upon him, Julia's power is particularly problematic. He is just beginning to date and to realize what it means to be a man; to see all of that stripped away by a faulty representative of the female sex makes an indelible impression upon his mind. It is in part because of his initial loathing for Julia that Hall desires so much to conquer her later on. The psychology is similar to that used in primitive societies that practice homeopathic magic—that which is of a potential threat to one can only be fully overcome when it has been reduced to insignificance, or at least when the threatened party has regained total control. Hall will later gain control of the center of Julia's sexual being just as the white males in Baldwin's "Going to Meet the Man" gained control over the black man's sexuality by castrating him. I contend that Hall is just as threatened, even by the child Julia, with the gem of the potential male-destroying power she wields.

I am not denying that Julia probably acted just as Hall has recounted her acting. The vividness with which the incident sticks in his mind—after twenty years—and the sense of his mental, if not physical, involvement in the scene suggest that it had had more meaning for him than perhaps he is willing or is able to admit. It defines in part his whole way of thinking toward Julia, and it provides the unconscious impetus for the formation of his attitude toward other women in his life. He is constantly aware of the need to be in control in all of his dealings with women, which is to some degree a measure of his desire to protect himself from all the Julias of the world at the same time that he would like to sneak up on them and forever remove that need for protection.

The extent of Julia's power not only as child preacher, but also as woman, is apparent at a Christmas dinner four years after the walkout. In the interim, Hall has been aware of Julia but has had little contact with her. Then, forced out of family commitment to attend the dinner when she is thirteen, he sees the continuation of the pattern that had been established earlier. Julia's control over her father is even more prominent. The frustration Hall feels and records in others only manifests what he himself feels; after recording what his mother and father feel about what is revealed to them, he allows himself one direct verbal assault upon Julia, which is revealing in several ways.

The problem is that Julia is not content to be a representative of God; she is trying to play God. Instead of taking Amy to a doctor to clear up problems that have resulted from a miscarriage years before, Julia, according to Joel, has "been fasting and praying—interceding with the Lord, to touch her mother's body" (p. 118). Joel has completely abdicated his role as head of the household and quietly follows what Julia wants. Julia's gall astounds Florence; how could the girl be so proud as to risk her mother's life in some flamboyant show of power from the Lord? And how, Florence asks and Paul wonders, can the full-grown Joel allow his daughter to run his household?[3] Amy's obvious physical deterioration forces Florence to confront Joel when Amy and Julia are out of the room:

> And Florence repeated, "Yes, I said *shit*, talking about *your* holy daughter, in *your* kitchen, on Christmas Day." She kept her voice low, but with an effort, and her voice was shaking. "You take your wife to a specialist, or *I* will. And I'll teach your daughter something about the laying on of *hands*." She stared at Joel. She said, with sorrow, "You and Amy should have done that a long time ago." Then she leaned down close to his face and whispered, "You goddamn, no-count fool, your wife is *sick!*" She looked at him with a look I had never seen on any face before: if it terrified me, I cannot imagine what it did to Joel. One saw in her face and heard in her voice that she did not want to say it, but she did: "And I'm not *sure* your daughter *wants* her to get well!" Then she watched his face, and her face softened. "Joel. Sometimes people who think they own the kingdom of heaven think they own everything—and every*body* else—too!" (p. 120) ·

More and more, Julia's excesses become Joel's weaknesses. He has lost his status of primary breadwinner, as well as that of father. Slowly losing his status as husband, he is becoming an appendage to Julia's anointment, which becomes more and more destructive. Paul tries to warn him: "I swear. I ain't never seen nothing like it. You both scared of that child. And you both done let something happen to that child— that ain't supposed to happen—to a child" (p. 127). Unfortunately, Joel is too weak to fight Julia—even if he wanted to.

Julia keeps herself away from the dinner guests, allowing her sick mother and Florence to make the last-minute preparations. She finally enters the kitchen and sits at the table, "arms folded, looking, at once, like a high priestess and a sullen girl" (p. 121). To her questions about her father's whereabouts, Hall responds as if Julia is the personification of disgust: "Your father and my father are sitting in the bar on the corner. You want to see him so bad, you drag your holy ass on down to the corner bar, you hear me, child?" (p. 121). Shocked Amy and stoic Florence help Hall restore his grownup posture, but he has let his mask slip long enough to show his true feelings toward Julia. Here is an individual he must force himself to remember is only thirteen years old, for what she is responsible for doing would suggest that she is much older. Hall's cursing of her is matched by his bestowing upon her "the most unsanctified look" (p. 122) he can manage in an effort to convince her that her "sanctified bullshit" did not reach him. He retreats when he realizes that he is dealing with Julia as an equal—because her power would suggest that—when in fact she is not equal to him, or at least that is the surface prompting of his retreat. Julia still holds for him, though, the same fascination and fear that she did earlier. He cannot truly conquer her in the same arena in which she operates, so he tells himself that she is only a child, calls her that, and tries to restore his status as an adult in her presence. Still, she has been able to unnerve him, to make him angry, to force him to relinquish his cool detachment. His objections to her are never couched in terms of questioning the validity of her religious conversion; they are always psychologically in terms of what a little girl is doing to usurp the roles of the men in her life. As he stands giving her that unsanctified look, Hall is tempted to say to her "that her daddy wasn't nothing in this world but her clown" (p. 122), but such an admission would again bring the confrontation to a level of equality and would emphasize again the power Julia has in having diminished the lines usually drawn between parents and children, between authority and lack of authority, between males and females.

That unconquerable center of Julia's being, backed by a religious conviction, keeps her power beyond suppression by Hall while it also suggests that she may suffer, but she will never be subdued. Her suffering begins with Amy's death, and it will continue through the guilt Julia shares with so many other black women in Baldwin's fiction. Amy dies after ugly scenes in which Florence and Martha, Hall's girlfriend, have tried to save her from Joel and Julia. On the occasion when they take the matter into their own hands and go to the Miller apartment to take Amy to the hospital, they find a cowardly Joel who sheepishly explains that Julia has taken Amy to a new church for a prayer meeting. Florence warns Joel again to "take your wife out of your daughter's hands" (p. 155). A passive Joel refuses and Amy is taken to a hospital, where Julia's fasting, praying, and washing of her mother's body cannot save her. Before she dies, though, Amy sees the truth about Julia and hints to her of the dreadful things to come: "You start fasting and praying—*today*—for your father, and for *you*. The Lord ain't pleased with you. He going to make you both to know it. How come you think you can fool the Lord? You might done had *me* fooled. But I *wanted* to be fooled! How come you think the Lord don't see? When *I* see!" (pp. 166–67). What Amy sees is the latent, potentially perverted relationship between Joel and Julia as well as the pride that has guided Julia's early years.

Her failure to save her mother forces Julia to see that she is a child who is subject to bereavement at the loss of her mother and that she is not a miniature version of God. It also shows that guilt in the female characters in Baldin's works is frequently induced by circumstances that are in reality beyond their control but for which they believe they have responsibility. Julia is a child, not a magician, or a high priestess, or a goddess; but she has come to believe that she has as much power through faith as others would believe she has. Amy's death convinces her that she has sinned, through pride, beyond forgiveness, that she has failed in an essential portion of her ministry. She has failed to save Amy, either literally or figuratively, and that means in the final analysis that she has failed to serve. She begins to feel as responsible for her mother's death as Elizabeth felt for Richard's—or at least that is what we can surmise from her actions.

Subconsciously, Julia gives up the ministry, although that decision will not be verbalized until later. Meanwhile, alone with her father (Jimmy has been sent to New Orleans to stay with their grandmother), she is a lonely fourteen-year-old in a huge brownstone that will shortly become a financial burden. Uncertain about growing up, hesitant about her ministry, and guilty about her mother's death, she passes judgment upon herself and willingly submits to her private purgatory, which is not proportionate to the wrongs she has committed. To this point, her sins have been caused by distortion of a personal relationship to God, leniency in Joel and Amy, Amy's need to believe coupled with Joel's greed, and, as we discover later, Julia's childish jealousy of Jimmy. Julia feels these reactions more than she is consciously aware of them. It will take many years and discussions with Hall before she recognizes all her thoughts. Meanwhile, these sins crystallize in her actions, and she loses herself in self-imposed punishment and atonement.

Two days after her mother's funeral, she hesitates, then voluntarily enters into an incestuous relationship with her father, which undermines her credibility as a black woman-child, but which puts her firmly in the tradition of Baldwin's guilty black women. At a time when she is confronting the terror of her self-delusions, her father insists that she return to preaching, emphasizing responsibility and the dead mother's expectations as the guiding motivations. "I think it's best . . . that you get back in the pulpit right away. It's a right long time you ain't been preaching—people keep asking me about you, girl, we got churches lined up for more than a year! And it'll help you get your mind off all this sorrow. You'll see. It's what your mother went away from here praying for—it was her last words to me. She was always so proud of you" (pp. 167–68). He insists upon beginning to make new commitments the next day and resists accepting Julia's refusal. Against her complaint that she has sinned and the Holy Ghost has left her, he emphasizes that she should put on a show, because "if you don't hit them churches, girl, how we going to eat? Tell me that. You know how much money *I* make—you been keeping this house going. You going to turn your father into a beggar now?" (p. 170). Taking advantage of her momentary hesitation, he appeals to her as man to woman, in classic blues tradition, not as father to daughter: "'You always liked to see me real sharp and pretty—I know you did. What you mean, you don't believe no more? Don't you believe in me?' 'I did it for you,' she said—and did not hear herself, did not know what she said. 'Then keep on doing it for me. Ain't but the two of us now'" (p. 171). He puts his arms around her to comfort her, and the comfort turns to incest. He initially has to slap her onto the couch, but she finally submits—physically, at least; her mental state is ambivalent.

A clear indication of the male/female dynamic at work in the book, the scene between Julia and her father further illustrates the serving position in which most Baldwin women find themselves. As a minister, Julia has served in the church, presumably saving whatever souls were inspired to come to Jesus through her. To her own mind, her credibility is lowest when the only value she has seen in herself has been dissolved in Amy's death. Joel now tries desperately to restore a serving posture in his daughter by convincing her that her worth may have been tarnished in the loss of her mother, but it can be restored to its gleaming status in serving her father by working to take care of him. Undoubtedly Julia is sorry that her father is left alone without her mother, as she herself has been left alone, but again the parent/child relationship is pushed beneath the surface by Joel and by Hall in favor of the male/female relationship. After all, *how* Joel makes the appeal is really Hall's language, not Joel's, because Hall is recreating the scene from the various bits of the story that he has been able to get from his family and friends. Being "pretty and sharp" is a line men use with women, not fathers with their daughters, and even the implicit notion that Julia should *work for* Joel is also out of the range of parent/child relationships. Restoration of the serving status Julia has been in and thereby restoration of a perverted sense of self-worth through "helping" her father are both accomplished in the participation in incest.

The ease with which Joel anticipates and rationalizes violating his daughter suggests that Amy's earlier suspicions were correct. She sensed more in Joel than perhaps he knew about himself; her death releases Joel from suppression. He tells Julia: "Nobody will ever have to know, baby, you'd be surprised; it happens all the time. Love is a beautiful thing, darling; something in every man, I believe, wants to turn his daughter into a woman. . . . You and the Holy Ghost been after my ass *awhile*; you wanted me, you got me" (p. 171). Julia steps away from her father, who elevates himself to a perverse assumption of control over her. He has become the physical lover comparable to the spiritual lover that Jesus is to those who totally commit their lives to him; he has secularly replaced the spiritual Jesus.

Julia voluntarily submits to her father's sexual advances for a period of months. She might find his touch loathsome, and she might hate herself, but she constantly gives in. Why? The ugliest possibility is that, in addition to her guilt, she enjoys the affair. As her father threw her on the sofa the first time, she felt that "something in her had always wanted this, but not this, not this, not this way, she wanted to say, *Please. Please wait*" (p. 171). Joel reinforces what he believes is a general desire in daughters for their fathers when he later offers Julia justification:

> "What's between you and me happens, happens all the time—this ain't the last time or the first time or the only time. I just ain't being a hypocrite about it—that's all. And you didn't call no cops on your daddy, did you? And you ain't going to, neither. *All* little girls wants their daddy—everybody knows that. I didn't do a damn thing but give you what you wanted. That's why you still here—*I* hear the way you call me Daddy!"   (p. 235)

to which Julia can only think:

> It was true—she became more terrified than ever, and said nothing. She murmured *Daddy* as he pounded into her, as she felt him shoot his semen into her: she was pleased to give him pleasure. His pleasure was over-whelming and terrifying, she could scarcely bear it, his pleasure left her alone in some dreadful place, and yet, something in her was pleased to give him pleasure. With all her heart, she wanted to flee—she could not move.   (p. 235)

A greater likelihood is that she sees her incestuous affair with her father as a deserved self-punishment, the ultimate flagellation for having committed the sin of pride and killed her mother. Is the horror of that "murder" more than the horror of taking her mother's place with her father? Somewhere in her mind are vestiges of the psychology that posit that one who is guilty must be punished for the crime he or she has committed. Julia's "crime," she believes, is in not saving her mother, and she has been unable to save her mother because she has strayed from the religious teachings that should have guided her life. Instead of putting them first, she has tried to put herself above them; therefore, God has caused her to fail in order to show her the fault inherent in her self-elevation. Youth, combined with an inability to think clearly through all the theological implications of her actions, leads Julia to condemn herself at this stage as thoroughly as some of the earlier Baldwin women condemned themselves for their actions.

In her earning ability, as in her sexual capacity, Julia becomes "wife" to Joel. She takes a job scrubbing floors after school to compensate for the loss of income from preaching and gives most of the money to her father. Still, the move to the brownstone is more than their meagre finances can afford. Joel has to pawn a favorite pair of cufflinks, and Julia feels "very sorry for him. She had nothing against him, nothing, either because she did not expect him to be other than he was, or because she was too beaten. She had to move, and yet, she waited" (p. 234). The waiting will prove more destructive than her preaching. The too early deflowering will eventually leave her barren; Joel's very act of drawing his daughter into womanhood ironically and temporarily guarantees that she will not experience it.

Joel's and Julia's involvement reinforces earlier scenes. The Sunday she stormed out of the Montana house was a portent of things to come. Before her departure, and shortly after Jimmy's stormy reaction to her, she had run to seek comfort in her father's lap. Like her heavenly Father, he had been her refuge from the troubles of the world. Her action evoked Hall's comment on the family when they were in church earlier: "Brother and Sister Miller came to our house, with their son and daughter: a young couple, merely, she very much in love with him, he very much in love with their daughter. They teased each other, and made a great fuss over Julia—who was a beautiful little girl. What surprised me was that she was a very cheerful little girl. She loved to laugh, especially in her daddy's lap, and her daddy loved to make her laugh" (p. 74). Hall says not that the man loves his daughter, but that he is *in love* with her, again an expression usually reserved for references to erotic love. Later, in the Montana home, Julia sits "on her father's lap, motionless, using him the way the Sphinx uses the plains of Egypt" (pp. 78–79). The lap sitting continues into Julia's adolescent years, making an apparently innocent action suspect by its intensity. When Julia is absent from her father, for even as short a time as an hour, she greets him with effusive hugs and expressions of longing upon his return. The first sexual violation of Julia begins when Joel takes Julia into his arms (a customary action with them) to comfort her. Arms she has found so safe earlier will become despicable to her, but it will be a long time before she finds the strength to extricate herself from their embraces.

Foreshadowing of the incest is coupled with the extended family's suspicions of what goes on in that lonely brownstone. Both Joel and Julia cease visiting the Montanas. Joel takes to drink, and Julia starts wearing makeup as well as high-heeled shoes. Florence perhaps suspects most clearly the nature of the relationship between Joel and Julia, but she has no proof and really does not want to confront the horror of her suspicions. She has failed to save Amy, her old friend's daughter, and she seems to have little hope of saving Julia. It is only when Julia becomes pregnant and her father nearly beats her to death that the suspicions of Florence and the neighbors reap tangible fruits.

Hall, a black man who must relate the violation of black female innocence by another black man, is thorough in dissociating himself from Joel. Lest the taint of perversion rub off on him, he carefully portrays what a despicable character Joel is. He makes Joel into a moral villain whose villainy must be viewed in isolation, not as a measure of all black men. From his very first scenes in the novel, Hall paints Joel as a man of questionable character. In moral contrast, Hall will later become Joel's alter ego. He will assume the role of father and lover to Julia in another "incestuous" relationship benignly designed, in part, to repair the damage Joel has done to his daughter.

Hall stresses the sexuality, laziness, ineffectualness, and spinelessness of Brother Miller.[4] Joel's sexuality represents the stereotyped image of the superstud who wins feminine favors as a result of flashy clothing and superficial charm. As Hall sits in church that Sunday listening to Julia preach, he observes her parents:

Her father made very little pretense—he didn't have to, being her father.
He was the zoot-suited stud of studs—a mild zoot suit, driving ladies wild
wondering what he'd be like wild. He had the cruel, pearly teeth, and the
short, black, tickling mustache, and that grin of the sinner man just waiting
for the touch which would bring him salvation, and thick, curly, *good* black
hair. His eyes were like Mexican eyes, and he seemed, in all things,
indolent, waiting for you to come to him.

I was not the only one who would see all this change, but, at that time,
Brother Miller had the world in a jug and the stopper in his lean brown
hand.   (p. 70)

The carefree, worldly image presented here makes Joel's monetary
hold on his daughter perfectly in keeping with his character. And we
are not unduly surprised when he resorts to his sexual "charm" when
economic persuasion fails.

Certainly we are inclined to share Hall's attitude toward a man who
would commit incest upon his adolescent daughter, but Hall's intense
dislike for Miller may also be tinged with jealousy. His severe evaluations of Miller pile up over a number of years, and most of the novel.
He calls him lazy (an accurate evaluation that Florence also shares)
and sees through his superficial motives about Julia's preaching:
"Without Julia's notoriety, and her earning power, Brother Joel Miller
would long ago have split the scene . . . Joel did not love his wife so
much as he loved his daughter because she put bread on the table"
(p. 102). When he sees him again at the Christmas dinner, he concludes: "Joel was still the zoot-suited stud of studs, fatigue beginning,
perhaps, to undermine the jawline, an embittered bewilderment
coming and going in his eyes, but the suit was navy blue, and so was
the knitted tie; the shirt was white, the cufflinks gleamed like gold. *A
pretty penny!* was the thought that came to me, like a messenger with
bad news" (p. 107).

The pretty penny is too spineless to save his wife from his daughter
and too ineffectual to take charge of his own household. He is, in fact,
uncomfortable in his own house: "Since it was the first time I had ever
seen him in his house, and since I was still, after all, very young, it
was almost as though I were looking at him for the first time. I may
have felt this because he seemed—somehow—so uneasy in his own
house. He seemed more like a guide. . . . Even the clothes that
Brother Joel Miller wore contributed to this airless, hothouse cli-
mate, for—they covered him: one did not wish to speculate on his
nakedness, or find oneself, in any way whatever, obliged to be a

witness to it" (p. 116). The man's moral deterioration is hinted at in
the slightly perceptible beginning of a physical deterioration and in
his general inability to control himself or his environment.

As Miller loses more and more control to Julia, Hall's judgments
become more explicit. He does not believe Joel is "much of a man"
because Joel does not "really seem to believe in anything, not even
long enough to fake it" (pp. 151, 152). After Joel impregnates Julia
and beats the baby out of her, and after Hall returns to New York from
a stint in the army, he makes clear the distinction between the
monster Joel and other black men, especially himself: "Joel appalled
the man in me, he made me sick with shame; but I had placed, with
speed, so vast a distance between his manhood and my own that he
could not threaten me, he had no power over me . . . I could divorce
myself from Joel" (p. 317). Why he even needs to consider the separation between himself and Joel makes his position questionable.

It is indeed hard for Hall to divorce himself from Joel, for he will
shortly find comfort in the very womb Joel has tried to destroy.
Meanwhile, Julia must find her own savior to lift her from the hell of
life with her father. In another ironic and incestuous twist, she is
helped along the road to recovery by engaging in a sexual act with
Crunch, who has been Arthur's first homosexual lover. At the time of
their encounter, Julia is fourteen, Arthur is sixteen and Crunch is
nearly twenty. Crunch, an oversized, lovable, good-natured lug,
stumbles into his affair with Julia; she literally begs him to seduce her.
By giving herself to another man, Julia believes, she can break the
awesome hold her father has over her. For the first time, she hints at
the relationship with her father, asks for help, and through tears,
tries to explain things to Crunch:

> "You don't know," she said, "how much I wanted to see you, how many
> times I've thought of you."
> "Of me? Why me?"
> "Lying next to my daddy, listening to him snore," she said. "I thought of
> you, oh, how I wished it was you!"
> Her tears began to fall again. He stared at her stupidly, saying nothing.
> "Don't look at me like that," she said. "It wasn't my fault, I swear it wasn't
> my fault, please be my friend."
> "Your father—?"
> "Don't tell. Don't tell, you hear? It wasn't his fault, either, he can't help it!"
> "Your father—?" He felt that he was about to throw up.
> "Yes. My father. He says it happens all the time." She looked up at him.
> "Does it?"

"I wouldn't know," he said—feeling colder and colder. . . . She moved, and buried her face in his chest. He put his arms around her, then she moved again and held him close.

"Oh, Crunch," she whispered. "Please make me well. Please touch me—take me—make me well." (pp. 238, 239)

Julia's innocent, childish question seems out of place with the grownup role into which she has been thrust; it focuses attention back to the fact that she is very much a child. Crunch is coaxed into making passionate love to her, which apparently accomplishes part of what she wants. When he asks how she feels afterward, she responds: "Saved." She makes Crunch into Jesus who saves by the giving of a liquid (blood/sperm) from his body. For the first time, she can confront her naked body "without shame or fear," for "what her father had stolen from her, Crunch had given back" (p. 241).

The healing, however, does not bring the total break. Crunch goes into the army and leaves Julia in the hands of Arthur, with the admonition that he be her friend. Arthur, who is unquestionably sensitive and loving (Hall's legendary portrait of him is at least), knows about Julia and Crunch, but Julia does not know about Arthur and Crunch. Crunch's two child lovers, therefore, mourn his absence in the room he has rented, the room to which Julia has begged to be taken. She hides out in the room away from her father as much as possible, but fear of spending nights alone almost always drives her home. She escapes further sexual violation if her father has gotten drunk and gone to pursue other women; if not, she endures his loathsome touch.

Joel's degeneration can be measured in his appearance one night when Arthur accompanies Julia home after they have gone to a movie together. In a drunken and jealous rage, Joel verbally assaults Arthur as someone Julia has picked up off the street. Before he sees or recognizes Arthur, though, he reveals much about himself: "He was wearing pajamas, carelessly, appallingly open, he was drunk, and he rushed toward Julia. 'I came home early, especially for you! I don't *never* see you no more, *where've you been?*'" (p. 274). When he becomes aware of Arthur, he turns on him: "'Who are you? What you doing here with my daughter?' He turned to Julia. 'You dragging them in off the streets now? . . . What you doing, coming in here this time of night, with my daughter? I don't want her fooling around with black scum like you? [*sic*] She got her *daddy* to look out for her'"

(p. 275). Julia makes him know who Arthur is, and his recognition brings knowledge of his nakedness, both literal and symbolic. He slinks out of their presence. What he has said, however, adds another dimension to the concept of father. In addition to the biological and the heavenly, Joel unknowingly provides the idea that he is pimp to his daughter, that he has made her into a whore who will go out to other men because he has directed her to that path. As her "daddy"—lover and pimp—he has initiated her for all the men who will come after him.

Julia wants to escape, but the slowness with which she goes about accomplishing her purpose brings further degradation; she is impregnated by her father. Rumor has it that the baby is Crunch's, but Julia admits to Hall, years later, that the baby was indeed her father's. Perhaps the tangible confrontation with his own sin causes Joel to go berserk. Perhaps he suspects that Julia has cheated on him. Perhaps he recognizes the irony of Julia having a child when Amy has died because she lost one. Anyway, he beats the baby out of Julia and almost kills her in the process. She screamingly calls for Florence, but the neighbors arrive before she does and give definite shape to the thoughts of incest that Florence has had earlier. She describes to Hall what she found upon arriving at the apartment.

> "Well, the skinny little thing had been beaten to an inch of her life. Her face, it wasn't no face, it was just a mess of blood and puffed-up flesh. Didn't have no lips, didn't have no eyes—just little dark slits where the eyes was supposed to be. I said, "Who did this?" I thought somebody had broke in and tried to rob them. . . . I wrapped up the child as best I could, in blankets—and the blood came seeping through those blankets, I just knew she was going to bleed to death." (p. 295)

But Julia survives and is whisked away to New Orleans to join Jimmy. Paul tracks Joel down and listens to a pathetic tale about someone breaking into the house and beating Julia in a robbery attempt. It is his story that sticks, Julia is thought to be the scandalous prostitute, and Joel is dismissed to haunting bars and chasing the women who "still like him" (p. 299).

Julia's initial extrication from the situation with her father, though not of her own volition, begins the process by which she will extricate herself from all the guilt associated with her mother's death as well as with the participation in incest with her father. Her baptism into the salvation Crunch offers is paralleled by the larger baptism: the sym-

bolic death that results from the father's beating and its continuation
in the prostitution in New Orleans is transformed into the new life of
Julia's modeling, her trip to Africa, and the final contentment she
finds as Hall watches her so peacefully turning the ribs at the barbecue that occurs near the beginning of the novel. Her rebirth is
what makes Julia different from the earlier Baldwin women. She
makes a complete change from one life-style to another, from one
very restricted way of thinking to larger, more functional ways of
thinking. She represents an escape, a freedom that looms large because of the path taken to reach it.

Although her transformation makes her different from the earlier
portraits of black women, there are other connections here with Julia
that have been hinted at before between earlier black women and the
men in their lives. Incestuous contact that is explicit and at times
brutal between Joel and Julia in *Just Above My Head* is a subtle
undertone in *If Beale Street Could Talk* between Tish and her father,
Joseph. The biblical parallel initially puts Joseph in the role of surrogate father, but incidents and comments throughout also point out
connections that could make Joseph the literal father if circumstances
were different. Tish, too, loves to sit on her father's knee in the
protecting gesture Joel has with Julia. The knee sitting portrayed is
especially noticeable in *If Beale Street Could Talk* because it takes
place in the present, when Tish is nineteen and pregnant. The scene
occurs after Sharon has announced Tish's pregnancy and before the
Hunts arrive. At her father's invitation to "sit down on your Daddy's
knee," Tish does precisely that: "I felt like a princess. I swear I did.
He took me in his arms and settled me on his lap and kissed me on the
forehead and rubbed his hand, at first roughly and then very gently
through my hair. 'You're a good girl, Clementine,' he said. 'I'm proud
of you. Don't you forget that'" (p. 60). Her response to sitting on his
lap is a mixture of innocence and sexual suggestions:

> That child in my belly was also, after all, *his* child, too, for there would
> have been no Tish if there had been no Joseph. Our laughter in that
> kitchen, then, was our helpless response to a miracle. That baby was our
> baby, it was on its way, my father's great hand on my belly held it and
> warmed it: in spite of all that hung above our heads, that child was prom-
> ised safety. Love had sent it, spinning out of us, to us. Where that might
> take us, no one knew: but, now, my father, Joe, was ready. In a deadlier and
> more profound way than his daughters were, this child was the seed of his
> loins. (pp. 60–61)

Valid to a point, the interpretation is nonetheless not exactly what one would expect a daughter to provide of her father, and her posture certainly is not an expected one.

Support Joseph provides is what Fonny is unable to; perhaps it is that reflection that inspires Tish's evaluation of Joseph later in the novel. She imagines Joseph and Frank together planning for Fonny's release and comments about Joseph: "He then looks, I swear to you,—and his hair is beginning to turn gray,—about thirteen years old. I thought once, I'm certainly glad I didn't meet him when he was a young man and then I thought, But you're his daughter, and then I dropped into a paralyzed silence, thinking: Wow" (p. 152). It is an innocent thought, she would suggest, yet she realizes that even innocent thoughts can be much too revealing. Another revealing connection occurs on the morning Joseph insists that Tish quit her job because Fonny needs her to bring the baby safely into the world. Tish bursts into tears; Joseph sits before her, she says, and "he kisses my tears" (p. 198). Again the action is one that is expected of a lover, not of a loving father. Baldwin has idealized this family relationship into sexual connotations that become explicit in *Just Above My Head*, suggesting that the ideas he develops there are ones he had long considered. Julia's relationship with Joel, no matter how destructive it turned out to be, is one to which Baldwin and Hall Montana are mutually attracted.

The next time Hall sees Julia, he will have an affair with her; she will be twenty-one and he thirty. His involvement with Julia needs to be set against not only his reaction to Joel, but his reaction to the other women in the novel. Hall sees himself as a man's man: confidant to his younger brother, exemplary son to his parents, able to show tears without being considered weak. He sees a definite place for women; they should be loved and protected, and they can possibly pursue careers of their own, but they should not consider themselves equal to men. Since Hall's narration reveals much about himself, the progressive impressions he gives to us about women should be considered within the chronology of the narration, not necessarily within the chronology of the years he covers, though, as we have seen with his evaluations of Joel, his attitudes have been formed early.

We first see Hall with Ruth, the woman he has met and married after the affair with Julia, and mother to his two children. He says he is "happy with her, simply" (p. 23). He also says earlier: "Ruth is the first real commitment I have ever made, outside of my commitment to Arthur, and this commitment was possible only because, loving me, she knew how much I loved my brother, and, loving me, she loved Arthur, too" (pp. 21–22), thus emphasizing the fact that Ruth's sharing of Hall's legendary esteem for Arthur is at least as important as his love for her (if indeed he really loves her). She is comforting (he calls her "mama," a suggestive reference) and tolerant of his lapses (she allows him to sleep on the day they are due for the barbecue at Julia's, promising to call to wake him when the preliminaries are near completion). Ruth is primarily an appendage, in place only in the guise of the roles she assumes: lover, wife, mother. Her marriage to Hall is a compliment to his good taste and his desire to settle down, not to any intrinsic qualities she has beyond those inherent in the general designation of woman. Ruth is the anchor he has settled for after the fun times and the flashy years.

If a male must engage in a heterosexual relationship, then perhaps that in which Hall is engaged with Ruth is most acceptable to him and to Baldwin. As we have seen earlier, for Baldwin, the bisexual males who engage in homosexual relationships perhaps have the most acceptable world. A male as sympathetic to homosexuality as Hall is would probably be even more conscious of not allowing women to dominate any relationship in which he would become involved. Ruth is the manageable compromise for which Hall has settled after his earlier affairs.

Many years before (but later in the chronology of the novel), Hall had been involved with Martha, who tries to help Florence rescue Amy. Of that involvement, he summarily concludes: "I knew I wasn't going to marry her" (p. 100). It is not so much his conclusion as his attitude after reaching it: Martha is convenient and good for him at this stage, but ultimately she will not do. The reason is not made clear, except for Hall's parodic references that Martha "tended to mourn." His family likes her and so do his friends; he himself cannot really find anything wrong with her. It is simply that he does not value her much. "Martha used to irritate me by leaving—or by seeming to leave—everything to me: she knew perfectly well that I was incapable of any other arrangement. But I pretended to believe, in those years, in a kind of doomed sexual equality as though the man and the woman held the same vision, carried the same load. This pretense simply revealed to Martha how little prepared I was to assume my own burden, that of the man, how little prepared I was to help her be a woman" (pp. 132–33). His attitude is presumptuous and vain, but it is within his innately given rights as a man to feel as he does, or so he believes. He keeps Martha in limbo when he joins the army: "Martha avoided asking me to marry her, I did not ask her to marry me. We— er, I—had the Korean war as our reason" (p. 158). Hall clearly does not care about the woman *as individual woman.*

Though she never explicitly states it, we can rather accurately surmise what Martha wants from the few times we see her. We know that she works in a hospital in what is apparently a relatively stable job. We know that her aunt has concluded that Hall and Martha would be a good match, and we know that Hall has fallen into the habit of staying over in Martha's apartment. All of these things point toward domesticity. So does Martha's joining with Florence to save Amy from Julia and Joel; she is concerned about saving the family and someday herself becoming a part of one. She does not push the issue of marriage, but that is clearly what she and her aunt want, and that is what is made clear by her attachment to Sidney, Hall's bartender friend, once Hall goes to Korea. Her job enables Martha to take care of herself, but she still desires a family and marriage. Hall's focus on his failure to propose reflects his awareness of what Martha truly wants, and it simultaneously reflects the very traditional trait Baldwin has built into her character in spite of her job security. The traditional role Hall sees for Martha is "right," from his point of view; he is simply not yet willing to join her in settling down.

His first glimpse of Amy at Julia's preaching continues his subordination of women; he pictures her as a luscious body ripe for his picking. "She had one beautiful ass, and high, tight demanding breasts, and long legs, and she always wore high heels—just to make sure you didn't miss those legs. When she got happy, she would stroke her breasts, and I would watch her thighs and her legs and that ass of hers as she started to shout, and I would get such a hopeless, unregenerate eighteen-year-old hard-on on in the holy place that you could certainly hear this sinner moan" (pp. 69–70). With Amy, as with Martha and Ruth, woman exists for man's pleasure, and Hall is sexually secure enough (so he would have us believe) not to alter that evaluation. He is the lion who wants the lioness in place: "I needed my own place, my own lair, *my* woman, *my* cubs" (p. 288). Made in reference to his need to leave his father's house after he returns from the army, this comment nevertheless extends beyond its immediate context.

The idea that woman exists for man's pleasure is complicated for

Hall by the fact that he fits into the category of man who also sexually desires to violate his gods. That idea in Baldwin's fiction goes back to the neighbors' response to Deborah's elevation to the status of virgin, to Frank and Alice Hunt's relationship, to the religious connotations of lovemaking between Fonny and Tish, and it culminates here in what Hall would like to do with Julia. By engaging in incest with her father, Julia has become as mysterious as the rape of Deborah made her—they are both harbingers of "source[s] of delight more bestial and mysteries more shaking than any a proper woman could provide" (p. 73). To become close to them, especially as Hall does with Julia, is to border on knowing the unknowable things identified with god-head. The "hard-on" Hall gets from watching Amy possessed by the god is ultimately akin to part of the feeling he has for Julia. In both instances, woman exists for the pleasure of the male figure, be that figure man or the woman who has been endowed with the power usually associated with (masculine) gods. The violation is a way of obtaining that power which emanates from some source other than the medium (woman) through whom it must be obtained. By desiring to make love to Amy and Julia, Hall desires to get closer to the masculine center of the universe.

Except for his mother, then, Hall has seduced or envisioned seducing every significant black woman in the novel. Toward his mother he is appropriately respectful, but she simply disappears from his narration around the time he is thirty. When the extended family relationships are considered, however, a parallel is drawn between Amy as surrogate mother to Hall and Florence as surrogate mother to Julia, though Florence is more motherly in relation to almost all the characters.[5] Technically, then, Hall's lust for Amy is an incestuous undercurrent to his affair with Julia. Add Hall's subconscious identification with Joel, who has violated his daughter, to his secret desire to violate a symbolic daughter with Julia—since he is nine years older than she—and the incestuous relationships and interrelationships become mind boggling.

With this background, and with total awareness of what has happened between Joel and Julia, Hall tells us he falls in love with her—abruptly (as can only happen in a Baldwin novel) and unintentionally, on their first date: "Somewhere between Sheridan Square and East 18th Street, Julia and I fell in love" (p. 351). Hall knows all the titillatingly lewd details of Julia's life, and she provides him with another on their first night out: she has worked as a prostitute in New

Orleans in order to earn money for Jimmy and herself to escape from their grandmother's household (Joel finally literally "turns her out"). Julia's survival in New Orleans has been heroic, and her general empathy for Jimmy has been admirable, yet it is not this context that Hall focuses upon; for him, Julia embodies all of his sexual fantasies and forbidden hopes. With her, he can descend to the depths of sexual degradation he envisions in his own mind and yet remain morally "clean." He says that he and Julia are good for each other, and perhaps in a way they are. The extent of his sexual fantasies about her, though, can be seen years later, even after his marriage to Ruth, when a gesture or a giggle from Julia would send him back to those passionate days they shared; his description of their sexual encounters (pp. 377–78) rivals anything Joel could envision with Julia, and would give a seasoned writer of pornography some competition. His first sexual encounter with Julia comes at the end of that date when they "fell in love." He has been away for a while and pleads with Julia to "welcome" him home. His need can be satisfied with a total stranger (a prostitute) or with someone with whom he feels so familiar and whose past he knows so well that dirt no longer seems like dirt (Julia). He can get the prostitute *and* the familiarity with Julia, and they spend a night together that is presumably satisfying to both.

Later, like concerned and tolerant parents, they watch over the budding affair between Jimmy and Arthur. (Hall is seven years older than Arthur and eleven years older than Jimmy.) Julia and Hall cannot call the relationship perverse because to do so would make perversity of their own relationship. Instead, they are all happy that their "family" is back together again. But their fabricated family structure falls apart when Arthur goes on a western tour, Jimmy goes to do civil rights works in the South, and Julia, for reasons not clearly defined, goes off to Africa. Alone in New York (except for his parents, who are diminishing as important influences in his life), Hall degenerates to mental and physical stupor—tears, improper diet, excessive drinking, inactivity. His pain at Julia's departure is physically apparent, but the reasons behind it are what he never faces squarely; the usually articulate Hall is atypically quiet in retrospection about the demise of his relationship. Eleanor Traylor extends this point to comment on "a certain myopia" in Hall, "which blinds him to the manifest ambiguities within himself." She adds that "Hall's ability to see *out* blurs, sometimes, his ability to see within."[6]

What he has told us earlier, however, might be instructive. At some

level, he is forced to confront the fact that he, for all his good intentions, has been less able to do for Julia what either Joel or Crunch did
for her. Certainly she left both of them as well, but he has never
caused the pain Joel has or played so definitely the savior role Crunch
has played. At least both of them touched and held on to Julia in ways
Hall is unable to.[7] Perhaps he feels Julia has reduced him to the status
of Joel, something from which Hall has sought consciously to dissociate himself. Perhaps she has equated him with Crunch, the sexually
usable "boy" for whom Hall and others have felt a great deal of pity.
Maybe Hall wanted to be *the* man in Julia's life, and, when she leaves
him, he is forced to realize that he is mere man, physically aligned
with the other men in Julia's life even if he believes himself morally
superior to them. Like a father, he wanted to save Julia, just as, like
"father" and "brother," he wanted to seduce her. Finally, his sorrow
may be a matter of pride. Julia leaves him; he does not leave Julia.
Therefore, she could be using him in the same way he has used
Martha and will use Ruth. He apparently believes that he should
have been the one to dissolve the relationship, not Julia.

The complicated relationship between Hall and Julia, and between and among other members of their families in the novel, can
best be explained by a parenthetical statement Hall makes. In the
long passage in which he describes making love with Julia, and at
the point he describes kissing her breasts, he says in a brief aside:
"(someone said that all love is incest)" (p. 377). The intended context,
of course, is that between mothers and their children, but the immediate context is lovemaking between Hall and Julia. A seemingly
insignificant aside, therefore, holds the key for putting the novel in
perspective and ultimately for understanding Hall. Julia's and Joel's
relationship is the only one in the novel that fits the definition of
incest as sexual contact between blood relatives; practically every
other relationship in the novel, though, is "incestuous."

Baldwin has prepared us in his earlier works for his thesis about
incestuous biological and extended family relationships. A quick review of them will illustrate how *Just Above My Head* is a culmination
of a thesis, not a new one. Notions of brotherhood and sisterhood
have pervaded all of Baldwin's works. Usually common in a religious
context, the titles have nonetheless taken on other overtones at
times. Such overtones in *Go Tell It on the Mountain* put Elisha's and
John's wrestling match in the church-cleaning scene in the context of
homosexual, thus incestuous, attraction. Elisha refers to John as his

"little brother" in the Lord and feels a responsibility for him even before John is converted. John, in turn, admires Elisha's holiness and often wonders about his private life beyond the church. The wrestling match evokes feelings of "wild delight" in John that come in part from his newfound strength in matching Elisha's, as well as from a sensation of being held tightly by a man. As they try to take advantage of each other, "Elisha's sweat was heavy in John's nostrils" (p. 53), which brings to mind the heightening of sexual interest with the smell of body odor. Here, the pounding wrestling contact is, unconsciously, acceptable physicality that substitutes for caresses.[8] After John's conversion, Elisha emphasizes that he is now John's "*big* brother in the Lord" (p. 220). Potential surfacing of sexual contact is repressed forever in the Brotherhood of the church, but it has been insinuated enough to support Baldwin's developing thesis.[9]

Questions that can be raised about earlier works also tie them easily to *Just Above My Head* and the theory of incest developed there. Would Florence, for example, prefer that Gabriel be her husband instead of her brother? While he has many faults, there is no denying that he *does* provide the stability, warped though it may be, that Florence has left home looking for and that she so much desires. Is John's desire for Gabriel's demise tied to an Oedipus complex?[10] Would he like to end his mother's suffering and assume his father's power by becoming *the* man in his mother's life?[11] Elizabeth emphasizes to him that he is her "right-hand man" and that she is "counting" on him. What exactly is the nature of that overwhelming loss Elizabeth feels at the separation from her father? Are there overtones of incest in that relationship? And what about Ruth in "Come Out the Wilderness"? What exactly is the feeling she has for her brother that haunts her through her relationship with Paul? Would she have preferred that her brother take her virginity, and would he in turn have preferred that? Similarly, would Ida have preferred Rufus as lover or husband rather than brother?[12] Her wish for escape through the mechanism of the prince in shining armor is as old as fairy tales, and that romantic aura is precisely what she uses to surround Rufus. She also embues him with the godlike ability to save, which is what Julia desires in some of her "brothers."

In *Another Country*, there is also a symbolic familial group that anticipates *Just Above My Head*. Vivaldo, Eric, and Rufus form a brotherhood of which Cass is symbolic sister, and the sharing of relationships between and among them anticipates the full-blown treatment in *Just Above My Head*. Cass and Vivaldo are attracted to each other, but both suppress their feelings out of respect for Richard; such restraint is not typical with any of the other characters. Eric and Rufus are lovers initially, and they are both friends to Vivaldo. After Rufus' death, Eric and Vivaldo become lovers. Cass, who has cried on Vivaldo's shoulder about her deteriorating relationship with Richard, in turn becomes Eric's lover. Although Richard is extremely angry about Cass's infidelity, Eric, Vivaldo, and Cass are ultimately very stoic about that as well as about their own intertwining relationships; they are all surprisingly humane and sophisticated about the sharing of bodies and beds.

Although Meridian Henry, black, and Parnell James, white, would both like to share Juanita's bed and affection in *Blues for Mister Charlie*, neither is confident or aggressive enough to follow through on his desire. Because they have been friends for years, Meridian and Parnell can be viewed as a kind of family; therefore, their desire for Juanita—and she is attracted to both of them—has overtones of incest. Such overtones become explicit when Richard, Meridian's son, arrives in town and renews a childhood romance with Juanita. Richard is the only one of the three who actually makes love with Juanita, but the relationships as drawn among the three men make the incestuous quality of their desires clear; the father and son are aware that Juanita has elicited their mutual love. Juanita thinks that there is "incest everywhere" (p. 126) when she imagines which man, Meridian and Parnell among them, she will end up "taking care" of after Richard's death and which one of them will help her "do it with love" (p. 126).

The incestuous connections extend to portrayals of some of the characters in *Tell Me How Long the Train's Been Gone*. At one point, Barbara, Leo, and Jerry all share a house when they are working in summer theater in New Jersey. Barbara and Jerry are lovers and share the downstairs bedroom; Leo sleeps upstairs. All three share food, social outings, and their desires to become successful in the theater; they therefore form a family group. Shortly, Barbara and Leo discover that they are in love, so Jerry and Leo symbolically exchange sleeping places. Jerry is depressed about the situation, but he does not become angry, and he is very generous in wishing the new lovers well.

Perhaps in an effort to tone down the romantic aspect of their relationship because of the guilt they feel about Jerry, Barbara and

Leo hide their feelings under the guise of "sister" and "brother." As they try to anticipate the problems in an involvement such as theirs, Barbara says to Leo: "Well. I hope you like having a sister—a white, incestuous sister. Doesn't that sound like part of the American dream?" (p. 211). Later, he asks her to allow him to kiss her "like a brother" (p. 214), and still later, he calls her "Sister Barbara"; she reciprocates with "Brother Leo" (p. 218). Very late in the novel, they kiss again "like brother and sister" and Leo reflects that "the incestuous brother and sister would now never have any children" (p. 336).

If Beale Street Could Talk, which is closest chronologically to Just Above My Head, is also closest in its treatment of the attraction between a "brother" and a "sister." Tish stresses the fact that she and Fonny have adopted each other to balance her lack of a brother, the indifference of Fonny's family, and the potential dangers of the street. They have grown up together as members of an extended family; she explains their early relationship: "I got to be his little sister and he got to be my big brother" (p. 17). When Fonny brings Tish home on the morning he asks for her hand in marriage, he says to Sharon: "She's always been my girl, you know that. And—I am not a bad boy. You know that. And—you're the only family I've ever had" (p. 104). Against Frank's depression later in the novel, Joseph uses the familial connection in urging him that they *must* get Fonny out of jail, because "that's our flesh and blood, baby: *our flesh and blood*. I don't know *how* we going to do it. I just know we have to do it" (p. 232). Everyone in the Rivers household accepts Fonny as family, and they similarly accept the innocent sisterly/brotherly connection that has blossomed forth into sexual love.

Julia and Hall also grew up like brother and sister, and their families are bound together by ties sometimes stronger than blood kinship. Florence Montana admits that she responds so thoroughly to Julia partly because of a girl child who has died at three, between Hall's and Arthur's births. Julia, therefore, becomes Florence's substitute daughter and Hall's sister. There is a double irony, then, in addressing the young evangelist in the respectful tones of "Sister Julia," for what would seem to be inviolate is not. Late in the novel, after their tumultuous sexual involvement and on the occasion when Hall meets Julia for dinner after her African trip, he says that they kiss each other in greeting "like brother and sister" (p. 523).

Jimmy has also been adopted into the Montana household as son and brother, but especially as brother. On that day when Amy slaps the five-year-old Jimmy, Hall holds him and wipes his tears away (the proud young Jimmy has refused to cry until they have gone out for ice cream), and Arthur works hard to make Jimmy laugh again and feels acutely the anguish of a younger brother. When Jimmy and Arthur become lovers, therefore, they already know each other as brothers; the double bond prevents Jimmy's desertion in the face of Arthur's many sexual improprieties in later years. Hall says at one point that if one "were to fail his lover, or his brother, he would then, somehow, have cut the cord binding us to life" (p. 261). He consistently sees himself, Julia, Jimmy, and Arthur as part of a family. Jimmy's pursuit of Arthur is put in that context:

> I could see how it all made perfect, idyllic sense to Jimmy, who would have a family again, or who would, perhaps, have a family for the first time. He would have Julia and me *and* Arthur, all of us belonging to each other. I could see, too, as Arthur couldn't, that Jimmy had probably had a crush on Arthur all his life. (p. 366)

Near the end of the book, when Hall is reconciled to the loss of Julia as a romantic partner, and after he has met Ruth, he says: "So there we were after all, the four of us, reunited, Julia, Jimmy, Arthur, me, bound together, as it now turned out, for life, and with the addition of Ruth, who arrived, simply, and transformed the space which had been waiting for her" (p. 540).

The four siblings of the two families are thus intertwined in various shades of the meanings inherent in the words "brother" and "sister." So are some of the other characters in the novel. Hall introduces Martha to Sidney, who is owner of a local bar that the Montanas and Millers occasionally patronize. Hall meets Sidney shortly after he turns eighteen and is allowed into the bar—on that fateful Christmas day of the scene at the Millers' when Joel, Paul, and Hall escape for a few minutes. As the older men talk, Sidney and Hall get acquainted, decide they like each other, and immediately become fast friends and brothers. Sidney meets Martha, dates her while Hall is in the army, and is planning to marry her by the time Hall returns. What Sidney and Hall have been to each other comes out in the farewell conversation he has with Martha:

> "Sidney was very nice during that whole time, and your mama liked him a lot. And that meant something, I must say"—she leaned forward, gesturing with her newly lit cigarette—"because I trust your mama."
> I said, I couldn't help it, "Sure. She treated Sidney like a son." Then I said, "I'm sorry. Go on."

"You should be," she said, refusing to be checked. "After all, you treat him like a brother." She paused, narrowing her eyes, both shrewd and mocking. "Don't you?"

She was calling up my promissory notes. "Yes," I said, "I do."   (p. 318)

What may have been a permissible violation under other circumstances reinforces the argument for incestuous relationships in this particular case.

Or consider the case of Ruth, whom Hall meets while Julia is in Africa. She is adopted into the Montana/Miller enclave and seems none the wiser about the interrelationships that have existed there. Rather, she is Julia's "bosom buddy," and her children are allowed to spend weekends at Julia's house. Hall creates a situation where two women with whom he has been intimate for extensive periods of time are in constant contact with each other (and he can still be aroused nostalgically during those moments of contact). Julia and Ruth are therefore sisters or co-wives[13] in their love affairs with Hall; one is symbolic and the other literal wife; and they are both mother to his children. In Julia, then, Hall's children have a sister, a mother, and an aunt; and, if Hall has made love to Julia because he could not make love to Amy, then perhaps a grandmother.[14]

Even the relationship in which Julia becomes involved in Africa has overtones of incest. The man is considerably older than she is and apparently reminds her of Joel. Julia has maintained earlier to Hall that, in spite of everything, she was still sympathetic toward her father: "It may sound funny . . . and nobody knows everything that happened—except me—but I don't have anything against him. Nothing at all" (p. 346). It is almost as if she is reliving the past with her African lover and hoping to reclaim that essential element of her own blackness that Joel has negated by violating history and culture. She tries to explain to Hall why she has left him and turned to the African:

"I said before—you're not history. You couldn't undo it. I couldn't lay it on you. Sometimes, you walk out of one trap, into another. I think I thought that *he* was history. Because he reminded me of my father. And because he was black, black in a way my father never was." And she smiled. "Perhaps I thought that *he* could undo it."   (p. 527)

He gives her, she says, the ability to look forward instead of backward. All that may be true; but it is because she sees him as a father image, as a potential healer, that she has been attracted to him in the first place.

The tainted condition Julia identifies as being purified only by a *blacker* blackness is reminiscent of *Another Country* and the indulgence in homosexuality between Eric and Vivaldo. To understand Ida's transgressions, Vivaldo must commit a greater one. To Julia, the sin of incest with one father can only be repaired by a greater sin with another, symbolic father, one closer to her ancestral origins (the man is also married and has children). To understand and expiate her own sin, therefore, Julia lowers herself further into symbolic blackness, which, at some level, reverses itself of negative connotations and ultimately purifies. Unlike Florence Grimes, who negates blackness, Julia wallows incestuously in the cultural blackness she associates with Africa.

All of these literal and symbolic incestuous actions that Hall plays with in the front mind of his narration are designed to conceal the essential truth of the novel: *Hall Montana has been hopelessly, sexually in love with his brother Arthur.* Subconsciously, however, that is the one truth he cannot admit and still retain his image of untainted manhood. He could only stand by, therefore, through Arthur's one-night stands until Jimmy came into Arthur's life, hopefully to stabilize his sexual habits.

Baldwin's attitude toward homosexual love between blood brothers, the kind that Hall envisions in *Just Above My Head*, was clearly established in *Tell Me How Long the Train's Been Gone*. Leo's brother, Caleb, released from jail after a false arrest for robbery and assault, comes home with an anguish so deep he cannot share it with his parents. When he and Leo retire to the room they share, great sobs overcome Caleb. Leo comforts him and falls asleep, only to awake to Caleb's embrace and sexual arousal. He is both "surprised" and "afraid" at his brother's excitement. Knowing what his brother "wants" and "needs," Leo's fear subsides, and the homosexual act occurs. Leo feels it is his responsibility to his brother to love him; he obtains a distinct "joy" from the encounter (pp. 162–63). Although he and his brother are later separated by Caleb's religious convictions, they have at least given physical expression to that peculiar dread and fear Hall knows is his in relation to Arthur.

Evidence for Hall's erotic love for his brother is supplied, first of all, by the extensive, almost unnatural quality of his grief upon Arthur's death. Ruth comes home to find him, he says, "naked, flat on my back, on the bathroom floor, my razor in my hand" (p. 15). In a grief too profound for mundane expressions, Hall is unable to cry about or speak of his brother for two years. Then, ostensibly prompted by questions from his son, he unravels the tale he relates to us. The telling is a blues composition on the pain of lost love, especially unrequited lost love. With the repetition of grieving expressions in the first three pages, Hall makes clear the legendary esteem in which he has held Arthur, but another note rings in his confession: "My brother. Do you know, friend, how a brother loves his brother, how mighty, how unanswerable it is to be confronted with the truth beneath that simple word? . . . And do you know, do you know, how much my brother loved me? how much he loved me! And do you know I did not know it? did not dare to know it: do *you* know? No. No. No" (p. 14). Like Tish in *If Beale Street Could Talk*, Hall early identifies with the reader because he will need a special understanding, for to have admitted the depth of love between brothers would have been to approach the forbidden and to deal with a reality his life-style will not admit. It is only late in the novel that he says his reflections are a "love song" to his brother (p. 497), and he intends that comment literally, not connotatively.

He feels an overwhelming responsibility as big brother, and he feels compelled to look out for Arthur. Being a big brother has mythical connotations that must be allowed for. Just as Arthur is afraid of possible rejection for being homosexual, Hall fears the same, but that fear is mitigated when the older brother, in typical mythical guise, can look after his younger brother and be tolerant and forgiving of his nontraditional inclinations. A noteworthy passage serves to make the point clear:

> Older brothers, younger brothers—this thought had crossed my mind as I watched Arthur watching Jimmy. It is taken for granted that the younger brother needs the older brother: this need defines the older brother's role, and older brothers remain older brothers all their lives—the proof being that they are always, helplessly, creating, for themselves, an older brother. No matter how desperately they may long for one, an older brother is not among their possibilities. But younger brothers also remain younger brothers all their lives, and either seek out older brothers, or flee from them. Loneliness being what it is—and wickedness being what it is—the role of the older brother is the easier role to play: it is easier to seem correct than to bear being corrected. The older brother's need, whatever it is, can always be justified by what he is able to dictate as being the need of the younger brother. (pp. 373–74)[15]

Hall's notions of fulfilling the mythical role of big brother are those tied to the responsibility of being a good son, carrying the burden his father explicitly has placed upon him for his brother's fate and that which his mother's actions imply. On his thirtieth birthday, he calls home from California and receives congratulations from his family. He openly asks: "You proud of me, Mama?" but thinks: "*Have I been a good son?*" (p. 328), a question that implies the "correctness" in his responsibility toward Arthur and his inability to admit that he has latent homosexual desires, especially toward his brother.

He admits to us, and hints to his son Tony, that he has engaged in homosexual activity in Korea.

> And I had fucked everything I could get my hands on overseas, including two of my drinking buddies. I had been revolted—but this was after, not before, the act. Before the act, when I realized from their eyes what was happening, I had adored being the adored male, and stretched out on it, all boyish muscle and throbbing cock, telling myself, What the hell, it beats jerking off. And I had loved it—the adoration, the warm mouth, the tight ass, the fact that nothing at all was demanded of me except that I shoot my load, which I was very, very happy to do. (p. 309)

The revulsion makes him reflect upon what need drives one to do and what women must feel when they are used, but he concludes: "*a stiff prick has no conscience*" (p. 309). His reflections do not raise him to another level of consciousness in dealing with women; however, his awareness of men loving men out of physical need can only intensify his premonition of the consequences if man loves man for open, unselfish, purely altruistic reasons in addition to the physical need. The public commitment would mean figurative or literal self-destruction.

Still, Hall has a split personality as it relates to homosexuality. Korea represents another place and time, with a different moral code. What was permissible there makes one a "sissy" or a "faggot" in the United States; that is, of everyone *except Arthur*. Arthur is pedestalized beyond judgment in Hall's mind. His ability to compartmentalize is amazing in its consistency. He elevates Arthur to the level of irreproachable purity, but his general attitude toward homosexuals is condescending and stereotypical. Since he is in advertising, he thinks at one point: "*hair color so natural only her hairdresser knows for sure*" and immediately concludes about the hairdresser: "who, probably, furthermore, like all hairdressers, is a faggot. Faggots, of course, never appear in this technicolored bazaar, except as clowns, or as the doomed victims of their hideous lusts" (p. 438). The "hideous lusts" of these "doomed victims" and "clowns" are what Hall escapes by keeping his desires suppressed and are what, paradoxically, could never apply to Arthur, his wonderful baby brother. His possible ironic adoption of these terms to effect the point of view of the ad world shows the extreme reaction he believes he could evoke if he were to admit to homosexuality. His imagining of the world's reaction to him is just as exaggerated as is the ad world's portrayal of homosexuals.

John S. Lash's argument about phallicism may be relevant to the distinction Hall makes between homosexuals as personified by his brother and "faggots." According to Lash, Baldwin makes a sharp differentiation between "phallic confrontation and overt effeminacy." On the one hand are men who seek other men in an act presented "as a normal or supernormal behavior pattern," and whose masculinity is not in question. On the other hand are the "sissies" or "freaks" who "advertise" by dress and mannerisms "their departures from sexual 'norms,'" who are exhibitionists, abnormal, unusual and deviate. These "simpering, limp-wristed poseur[s]" are looked down upon by the true phallicists as well as by the heterosexuals. The argument is appealing except for Hall's uncertainty about his own sexuality. He cannot clear his mind of at least some of the mental baggage that suggests that homosexuals, regardless of the fine distinctions, are basically "freaks." [16]

Arthur lives the homosexual life that closet homosexual Hall never could. In describing Arthur's and Crunch's youthful love affair, Hall maintains that they lived dangerously and openly with their love because youth protected them; they were too young to be aware of the emotionally painful atmosphere by which they were surrounded. Even in youth, Hall is already too old to enjoy that kind of freedom because he is acutely aware of the emotional and societal consequences of male/male love, and he is coward enough to allow those potential consequences to control his life. So he lives a secret life, fantasizingly, in his brother's sexual adventure. The minute, graphic detail with which he describes Arthur's affairs suggests that he thoroughly enjoys the telling of those encounters. They may be painful, but they are also pleasurable. Such is the paradox of the blues: laughing to keep from crying. The voyeuristic pleasure may be evoked, but it cannot be sustained; ultimately, Hall must live with now. Yet the rambling and seemingly unstructured narrative that he relates allows him to enjoy the transitory pleasure of the painful love he has for Arthur through at least one last climactic purgation. When his tale is over, his release is in tears, not in semen, but the double entendres that have paraded aggressively throughout the novel make it clear that the climax is between Hall and Arthur.

A man whose vision is so severely limited by his own sexuality and his own repressions cannot be expected to provide the whole truth about anyone in the novel, and certainly not about Julia, the major character among the black women. From the point at which Julia's actions "frightened" Hall to his affair with her and her departure for Africa, to her stubborn and enigmatic refusal to blame her father, to her reconciliation with Hall, he cannot fully decipher what she is about. He can always see in her the "child's smile" (p. 34) that belies her history, but he never fully understands the complexities that compose it. She is metaphorically above his head. A phrase from a traditional song about music in the air and heaven, the title also suggests that which cannot be touched and that which cannot be understood. Arthur, who cannot be touched sexually by Hall, is like the weight of the ceiling that symbolically presses down upon him in the first few pages. Julia, whose body Hall has touched many times, remains a mysterious entity. She has something intangible that cannot be taken. Hall concludes about her: "It is astounding to behold—endure—a beauty to which you are forever and inexorably connected, and which will never, never, never belong, submit, to you. It shakes one mightily to confront the vulnerability before which stone and steel give way" (p. 525).

Julia's elusiveness solves many but not all of the problems of how black women are treated in Baldwin's fiction. Her case perhaps represents more a limitation of Hall's skills as narrator and as a human being than praise for the virtues of Julia as woman, though that certainly emerges. As black woman, Julia still begins in a *serving* position; she serves in the church, and she serves to allow a confused Hall Montana to try to understand his own life and that of his brother. Her serving might be more complex than that of the other women, but it is still there. She cannot be possessed, but she is also not willingly elevated above that second-class status of offering some assistance to the men in the novel; her rise is in spite of Hall.

Nonetheless, in some ways, Julia finally becomes the freest of Baldwin's black female characters, because she at least frees herself of the church and of the males and male lovers in her life. In extricating herself from the church, she frees herself of the guilt that has limited the growth of so many of the other black female characters in Baldwin's fiction. By denying that her physical participation in acts others would consider sinful represents a tainting of her soul, Julia succeeds in negating the assumption that women are innately, inherently guilty of some act for which they need constantly to atone. By denying the power of church strictures to guide her life, she succeeds in putting the church in a compartmentalized perspective that no black woman presented prior to this point has been consistently able to do. By setting up her own rules for living, she gains the respect of Hall and of the reader, for even as she prepares that delicious barbecue for Hall and his family, she is doing it in her space and on her own terms instead of going to Hall's house. Her modeling job has enabled her to maintain the self-sufficiency that Martha could not envision even with her secure job at the hospital. Her trip to Africa and her broadening of cultural experiences indicate, in their very geographical distancing, the degree of the mental change in Julia. That church that she grew up in would probably never mention Africa, except as a place where missionaries (some perhaps from its own group) went to Christianize the savages. Julia's visit to Africa, therefore, shows not only the geographical distance, but the great psychological distance between herself and black women in Baldwin's earlier fiction.

In extricating herself from the males and male lovers in her life, Julia achieves a healthy state of singleness that no other black woman in Baldwin's fiction has been able to achieve. Leaving the church frees her from the most dominant of male images, that of God. She is forever concerned about Jimmy's welfare, but the novel goes beyond the point where she is mundanely tied to having his best interests as her major ones. When she frees herself of her father, of Crunch, of Hall, and of the African lover, she manages to find a contentment that most of the other black women in Baldwin's fiction do not. She is no longer the seeker; she is the sought. Hall constantly seeks to understand her in an effort to understand himself and to understand Arthur. To him, Julia will always be the individual who has "looked upon chaos" and survived. In contrast, Hall will forever be the individual who did not dare to look upon chaos because he knew from the beginning that he could not survive it. Unlike Hall, who continues to believe that vicarious experience can serve equally well as empirical experience, Julia, like Zora Neale Hurston's Janie Crawford, has "been there to know there."

CONCLUSION

The natural tendency that results from such a study as this one is the desire to speculate on where the author will go from this point on in relation to the topic covered. The wiser course, however, is to resist that temptation, to insist that the lens of the future is too cloudy for any clear perception. It is doubtful if Baldwin will ever get completely away from the religious background that shaped his early years, but what he has written so far is not enough for one to feel confident in suggesting that the secular course will become more prominent in his works. Suffice it to say that his dissatisfaction with the religious world has become apparent, and he has created characters who react sufficiently to that world.

There is also a tendency in a study like this to bring the author's personal life to bear upon the discussion. In practically all of the lectures I gave on this topic prior to the appearance of this book, someone in the audience asked how I thought Baldwin's life-style explained his portrayal of black women. I can only say here what I said again and again in those lectures; too much of what Baldwin has written has been explained away, commented upon, or otherwise treated in the context of his personal life, and too many of his essays have been used to interpret the literature. I have tried to resist that urge in this study, except for the elements in *Go Tell It on the Moun-*

tain that are factually tied to Baldwin's biography. Otherwise, I have tried to remain within the realm of the created works for my discussions and to allow commentary to evolve from within the text instead of superimposing external notions onto the text.

There is also a tendency for people to castigate Baldwin for his treatment of black women, to believe that his trespasses are somehow larger than those of other black male writers. If we look at the characters in *Go Tell It on the Mountain* and other of the early fiction, we see women who may be somewhat stereotyped, but there is a ring of familiarity in Baldwin's presentations of them. Baldwin has at least been willing to attempt to treat black female characters; his accomplishments are not nearly as problematic as they may seem at a cursory glance, and his faults are not nearly as glaring when he is compared with other black writers.

Of the three major black male writers who are usually pointed out in America—Richard Wright, Ralph Ellison, and James Baldwin—Baldwin has made a much more consistent attempt to portray black women than either of the other two. When we think of Richard Wright, the portrait of black womanhood that immediately comes to mind is that of Bessie Mears, the drunk, victimized, desperate young woman in *Native Son* who is killed by Bigger Thomas and whose body serves as a piece of evidence in the case concerning Mary Dalton. When we think of the Invisible Man, we think of his sexual inactivity as a preclusion to serious portraits of black womanhood, and we turn instead to Mary Rambo, the mothering saint who nurses him back to health after his fiasco in the paint factory. Baldwin has given more serious attention, over a long period of time and through many more works, to portraits of black women. Again, attempts to castigate his accomplishments come from sources external to the works themselves, or from the characters' preferences in several of the works for homosexual rather than heterosexual liaisons. Too readily do critics extend the characters' preferences to easy evaluations and generalizations throughout the canon of Baldwin's works.

I have endeavored to treat Baldwin's attempts as well as his accomplishments in the presentation of black female characters in his fiction, and the question now turns to what overall assessment can be made of such treatment. The earliest history of Baldwin's fiction is the history of a group of people in conflict with each other and in conflict with themselves. Those conflicts can center upon the stressful relationship between the individual and his god, and how it manifests itself in the pull between conscience (duty) and desire (pleasure). They can also center upon the conflicts between males and females and, in the context of this study, this is the consideration that will be developed here. The works examined in this study may be viewed in another progression, therefore, one that traces the resolution of conflict between males and females in Baldwin's fiction, particularly between black males and females. The question again centers upon value—how much value black women have to the males in their lives and how much value they can see in themselves without the yardstick of masculine evaluation. A corollary part of the question is to consider the circumstances under which black men and black women in Baldwin's fiction are at peace.

The black women who seem to be least problematic in their creation, and consequently in their relationship to the males in their lives, are the ones who stay within the limitations of the roles that have been carved out for them. Whether or not they may wholeheartedly acquiesce in the positions in which they find themselves, they nevertheless consent to subordinate themselves to the males. Black women in Baldwin's fiction become problems for the male narrators and the male characters in direct proportion to their desire to want more out of life than being wives, mothers, sisters, and lovers. That pattern, as pointed out, begins in the characters of Elizabeth and Deborah; it culminates in the characters of Martha, Florence, and Ruth in *Just Above My Head*. Martha, for all her working to support herself, really desires to be a wife and mother above all else. Ruth becomes the willing appendage to Hall Montana and readily acquiesces in everything he wants, including maintaining close contact with Julia. Florence Montana, like Sharon Rivers, is the idealized mother figure once again. She is ever supportive, ever understanding, ever so much an expected part of the backdrop to her family's existence that she hardly demands comment and attention except in relation to them. When she is no longer needed, she simply disappears from the novel.

The women who help and serve, therefore, are in place to Baldwin and to his narrators. We may also turn this question around and say that the men who are most in place to the women in the fiction are the ones who also fulfill the traditional roles that the women's characters necessitate as complements to themselves. Consider the evidence: Florence wants Frank to be "the husband she had traveled so far to find"; all of the conflict between them is tied to the fact that Frank's notion of being a husband differs drastically from the very traditional image that Florence has of the husband who will love her dearly, save his money to buy a house, and be the model of nonsmoking and nondrinking. Elizabeth's greatest desire is that Gabriel will revert to the loving, attentive husband and father she envisioned him being when she first met him. Her conflict with Gabriel again centers upon the clash between each of their expectations of what the other should do in the very traditional role of husband and wife.

That problem is similarly manifested with Ruth and Ida. Ruth wants faithfulness and commitment in her relationship with Paul, both of which are very traditional expectations of men and women involved in romantic relationships. Even though she is not married to Paul, she wants the security that such an implied relationship would bring. So, too, with Ida. In spite of her actions, loyalty and commitment are still the guiding factors in her relationship with Vivaldo. Though she herself may not yet be willing to submit herself to the same rules, she nevertheless desperately wants Vivaldo to make such a lasting commitment to her. Again, this is marriage in the mind, if not in the courts.

And the pattern continues throughout Baldwin's fiction. Not a single one of his black women wants a casual relationship, a one-night stand. All want very traditionally sanctioned one-man/one-woman relationships. That wish is at its most easy realization in *If Beale Street Could Talk*. There both Sharon and Tish have the kind of relationship that some of the earlier women may have wanted. Though Sharon and Joseph are married and Tish and Fonny are not, the same evaluation applies to each. Sharon is content because Joseph is in place as supportive, loving husband. Tish is equally content to know that Fonny's commitment is to her and the baby; the ugliness of working to get him out of jail is merely the unpleasantness that surrounds that very traditional pattern.

Like the women, therefore, the men who submit to their roles are the ones who are most attractive to the black women in Baldwin's fiction. There is a major difference in the roles the men play and those played by the women, however. The men have more choice in their desire to submit or not: Gabriel chooses Elizabeth, Paul chooses Ruth, Vivaldo chooses Ida, Hall chooses Ruth; the men choose the women, not vice versa. That, too, is a part of the tradition that Baldwin recognizes as creating much turmoil, but one to which he nevertheless adheres again and again in his works.

The men can move beyond the traditional restraints and be readily forgiven; the women cannot. Those who move beyond their place are the problems in Baldwin's fiction, and the one major problem we have thus far in the Baldwin canon is Julia Miller. Asserting through actions rather than argument what she wants to do with her life, Julia moves beyond the roles of wife and lover, and by the end of the novel her role as sister is somewhat muted. In Julia, therefore, Baldwin has created a representation of that part of womanhood that man might wish to suppress, but that he also, paradoxically, wishes to be in touch with. The other women—the faithful wives, the adoring sisters, the sacrificing mothers—lose interest for him in direct proportion to their abilities to fulfill the functions for which they have been created in the works in which they appear. But Julia is that "something else."

Perhaps Baldwin believes that the only way to make woman totally acceptable is to make her more than human. He does not place Julia in the realm of the gods, but he makes her inaccessible through the usual channels of human intercourse. It is her unconquerable center, which is everlasting at the same time that it is vulnerable, that most attracts Hall to her. What Julia ultimately is may be a key to understanding where Baldwin believes women, and particularly black women, ultimately are. Julia resists categorization; she resists the concept of place, and she thereby becomes simultaneously attractive and repulsive to Hall. She bolsters his ego at the same time that she threatens his freedom, and he in turn is both attracted to and repulsed by that possibility for being overcome. Julia and Hall represent the stage at which black men and black women can lay down their weapons and end their battles.

The black men and women are at peace in Baldwin's fiction when they are out of each other's presence, when they have glorified, larger-than-life romances, or when they have truly platonic relationships. The tide turned with the presentation of the characters in *If Beale Street Could Talk* and crests in *Just Above My Head*. Fonny and Tish are presented from their childhood as being mythically chosen for each other; they are the Romeo and Juliet of the neighborhood even before they know the origin of those names. They are selected as if their marriage has been made "in heaven," and neither rejects the other in an attempt to deny that otherworldly solidification of their relationship. The novel becomes a fairy tale in the quest tradition. Fonny, currently lost to Tish and physically separated from her, can only be restored to his place in the tale if Tish undertakes the "journey" of freeing him from jail. Her journey involves obstacles as severe, comparatively speaking, as Scylla and Charybdis were to Odysseus. Because, in this context, the issue of saving Fonny becomes larger than the mundane, day-to-day realities of a romantic relationship, no meaningful conflict is allowed to surface between the two individuals involved in the relationship.

The religion of love that Baldwin allows Fonny and Tish to create through their lovemaking adds yet another dimension to the super-realistic quality of their relationship. Like Joseph and the Virgin Mary, they have been chosen for a special mission. Through them, love can be recaptured from perversion and sex can be made holy. In the face of such mythic creations, Fonny and Tish as individual black man and black woman become much smaller; microscopic almost, in comparison to Elizabeth and Gabriel or to Florence and Frank, yet larger than all of them in their message of peace and universal brotherhood.

Sex that was transformed into godhead in *If Beale Street Could Talk* is eliminated altogether in *Just Above My Head*. Realizing that he perhaps could not keep his characters at the level of the gods and still enable them to live in this world, Baldwin initially returned to the worldliness of sex in *Just Above My Head* as well as to some of the familiar conflicts between males and females that were visible in his earlier fiction. In the conclusion of the novel, however, Baldwin leaves Julia, though in this world, yet beyond the petty realities of role playing and sex. The brotherhood he had underscored with Tish, Fonny, their families, and the Puerto Ricans in *If Beale Street Could Talk* is picked up again with the extended families in *Just Above My Head*, particularly as it is manifested at the end of the novel with Hall's family and with Julia and Jimmy.

Having moved beyond sex, wives, mothers, sisters, and lovers, the major black male and female characters in *Just Above My Head* are truly at peace when they have transcended physical contact (though Hall has not yet transcended desire) and can also exist at an implied larger-than-life level. Julia has gone through many storms to arrive at the calm she manifests on the day of the barbecue. And Hall has gone through a lot to realize that Julia can no longer be possessed physically. They have given up each other's bodies for mutual respect and peaceful coexistence. Lest we conclude that such a platonic view might suggest the end of the family, keep in mind that Hall still has Ruth and his children, Odessa and Tony. He has them, and he has

Julia. Somewhere in the midst of that seeming overdose is the suggestion that perhaps the extended family, the communal family, minimizes the acute tension that individuals feel who are isolated in nuclear families. Remember, again, that Florence and Elizabeth are in many ways isolated; especially is this true of Florence and her desire to escape from "niggers." Ruth voluntarily gave up her repressive nuclear family, and Ida voluntarily left Harlem to escape what she imagined would be confinement from her environment if she remained within her nuclear family. The concept of the extended family—across oceans, across nations and nationalities, across sexes—as a viable alternative to the restrictions of the nuclear family surfaced in *If Beale Street Could Talk* with Fonny and Frank becoming a part of the Rivers family, and with the Puerto Ricans in New York adopting Tish and Fonny. Conflicts that may arise ultimately seem small because the support group is larger; such is the case with the extended families in *Just Above My Head*. Before the establishment of peace, however, it must be clear who can touch whom, who must play which roles for whom, and what all expectations are. It is only after all those things have been clarified that Hall and Julia can be so peaceful with each other. They have sacrificed parochial experience for international experience, and they have thereby broken free of some of the restraints that so characterized the interactions between black men and black women in Baldwin's earlier fiction. Their situation does not allow us to conclude that the black man has completely given up his desire for mastery over black women; it does suggest, however, that at least one kind of black woman has escaped from the limitations of that desire. Hall and Julia may or may not point the way to the future in Baldwin's works, but they do show that at least one healthy pattern of resolution to the conflicts between black men and black women in Baldwin's fiction has been meticulously worked out.

N O T E S

I N T R O D U C T I O N

1. These are Carolyn Wedin Sylvander's *James Baldwin* (New York: Ungar, 1980), Louis H. Pratt's *James Baldwin* (Boston: Twayne, 1978), and Stanley Macebuh's *James Baldwin: A Critical Study* (New York: Joseph Okpaku Publishing, 1973). In none of these studies do the women characters emerge for special consideration. In their treatments of some of the short stories, women characters are not mentioned. A fourth book-length critical study, now available in English, was originally done by a Swedish scholar. See Karin Möller, *The Theme of Identity in the Essays of James Baldwin* (Göteborg, Sweden: Acta Universitatis Gotogurgensis, 1975).

2. See Fern Marja Eckman, *The Furious Passage of James Baldwin* (New York: Evans, 1966).

3. Baldwin has published six novels and one collection of short stories. He has also published a children's book, *Little Man, Little Man* (Dial Press, 1976).

4. Keneth Kinnamon, *James Baldwin: A Collection of Critical Essays* (Englewood Cliffs, N.J.: Prentice-Hall, 1974) and Therman O'Daniel, ed., *James Baldwin: A Critical Evaluation* (Washington, D.C.: Howard Univ. Press, 1977).

5. See Jacqueline E. Orsagh's "Baldwin's Female Characters—A Step Forward?" in O'Daniel, pp. 56–68. Orsagh treats both black women characters and white.

6. I treat all of the novels except *Giovanni's Room* (Dial Press, 1956), which has no black characters, and *Tell Me How Long the Train's Gone* (Dial

Press, 1968), where a white woman is the central character in the life of Leo Proudhammer, the black male protagonist.

7. James Baldwin, *Go Tell It on the Mountain* (Knopf, 1953; rpt. New York: Dell, 1974), p. 16. Further references to this source will be parenthesized in the text.

8. James Baldwin, *Another Country* (Dial Press, 1962; rpt. New York: Dell, 1963), p. 293.

9. James Baldwin, *The Amen Corner* (New York: Dial, 1968), p. 97. Further references to this source will be parenthesized in the text. Sister Margaret, as pastor of her church, could be drawn in part from the woman preacher who influenced Baldwin. See *The Fire Next Time* (New York: Dell, 1963), pp. 43–44.

10. James Baldwin, *Blues for Mister Charlie* (Dial Press, 1964; rpt. New York: Dell, 1970), p. 46.

CHAPTER ONE

1. I use the term *fundamentalist* to suggest the stronghanded, literal way in which members of the church are asked to apply the scriptures to their lives, not to suggest a specific denomination. Though internal evidence suggests that the church Baldwin presents in the Harlem scenes in *Go Tell It on the Mountain* is Holiness, that same conclusion cannot be drawn about the church in which Gabriel participates in the South, which is probably Baptist in its emphasis upon revival, confession, and baptism. And other conclusions could probably be drawn about the church in which Julia grows up in *Just Above My Head*. My emphasis, rather than on denomination, is on the close relationship between the Bible and how one lives, and the insistence in various churches that members be directly accountable to the membership for their various transgressions. For example, a sinner would be required to confess before the entire congregation if she had a child out of wedlock; members who were caught "walking disorderly," as Elisha and Ella Mae are in *Go Tell It on the Mountain*, would be reprimanded before the entire congregation.

2. James Baldwin, *Go Tell It on the Mountain* (Knopf, 1953; rpt. New York: Dell, 1974), p. 70. Further references to this source will be parenthesized in the text.

3. The nicknames recall those Baldwin himself suffered when he was growing up; perhaps, in a positive inversion, he is trying to show that he can now use those names without feeling pain or that, by placing them in a romantic context, the sting of venom they carry will be diminished. One of Baldwin's fellow students from junior high school remembered students "screeching" "Bug eyes!" at Baldwin (Fern Marja Eckman, *The Furious Passage of James Baldwin* [New York: Evans, 1966], p. 44). Eckman records, too, that he was called "Froggy" and "Popeyes" (p. 48). Carolyn Wedin Sylvander also records in *James Baldwin* (New York: Ungar, 1980) that Baldwin was called "Froggy" and "Popeyes" (p. 5).

4. The best examples of Baldwin's discussions of his relationship to his stepfather appear in *Notes of a Native Son* (Boston: Beacon Press, 1955). See also Eckman, *The Furious Passage of James Baldwin* (New York: Evans, 1966), chap. 1, especially pp. 5–9.

5. In almost all of his fiction, Baldwin has a scene in which a character remembers a hostile or violent incident that occurred in the South, or he has characters whose deficiencies in personality can be traced back to their youth in the South. Baldwin's black emigrants from the South almost always have an intolerable stench of inadequacy that he identifies with their origins. For a discussion of this phenomenon from the black male characters' perspectives, see Trudier Harris, "The South as Woman: Chimeric Images of Emasculation in *Just Above My Head*," *Studies in Black American Literature*, ed. Joe Weixlmann and Chester J. Fontenot (Greenwood, Fla.: Penkevill Publishing Co., 1983), pp. 89–109.

6. Shirley S. Allen discusses the use of the narrator in her article, "The Ironic Voice in Baldwin's *Go Tell It on the Mountain*," in Therman O'Daniel, ed., *James Baldwin: A Critical Evaluation* (Washington, D.C.: Howard Univ. Press, 1977), pp. 30–37.

7. Jacqueline E. Orsagh, "Baldwin's Female Characters: A Step Forward?" in O'Daniel, pp. 56–68.

8. George Kent, "Baldwin and the Problem of Being," in *Five Black Writers*, ed. Donald B. Gibson (New York: New York Univ. Press, 1970), p. 151.

9. Shirley S. Allen, "Religious Symbolism and Psychic Reality in Baldwin's *Go Tell It on the Mountain*," *College Language Association Journal* 19 (December 1975): 189.

10. See Trudier Harris, "The Eye as Weapon in *If Beale Street Could Talk*," *Melus* 5, iii (fall 1978): 54–66 for a discussion of how sex transcends its physical context to become religious and political. See also Trudier Harris, *Exorcising Blackness: Historical and Literary Lynching and Burning Rituals* (Bloomington: Indiana Univ. Press, 1984) for a discussion of the political power of sexuality in "Going to Meet the Man."

11. Kent, p. 151.

12. Eckman states that "Set thine house in order" was the last sermon Baldwin preached before his departure from the ministry (p. 82). The finality of some impending change also applies to Florence. The sermon is also the one Sister Margaret Alexander uses in *The Amen Corner* (New York: Dial, 1968), pp. 9, 10.

13. Surprisingly, Deborah is also included in Orsagh's discussion of the women in Baldwin's works, but there is no evidence in the novel of Deborah taking a single action; she is acted upon in the rape, she reacts to Gabriel's proposal of marriage, and she prefers to react to Gabriel's infidelity with Esther instead of taking whatever small action she could against it.

14. *Blues for Mister Charlie* (Dial Press, 1964; rpt. New York: Dell, 1970), Act III, p. 125.

15. Charles Scruggs, "The Tale of Two Cities in James Baldwin's *Go Tell It on the Mountain*," *American Literature* 52 (March 1980): 12, provides an interesting interpretation of the suicide. He suggests that it is the store-

216 NOTES TO PAGES 57–97

owner's comment to Richard during the lineup—"You black bastards, you're all the same"—that leads to his suicide, not the beating; the comment makes him realize that "no matter how smart he is, he remains a 'nigger.'" Even if we accept this interpretation, we can still see that the basis of Richard's action is nonetheless tied to a weakness of spirit.

16. Scruggs suggests (ibid., p. 15) that Elizabeth's thoughts of Richard, especially of the book he was reading when they met, indicate her fear that the sensitive, humanistic part of John that is most like Richard has been submerged forever. Therefore, she cries and thinks of Richard because John has adopted Gabriel's "gloomy religion."

17. Baldwin comments in *The Fire Next Time* on a similar competition between his father and himself. "And I don't doubt that I also intended to best my father on his own ground"—by becoming a member of the church and a "Young Minister" (New York: Dell, 1963), p. 48.

CHAPTER TWO

1. Although *Going to Meet the Man* was published in 1965, six of the eight stories had been published prior to 1962, when *Another Country* appeared. I am retaining the chronology of most of Baldwin's fictional creations, then, by discussing the collection of short stories before the novel. The Dell paperback edition of *Going to Meet the Man* is the one used for quotations throughout this book.

2. "The Rockpile," along with the title story, "Going to Meet the Man," first appeared in the collection in 1965. The repeat of characters from *Go Tell It on the Mountain*, however, suggests that the story was written earlier.

3. "The Outing" was published in *New Story* in 1951.

4. Baldwin recognizes the secular and sacred qualities of the rocking concept in *The Fire Next Time* (New York: Dell, 1963), pp. 49–50. In *The Amen Corner* (New York: Dial, 1968), he described a service not only as "loud," but as "violent" (p. 10). At another point in "The Outing," the saints talk about the spirit having "jumped" on them (p. 29), an aggression usually not assigned to things holy and that indeed has almost a mugging connotation.

5. "Sonny's Blues" first appeared in *Partisan Review* in 1957.

6. The exposed communication—through music—between Sonny and his brother, which makes for a new understanding between them, anticipates ideas Baldwin develops in *Another Country*. For a discussion of how the blues functions "as an art of communication," see John Reilly's "'Sonny's Blues': James Baldwin's Image of Black Community," in Therman B. O'Daniel, ed., *James Baldwin: A Critical Evaluation* (Washington, D.C.: Howard Univ. Press, 1977), pp. 163–69.

7. "Come Out the Wilderness" first appeared in *Mademoiselle* in 1958.

8. The reference to the "funnyface" recalls again the nicknames used in *Go Tell It on the Mountain*, obviously used here in a less than complimentary way.

CHAPTER THREE

1. James Baldwin, *Another Country* (Dial Press, 1962; rpt. New York: Dell, 1963), p. 250. Further references to this source will be parenthesized in the text.

2. Many critics have commented upon or directly complained about such occurrences in the novel. "As for sexual episodes," writes Colin MacInnes, "although there are glorious moments . . . the effect is frequently turgid and high-flown: the worst passages being almost like inflated parodies of the best"; see "Dark Angel: The Writings of James Baldwin" in Donald B. Gibson, *Five Black Writers* (New York: New York Univ. Press, 1970), p. 135. In *The Furious Passage of James Baldwin*, Fern Marja Eckman comments: "Undeniably there are powerful and beautiful passages in *Another Country*. Just as undeniably, the less standard varieties of sex are consistently sugared over and sentimentalized, with many—but not all—of the couplings between homosexual and heterosexual, Negro and white, in most of their possible equations, glorified as the apotheosis of love" (New York: Evans, 1966, p. 165). Eugenia Collier maintains that *Another Country* has "something offensive for everyone," including "the sordidly graphic descriptions of sex"; see "The Phrase Unbearably Repeated" in Therman B. O'Daniel, ed., *James Baldwin: A Critical Evaluation* (Washington, D.C.: Howard Univ. Press, 1977), p. 38.

3. Eckman (p. 113) mentions the suicide of Baldwin's friend, Eugene Worth, who, like Rufus, jumped off the George Washington Bridge. See also p. 162.

4. See George Kent, "Baldwin and the Problem of Being," in Gibson, *Five Black Writers*, p. 156; MacInnes, p. 136; and Fred L. Standley, "*Another Country*, Another Time," *Studies in the Novel* 4 (Fall 1972): 506.

5. Eckman, p. 159.

6. See Stanley Macebuh, *James Baldwin: A Critical Study* (New York: Joseph Okpaku Publishing, 1973), p. 87.

7. See Jacqueline E. Orsagh, "Baldwin's Female Characters: A Step Forward" in O'Daniel, pp. 62–65.

8. Donald B. Gibson, "James Baldwin: The Political Anatomy of Space," in O'Daniel, p. 12.

9. John S. Lash maintains that Rufus "has on occasion sought refuge from the whiplashes of the Negro life in New York in sexual indulgences with Vivaldo Moore, his best friend," but there is no explicit evidence in the novel to validate that statement; see "Baldwin Beside Himself: A Study in Modern Phallicism," in O'Daniel, p. 53.

10. Lash suggests that Eric is "the phallicist to whom men—and one woman—turn in their hours of bafflement and exaltation, the ministering angel, as it were, of the phallic god residual in the flesh of every man" (ibid., p. 50). He also maintains that "phallic confrontation" between men in Baldwin's works is "a normal or supernormal behavior pattern" and that Baldwin distinguishes between "phallic confrontation and overt effeminacy." Gibson also discusses the sometimes negative attitude Baldwin has toward

homosexuality. Of *Giovanni's Room*, he asserts: "The novel makes clear the author's disgust with fairies, with males who assume feminine guise of dress or manner, and with males who are not at least bisexual" (ibid., p. 9). In *Another Country*, all of the prominent male characters who engage in homosexual acts—Rufus, Vivaldo, Eric—are bisexual. The ultimate fulfillment of sexual contact is between Eric and Yves, whose name, as Lash points out, is significantly pronounced "Eve," reinforcing the sometimes paradisial contact between males and males.

11. The level of communion between Eric and Vivaldo anticipates the religion of love through sex that Fonny and Tish will create in *If Beale Street Could Talk*.

12. See Gibson, "James Baldwin: The Political Anatomy of Space" in O'Daniel, p. 13.

13. Macebuh calls Vivaldo's role "priestlike" in the face of Ida's confession (p. 95).

14. Macebuh, p. 88.

15. Eckman comments on the alternative ending Baldwin had planned for the novel and for Ida: "And Ida herself, the figure with whom Baldwin was most concerned, simmering with his own rage, swathed in his own bafflement, was to have wound up as a patient in a psychotic ward, a fate reserved in the published version for a white girl" (p. 159).

16. Addison Gayle maintains that the assimilationist approach to the novel demands that blacks give up their blackness. "Strip away the more sensational features of *Another Country*," he writes, "and the integrationist ethic is revealed; to be elevated to human kind, Blacks must be made one with the society, must desert the legacy of the cultural past." Gayle, *The Way of the New World* (Garden City, N.Y.: Doubleday, 1976), p. 267.

CHAPTER FOUR

1. James Baldwin, *The Fire Next Time* (New York: Dell, 1963), pp. 57-58. Further references to this source will be parenthesized in the text.

2. William Edward Farrison, "If Baldwin's Train Has Not Gone," in Therman B. O'Daniel, *James Baldwin: A Critical Evaluation* (Washington, D.C.: Howard Univ. Press, 1977), p. 79. Farrison's comment must be put in the context of his general approach to Baldwin in the article; he is offended by Baldwin's "greatly overworked four-letter words" and by the "plethora" of sexual acts in which a novel like *Tell Me How Long the Train's Been Gone* "needlessly abounds." Farrison superimposes a rather straitlaced morality onto Baldwin's novels and sees *If Beale Street Could Talk* not as a culmination of the writer's talent to that point, but as a diminution. John W. Aldridge, "The Fire Next Time?" *Saturday Review/World* (June 1974): 25; John McCluskey, essay review of *If Beale Street Could Talk* in *Black World* (December 1974): 51-52, 88-91.

3. Perhaps the most serious and detailed treatment of women in a Baldwin novel is that offered by Hortense Spillers on *If Beale Street Could Talk*. See

"The Politics of Intimacy," in *Sturdy Black Bridges*, ed. Roseann P. Bell, Bettye J. Parker, and Beverly Guy-Sheftall (Garden City, N.Y.: Doubleday, 1979), pp. 87–106.

4. Baldwin apparently had firsthand knowledge of this kind of parental separation. One of his friends recalled Baldwin's mother addressing his father, David Baldwin, as *Mr.* Baldwin; Fern Marja Eckman, *The Furious Passage of James Baldwin* (New York: Evans, 1966) p. 72. Mrs. Hunt and David Baldwin have in common the religious fanaticism that separates them from their offspring.

5. James Baldwin, *If Beale Street Could Talk* (New York: Signet, 1975), p. 26. Further references to this source will be parenthesized in the text.

6. Trudier Harris, "The Eye as Weapon in *If Beale Street Could Talk*," *Melus* 5 (Fall 1978): 54–66 refers to the act as a form of religion.

7. Donald B. Gibson, *The Politics of Literary Expression: A Study of Major Black Writers* (Westport, Conn.: Greenwood Press, 1981), p. 120.

8. James Baldwin, *Go Tell It on the Mountain* (Knopf, 1953; rpt. New York: Dell, 1974), p. 121. Leo Proudhammer, in *Tell Me How Long the Train's Been Gone* (Dial Press, 1968; rpt. New York: Dell, 1970), says that "the theater began in the church," p. 323. Further references to this source will be parenthesized in the text.

9. James Baldwin, *The Devil Finds Work* (New York: Dial, 1970), p. 29. Eckman quotes Baldwin as saying: "Being in the pulpit was like being in the theater. . . . I was behind the scenes and knew how the illusion worked" (pp. 72–73). Baldwin also refers to his role in the church as a "gimmick" and to the church business as a "racket"; see *The Fire Next Time* (New York: Dial, 1963), pp. 38, 44.

10. Critics who suggest that Frank commits suicide because he is despondent over the loss of his job fail to consider the negative effect of his wife and daughters upon his mental attitude. (Frank has been fired for stealing items to sell to help meet Fonny's bail.) Since they are so unconcerned about Fonny, Frank realizes that losing his job posssibly means that Fonny will remain in jail. The lost job is therefore the catalyst to suicide, not the cause. Fonny has emphasized that Frank stayed with Mrs. Hunt only because of him; when it seems to Frank that his one reason for staying will be forever out of his reach, he kills himself. McCluskey calls Frank's suicide "one of the least convincing acts of the entire novel," asserting that it goes against the optimistic current. *Black World*: 89.

11. Perhaps the relationship between the parent and the child works so well because the offspring are female, not male. The counterpart in the idealized male parent/male offspring relationship is suggested in Frank and Fonny, but the focus of the novel does not provide for much concentration on them as parent and child.

12. Craig Werner provides interesting commentary on the economics at work in the novel. He sees it in part as a culmination of Baldwin's attitude toward the society in which black people constantly come in in second place. Baldwin offers in *If Beale Street Could Talk*, Craig Werner suggests, a "concrete tactical suggestion" for those who are economically deprived; "the

oppressed" should "*use* the system whenever possible, play on its built-in weaknesses," as Joseph and Frank obviously do. Werner, "The Economic Evolution of James Baldwin," *College Language Association Journal* 23 (September 1979): 27.

13. The impending birth is considered to be the most important issue here. It ties to Baldwin's belief about saving the children and to the Mary, Joseph, Jesus analogy that permeates the story. See Louis H. Pratt, *James Baldwin* (Boston: Twayne, 1978), pp. 28–29.

14. The sacrament here ties in with the imagery of a holy conception between Fonny and Tish, with Joseph, like the biblical Joseph, serving as surrogate father to the child in the absence of Fonny, its real, holy father.

15. Aldridge, pp. 24–25.

16. Baldwin discusses this connection between blacks, Puerto Ricans, and other minorities in *No Name in the Street* (New York: Dial, 1972), p. 149. Remember, it was a little Puerto Rican girl who sparked Ernestine's commitment, and it is Puerto Ricans Tish imagines being in the same predicament as Fonny.

17. Carolyn Wedin Sylvander, *James Baldwin* (New York: Ungar, 1980), p. 84.

18. Pratt discusses in detail Baldwin's conflict with the Black Aesthetic nationalist critics such as Amiri Baraka and Eldridge Cleaver. They insisted, in the 1960s, that Baldwin hated himself and other blacks. The excessively positive images of the prominent black characters in *If Beale Street Could Talk* could be in part a bowing to that criticism; see pp. 23–27, 125–129. It could also be a result of the extended conversation on black men and women that Baldwin had with Nikki Giovanni in November of 1971; see James Baldwin and Nikki Giovanni, *A Dialogue* (London: Michael Joseph, 1975).

19. Tish as narrator is one of the things John McCluskey finds attractive about the novel; he likes "the simplicity and authenticity of the voice" but recognizes "it cracks on occasion." See McCluskey's essay review of the novel in *Black World* 24 (December 1974): 90.

20. Most importantly, she is the *body* through which Fonny's baby will be brought into the world.

CHAPTER FIVE

1. The novel was published in 1979, but the Dell 1980 paperback edition is used for quotations here; references will be parenthesized in the text.

2. See Trudier Harris, "Tiptoeing Through Taboo: Incest in Alice Walker's 'The Child Who Favored Daughter,'" *Modern Fiction Studies* 28, iii (Autumn 1982): 495–505, for a discussion of subjects, particularly incest, that black writers are reluctant to treat.

3. Joel has allowed Julia to control the running of the household to such an extent that he goes behind her back to drink wine.

4. The "Brother" title will be significant later on.

5. In that distressing phone call she makes to Florence after she is beaten, Julia screams "Mama Montana! Mama Montana!" (p. 295).

6. Eleanor Traylor, "James Baldwin's *Just Above My Head*," *First World* 2, iii (1979): 40–43.

7. As family, though, certainly Hall hangs on to Julia much longer than the other men.

8. Stanley Macebuh discusses the homosexual attraction between Elisha and John in *James Baldwin: A Critical Study* (New York: Joseph Okpaku Publishing, 1973), pp. 52, 54, 61–62, and 67. See also Michel Fabre, "Fathers and Sons in James Baldwin's *Go Tell It on the Mountain*," in *James Baldwin: A Collection of Critical Essays*, ed. Keneth Kinnamon (Englewood Cliffs, N.J.: Prentice-Hall, 1974), pp. 127–28; Fern Marja Eckman, *The Furious Passage of James Baldwin* (New York: Evans, 1966), pp. 30–31; and George E. Bell, "The Dilemma of Love in *Go Tell It on the Mountain* and *Giovanni's Room*," *College Language Association Journal* 17 (March 1974): 401–2.

9. Several critics who recognize the homosexual attraction between John and Elisha suggest that John's conversion is a signal to a development of the relationship. My position, which is just the opposite, is shared by Charles Scruggs, who suggests that "from Baldwin's point of view, the church allows the two boys to express their love for one another within an ordered framework; it metamorphoses a potentially illicit passion into something transcendental." See Scruggs, "The Tale of Two Cities in James Baldwin's *Go Tell It on the Mountain*," *American Literature* 52 (March 1980): 14–15.

10. Fabre, pp. 122, 126, 129.

11. Charlotte Alexander is one critic who ponders this possibility, in "The 'Stink' of Reality: Mothers and Whores in James Baldwin's Fiction," in Kinnamon, p. 92.

12. Therman O'Daniel, in "James Baldwin: An Interpretive Study," *College Language Association Journal* 7, i (September 1963) makes the following comment about the relationship between Ida and Rufus: "There is no specific mention of incest in *Another Country*, but again, Ida's strong devotion to Rufus, before and after his death, is reminiscent of similar sister-brother or other family attachments in Greek drama" (p. 46).

13. I am grateful to Professor Susan L. Blake of the English Department of Lafayette College, Easton, Pennsylvania, who, in an early reading of this chapter, offered the term "co-wives" to describe the relationship Julia and Ruth have to Hall.

14. And what do we do with the fact that Jimmy refers to Ruth as "Mother Mattie"? P. 536.

15. Baldwin has discussed his position as older brother in his family in several of his autobiographical essays. Carolyn Wedin Sylvander, in *James Baldwin* (New York: Ungar, 1980), also discusses Baldwin's position; see especially pp. 4–9. Eckman also details Baldwin's relationship to his younger sisters and brothers.

16. Lash, "Baldwin Beside Himself: A Study in Modern Phallicism," in O'Daniel, 47–55.

SELECTED BIBLIOGRAPHY

Aldridge, John W. "The Fire Next Time?" *Saturday Review/World* (June 1974): 20, 24–25.

Allen, Shirley S. "Religious Symbolism and Psychic Reality in Baldwin's *Go Tell It on the Mountain.*" *College Language Association Journal* 19 (December 1975): 173–99.

Baker, Houston A., Jr. "The Embittered Craftsman: An Essay on James Baldwin." *The Journal of African-Afro-American Affairs* 1 (June 1977): 28–51.

Baldwin, James. *Go Tell It on the Mountain*, Knopf, 1953; rpt. New York: Dell, 1974.

————. *The Amen Corner.* New York: Dial, 1968.

————. *Another Country.* Dial Press, 1962; rpt. New York: Dell, 1963.

————. *Going to Meet the Man.* Dial Press, 1965; rpt. New York: Dell, 1969.

————. *Tell Me How Long the Train's Been Gone.* Dial Press, 1968; rpt. New York: Dell, 1972.

————. *If Beale Street Could Talk.* Dial Press, 1974; rpt. New York: Signet, 1975.

————. *Just Above My Head.* Dial Press, 1979; rpt. New York: Dell, 1980.

————. *Blues for Mister Charlie.* Dial Press, 1964; rpt. New York: Dell, 1970.

————. *Notes of a Native Son.* Boston: Beacon Press, 1955; rpt. New York: Bantam, 1968.

————. *Nobody Knows My Name.* New York: Dial, 1961.

————. *The Fire Next Time.* Dial Press, 1963; rpt. New York: Dell, 1972.

————. *No Name in the Street.* New York: Dial, 1972.

————. *The Devil Finds Work.* New York: Dial, 1976.

———— and Margaret Mead. *A Rap on Race.* New York: Dell, 1972.

———— and Nikki Giovanni. *A Dialogue.* London, Michael Joseph: 1975.

Bell, George E. "The Dilemma of Love in *Go Tell It on the Mountain* and *Giovanni's Room.*" *College Language Association Journal* 17 (March 1974): 397–406.

Bigsby, C. W. E. "The Divided Mind of James Baldwin." *Journal of American Studies* 13 (December 1979): 325–42.

Cruse, Harold. *The Crisis of the Negro Intellectual.* New York: William Morrow Company, 1967.

Dance, Daryl. "James Baldwin." In *Black American Writers: Bibliographical Essays, II: Richard Wright, Ralph Ellison, James Baldwin, and Amiri Baraka,* ed. M. Thomas Inge, Maurice Duke, and Jackson R. Bryer. New York: St. Martin's Press, 1978.

————. "You Can't Go Home Again: James Baldwin and the South." *College Language Association Journal* 18 (September 1974): 81–90.

Eckman, Fern Marja. *The Furious Passage of James Baldwin.* New York: M. Evans and Company, 1966.

Foster, David E. "'Cause my house fell down': The Theme of the Fall in Baldwin's Novels." *Critique: Studies in Modern Fiction* 13 (1971): 50–62.

Freese, Peter. "James Baldwin, 'Going to Meet the Man' (1965)." *The Black American Short Story in the 20th Century,* ed. Peter Bruck. Amsterdam: Grüner, 1977, pp. 171–85.

Gayle, Addison, Jr. "A Defense of James Baldwin." *College Language Association Journal* 10 (March 1967): 201–8.

————. *The Way of the New World: The Black Novel in America.* Garden City, N.Y.: Doubleday, 1976.

Gibson, Donald B. *Five Black Writers.* New York: New York University Press, 1970.

————. *The Politics of Literary Expression: A Study of Major Black Writers.* Westport, Conn.: Greenwood Press, 1981.

Graves, Wallace. "The Question of Moral Energy in James Baldwin's *Go Tell It on the Mountain.*" *College Language Association Journal* 7 (September 1963): 215–23.

Gross, Barry. "The 'Uninhabitable Darkness' of Baldwin's *Another Country*: Image and Theme." *Negro American Literature Forum* 6 (Winter 1972): 113–21.

Harper, Howard. *Desperate Faith: A Study of Bellow, Salinger, Mailer, Baldwin and Updike.* Chapel Hill: Univ. of North Carolina Press, 1967.

Harris, Trudier. *Exorcising Blackness: Historical and Literary Lynching and Burning Rituals.* Bloomington: Indiana Univ. Press, 1984.

————. "The Eye as Weapon in *If Beale Street Could Talk.*" *Melus* 5 (Fall 1978): 54–66.

————. "Tiptoeing Through Taboo: Incest in Alice Walker's 'The Child Who Favored Daughter.'" *Modern Fiction Studies* 28 (Autumn 1982): 495–505.

————. "The South as Woman: Chimeric Images of Emasculation in *Just*

Above My Head." *Studies in Black American Literature*, ed. Joe Weixl-
   mann and Chester J. Fontenot. Greenwood, Fla.: Penkevill Publishing
   Co., 1983, pp. 89–109.
"James Baldwin." *Contact* 9 (January–February 1984): 14–17.
Kinnamon, Keneth, ed. *James Baldwin: A Collection of Critical Essays*.
   Englewood Cliffs, N.J.: Prentice-Hall, 1974.
Klein, Marcus. "James Baldwin: A Question of Identity." *After Alienation*.
   New York: World, 1962.
Lee, Brian. "James Baldwin: Caliban to Prospero." In *The Black Ameri-
   can Writer* 1, ed. C. W. E. Bigsby. Baltimore: Penguin Books, 1969,
   pp. 169–79.
Lobb, Edward. "James Baldwin's Blues and the Function of Art." *Interna-
   tional Fiction Review* 6 (Summer 1979): 143–48.
Macebuh, Stanley. *James Baldwin: A Critical Study*. New York: Joseph
   Okpaku Publishing, 1973.
Margolies, Edward. *Native Sons: A Critical Study of Twentieth-Century
   Negro American Authors*. Philadelphia: J. B. Lippincott, 1968.
McCluskey, John. *"If Beale Street Could Talk."* *Black World* 24 (December
   1974): 51–52, 88–91.
Moore, John Rees. "An Embarrassment of Riches: Baldwin's *Going to Meet
   the Man.*" *Hollins Critic* 2 (December 1965): 1–12.
O'Daniel, Therman B., ed. *James Baldwin: A Critical Evaluation*. Washing-
   ton, D.C.: Howard University Press, 1977.
―――. "James Baldwin: An Interpretive Study." *College Language Associa-
   tion Journal* 7 (September 1963): 37–47.
Pratt, Louis H. *James Baldwin*. Boston: Twayne Publishers, 1978.
―――. "James Baldwin and 'the Literary Ghetto.'" *College Language Asso-
   ciation Journal* 20 (December 1976): 262–72.
Schero, Elliott M. *"Another Country* and the Sense of Self." *Black Academy
   Review* 2: 91–100.
Scruggs, Charles. "The Tale of Two Cities in James Baldwin's *Go Tell It on the
   Mountain.*" *American Literature* 52 (March 1980): 1–17.
Spillers, Hortense. "The Politics of Intimacy." In *Sturdy Black Bridges:
   Visions of Black Women in Literature*, ed. Roseann P. Bell, Bettye J.
   Parker, and Beverly Guy-Sheftall. Garden City, N.Y.: Doubleday, 1979.
Standley, Fred L. *"Another Country,* Another Time." *Studies in the Novel* 4
   (Fall 1972): 504–12.
―――. "James Baldwin: The Artist as Incorrigible Disturber of the Peace."
   Southern Humanities Review 4 (Winter 1970): 18–30.
―――. "James Baldwin: The Crucial Situation." *South Atlantic Quarterly*
   65 (Summer 1976): 371–81.
―――― and Standley, Nancy V. *James Baldwin: A Reference Guide*. Boston:
   G. K. Hall, 1980.
Sylvander, Carolyn Wedin. *James Baldwin*. New York: Ungar, 1980.
Thelwell, Mike. *"Another Country:* Baldwin's New York Novel." In *The Black
   American Writer* 1, ed. C. W. E. Bigsby. Baltimore: Penguin Books,
   1969, pp. 181–98.

Traylor, Eleanor. "James Baldwin's *Just Above My Head.*" *First World* 2 (1979): 40–43.

Vopat, James B. "Beyond Sociology? Urban Experience in the Novels of James Baldwin." In *Minority Literature and the Urban Experience,* ed. George E. Carter, James R. Parker, and Sara Bentley. La Crosse, Wisc.: Institute for Minority Studies, 1978.

Wasserstrom, William. "James Baldwin: Stepping Out on the Promise." In *Black Fiction: New Studies in the Afro-American Novel Since 1945,* ed. Robert A. Lee. New York: Barnes and Noble, 1980.

Weatherby, William J. *Squaring Off: Mailer vs. Baldwin.* New York: Mason Charter, 1977.

Werner, Craig. "The Economic Evolution of James Baldwin." *College Language Association Journal* 23 (September 1979): 12–31.

Williams, Sherley Anne. *Give Birth to Brightness: A Thematic Study in Neo-Black Literature.* New York: Dial, 1972.

INDEX

Black Women in the Fiction of James Baldwin has been typeset in ten point Caledonia type with two points of spacing between the lines. Weiss II initials were selected for display. The book was designed by Judy Ruehmann, composed by G&S Typesetters, Inc., printed offset by Thomson-Shore, Inc., and bound by John H. Dekker & Sons. The paper on which the book is printed is designed for an effective life of at least three hundred years.

THE UNIVERSITY OF TENNESSEE PRESS : KNOXVILLE